SHE TEACHES ME STILL

SHE

TEACHES
ME STILL

A Memoir of Phyllis Strong Le Peau

Andrew T. Le Peau

FILL US PUBLISHING

Downers Grove
Illinois

Interior photos provided by Diane O'Day, Paul Bertsch, and Andrew T. Le Peau.
Cover photo: John Economides
Cover design, interior design, and typesetting: Cindy Kiple
Publishing services: Marcus Constantino, LLC, marcuscostantino.com

ISBN 979-8-9936718-1-9 (paperback)
ISBN 979-8-9936718-2-6 (ebook)
ISBN 979-8-9936718-3-3 (audiobook)

Printed in the United States of America

To everyone who has a Phyllis story

"When our children ask us about who they are,

we respond by giving them stories . . . because

stories–those memories–drive deeper into our

hearts than any abstract proposition.

They give us an identity."

Sarah Irving-Stonebreaker,
Priests of History

"We must absorb history . . . to know

who we are and how we should act."

Leszek Kolakowski

CONTENTS

1

MEETING

Phyllis Jeanne Strong and I are high the first time we meet—at 9,100 feet above sea level to be exact. It is Thursday, August 9, 1973.

I had my last final at the University of Denver the day before, on August 8. I will be graduating August 10 on the lawn in front of the towering, stately Mary Reed Hall which has been the landmark building on campus for decades. The reason for the summer commencement is that I had realized I could graduate in three years if I took a summer term to finish the courses I needed.

But this day between my last final and my graduation is free. A college buddy, Mike Clark, wants to see some people at Bear Trap Ranch (the Rocky Mountain campground run by InterVarsity Christian Fellowship). We had both been in the InterVarsity chapter at DU, and I was to start my new job with InterVarsity as campus staff in St. Louis the following week. Mike asks if I would like to come along for the ride. I say sure.

We drive for an hour due south from Denver on I-25 and then wind our way west up the Old Stage Road for about thirty minutes. The road twists as it rises three thousand feet above Colorado Springs. It's a heart-stopping nine-mile drive for some. Since the dirt road is at times only one lane wide, cars often must stop to let oncoming vehicles pass. The curves can be so sharp that drivers can't see around the turns. They need to honk their horns as they approach each blind curve to alert potential oncoming traffic.

The excitement of the drive is enhanced because no guardrails separate drivers from drops of several hundred feet into the otherwise picturesque mountain valleys. The only thing protecting cars from a rapid descent is a two-foot-high berm, a ridge of dirt and gravel along the downhill side of the entire road. This is created by road graders which service the road when rain and melting snow create deep ruts and washboard conditions.

The Old Stage Road is even more exciting in winter when it enjoys an abundance of snow and ice. But since this is August, no tire chains are needed, and Mike and I can forego that extra rush of adrenaline. In any case, since we have made the trip many times before, the two of us simply enjoy the scenery and the conversation.

Over the previous three years I had been to Bear Trap nine or ten times. That's where InterVarsity held its fall and spring weekend conferences for students in Colorado, Wyoming, and New Mexico. At each conference I learned more about Bible study, about prayer, about reasons for faith, about leading small groups, about being a disciple.

Also in the summer of 1971, after my freshman year, I attended InterVarsity's month-long leadership training program at Bear Trap with about seventy other students from around the country. Several of these later joined InterVarsity staff, became missionaries, or pastored churches. Some married each other.

One of the students who eventually became a pastor in New York was a couple of years older than me. He came from Lehigh Valley, Pennsylvania, and attended Bucknell University. Most students were from the central part of the country, so I asked him how he ended up coming all the way to Colorado when InterVarsity had other programs much closer to his home. He said it just fit his schedule better. Decades later he would write a number of best-selling books. His name was Tim Keller.

As Mike and I enter Bear Trap, we see the few dozen buildings, mostly small log cabins, which make up the ranch. These are situated in a small, narrow valley surrounded by peaks that rise one, two, or three thousand feet above the valley it sits in. I have climbed Sugarloaf, Devil's Slide, and Mt. Vigil many times. Nothing is flat in Bear Trap. People joke that you always have to walk uphill anywhere you go. It certainly feels that way since the thin air in the high altitude makes breathing difficult for those who aren't acclimated.

After Mike and I park and get out of the car, I am struck again by the sharp, cool air laced with the intense scent of Ponderosa Pine, Lodgepole Pine, and Spruce-Fir that populate Pike National Forest. It is at once fresh and pungent, penetrating everything. I always associate that smell with this place.

While Mike has his meetings, I am free to wander and chat with others. I bump into a friend who says I should meet Phyllis Strong because the two of us will be working together for InterVarsity in St. Louis. Phyllis was already part of Nurses Christian Fellowship, the nurses division of InterVarsity, and was staffing the camp then in progress at Bear Trap.

In a few minutes we are introduced to each other while standing with several people outside in a group between the dining hall and a large bell which sits up on two pairs of hefty, roughhewn poles. The sun shines brightly as it usually does at midday until the late afternoon clouds and rain roll in from the west like clockwork over the Rockies.

Phyllis and I chat for perhaps five minutes. I notice her wide smile and of course her red hair. She seems tall but it is hard to tell exactly because, it being Bear Trap, everything is on a slant, and I am on the downhill side of the conversation. I can tell she is older too, at least older than I am. I am just twenty-one and anyone over thirty seems very old. Later I learn she is twenty-nine.

Sometimes people talk about love at first sight, of an immediate connection, of sparks flying when they first meet someone. While I enjoy that first encounter, I have no dramatic reaction. And Phyllis doesn't either. Maybe that is because our first meeting is so brief. Maybe it is the age gap. Maybe it's just that sometimes there is no immediate flash of fire between two people.

As I step away, I don't know that Phyllis and I will return together to Bear Trap many times—with four children in tow! I would likely have run scared if someone had told me.

I have no inkling of the massive impact this woman will have on my life over the next five decades. I don't know the joy and fun she will bring to this guy who in college was nicknamed "the melancholy Frenchman." I don't realize how she will encourage my love for laughter. As someone who takes himself too seriously, I certainly don't know that she will teach me how healthy (and funny) it is to laugh at yourself.

I have no idea that she will nurture in this introvert a habit for hospitality and for creating welcoming spaces for people. I would never have guessed how much I, who am so task-oriented, will learn from this consummate people-person. I am unaware of how much wisdom and compassion she has to teach a book-smart person like me.

I am clueless that Phyllis will show me ways to love others with the love of Jesus in a way that they will find so appealing. Nor do I know how she will teach me the importance of forgiving, of reconciling, of having adventures, and of taking risks.

I don't know that this is the most alive person I will ever meet.

2

BEGINNING

Right after graduation from the University of Denver, I packed up my books and belongings, and returned to Minneapolis. My parents had not come to graduation. My dad was well into his seventies at that point, and a thousand-mile trip for a one-day event was just not their style. When I got home, they pitched in to help me get a car—a new, light green, no-frills Chevy Nova. I was lucky it had a radio.

They weren't thrilled with the idea of my working for InterVarsity—because as a Catholic my mom wasn't sure about this Protestant (I called it "interdenominational") organization, and because for my dad ministry wasn't a "real" job. But they helped anyway.[1]

Just a few days later, early in the morning, I drove away from the only home I'd ever known. I had a sense of excitement about going out on my own and starting a new adventure. But I remember my parents standing together a bit forlornly on the porch watching me go. I sensed a certain sadness in them, perhaps because of their doubts about my job. Only years later did I realize another reason. Their last child was leaving home.

I drove to St. Louis where I was to work primarily with the InterVarsity chapters at Washington University (Wash U.) and across the river at Southern Illinois University Edwardsville. I spent the week getting settled. I stayed a few days with my sister, Mary, her husband Kirby, and their nine-month-old daughter, Kim, in their small house in Jennings, a community tucked between St. Louis and Ferguson.

My first official day on the job was Wednesday, August 15, 1973. I met with my supervisor, Paul Woodard, the area director for Missouri, Kansas, and Nebraska. He had interviewed me (yes, at Bear Trap Ranch) back in June. After hiring me, he and his wife Kathy helped me find a place to live. It was a large, old brick house just north of Forest Park (site of the 1904 St. Louis World's Fair). The three other guys renting it were current or former students in the chapter at Wash U.

My major orientation was at the end of the month, a four-day area team meeting held in Lincoln, Nebraska. George and Barbara Stulac, who were staffing the InterVarsity chapter there, hosted the group of ten or twelve of us. And of course, Phyllis was there. Though as part of Nurses Christian Fellowship she technically didn't belong to the campus division, Paul had welcomed her and an NCF intern to the team.

Phyllis was the life of the party. She loved games and made sure we played a board game version of Royal Rummy, which I later learned was a staff-team tradition. It was cut-throat competition in the most fun way possible. She laughed and laughed when, in the middle of the game, George said with mock melancholy, "I've never won a game of Royal Rummy in my life, you know." But he won that night.

During one of our work meetings, we were discussing some plan or issue when Phyllis voiced a different viewpoint from what others had expressed. "And," she said, "I do so hesitantly because I respect you all so much."

A bit later in the discussion I explained why I agreed with her, adding. "And, Phyllis, I'm sure you're glad to hear that from someone you respect so much." The group howled in laughter, just the effect I was looking for since clearly she barely knew me and couldn't have formed much of an impression one way or another.

But I was pleased with her half-embarrassed enjoyment at the joke.

Afterward I wrote my first weekly report for Paul. In it I summarized my experience at the staff meeting and gave one-sentence sketches of several who were there, including this: "Phyllis is a real looney-bin. I'm very glad she's in St. Louis. She does the group good."[2] I suppose I could claim to have a sixth sense for first impressions. The truth is that Phyllis was just so transparent, so open, and so without guile that everyone could see what a joyful free spirit she was.

Just a few weeks later, Phyllis taught me for the first time. The topic was caring for people in times of trouble, sickness, grief, and death.

In October and November Phyllis led a course at Memorial Presbyterian Church in St. Louis called Love That Heals which met one evening a week for six weeks. The material was developed by Bonnie Miller and other Nurses Christian Fellowship staff in the context of the medical world where people are frequently dealing with significant, sometimes critical, physical needs. What every nurse knows is that other deep issues often arise at such times. The seminar was designed, however, for anyone who wanted to learn how to care better for people emotionally, spiritually, and physically. (This course became the core of the eight guides in the Caring People Bible Study series that Phyllis developed in the early 1990s for InterVarsity Press.)

I attended each of the sessions and tried to do the homework as best I could. But most of it was outside my comfort zone. Yet the lessons I learned during that seminar (and of course reinforced by Phyllis over the years) stuck with me. "Visiting people in the hospital can be hard," she said. "But even for someone in a coma or someone who is not responsive, their hearing is considered the last sense to go. You can still talk to them."

We were to visit people in assisted living communities. "It's not hard talking to old people. They love to tell their stories from the past. Just ask them about growing up." And Phyllis told us, "Everyone wants to talk about themselves. They will feel cared for if you just listen. All you have to do is ask questions."

The simplicity of this advice rang true. I was so much in my head in those days (as I probably still am), that connecting with people on a personal level was hard. I liked debating ideas and sharing things I was learning. To give people, in a non-threatening way, the opportunity to talk about themselves was unexplored territory for me, strange and intimidating. Phyllis made it all seem so natural in her presentation and in her example.

By that time we had already developed a pattern of cheerful banter. So about ten minutes before the first gathering of about thirty people, I walked up to the front to ask how she felt. "Oh, I guess I'm a bit nervous," she said.

"Well," I responded with a twinkle clearly glimmering in my eye, "you have every reason to be." She was both shocked and delighted. That became a catchphrase in our relationship that always brought smiles to us.

The six weeks were eye-opening for me. I had little experience and less natural ability in showing empathy. The assignments each week to put what we were learning into practice felt as appealing as chewing charcoal. In truth, I was the one who was nervous.

John and Patti Strong also attended. John, Phyllis's cousin, was like a brother to her since the two of them had grown up near each other. She instantly considered Patti a sister. After that first evening of the seminar, Patti said to Phyllis, "I saw you and Andy joking before things got started. What's going on between you two?"

Suddenly and unexpectedly, tears began welling in Phyllis's eyes. "Oh," she said, "he'd never give me a second look." It was true that nothing was going on between us, but Patti knew Phyllis well enough to sense something in her before Phyllis even did in herself.

⁌ ⁌ ⁌

The next month the two of us attended the InterVarsity Missions Convention at Champaign-Urbana, Illinois, held December 27-31, 1973. About 15,000 students, staff, and missionaries descended on the campus of the University of Illinois for the event which was held there every three years.

I had spent Christmas in Minneapolis with my folks and flew to O'Hare the morning of December 26. Several Greyhound-type buses were chartered to take staff on the two-and-a-half-hour ride to the campus. Shortly after lunch we loaded up and got going.

Soon snow started falling. About an hour into the trip, I could see from my vantage point on the right-hand window seat near the middle of the bus that a car a few hundred feet in front of us was spinning out of control. I heard the bus driver immediately downshift as he began to brake. But we were sliding with the back of the bus heading for the out-of-control car, which was going toward the grassy median. On impact the bus rebounded the other way. It twisted and immediately all the windows in the bus exploded. People were flying through the air and the bus landed on its left side in the grass just off the shoulder of the road. There was an eerie moment of silence before people began to pick themselves up. The bus driver began lifting people up to the door, which was now facing skyward.

I could hardly take in that two passengers were killed immediately, one of whom was Susan McClure, who had been sitting in the window seat across the aisle from me. A few others were injured and taken to hospitals. All of us were stunned. Arrangements were made later that day to take us to a hotel in Champaign. I called my parents to let them know I was uninjured, in case the story made the news in Minnesota. But it hadn't.

The next day most of the others on the bus and I plunged into helping get thousands of students registered, settled in, and oriented to the week ahead. I suppose the idea was that for the moment it was better for us, if we were able, to be busy rather than dwell on the tragedy.

During the week I bumped into Phyllis, which was remarkable given the vast size of the conference. She was deeply concerned about me and so glad that I was all right.

The week immediately following the Urbana convention, InterVarsity held another conference in town for its three or four hundred staff. The idea was to save travel money since we were all together anyway. But we were so exhausted, I'm not sure how much it benefited us.

January 2 was Phyllis's birthday. I had heard from other members of our team that she was not feeling great about this particular birthday, however. She was turning thirty. Perhaps being unmarried added to her discomfort. But I had already gotten a birthday card and a Baskin-Robbins gift certificate for her. So I found her in the crowd and quickly and quietly gave the envelope to her. "I know you're not thrilled about your birthday, but I already had this for you and wanted to give it to you," I said. She smiled broadly, of course, hugged me, and said she was happy to get it.

A few weeks after we got back to St. Louis, I called to say I wanted to get together for a meal with each of the InterVarsity staff in town, making clear in a lighthearted way that this was just to get to know everyone better. We found a day that fit our calendars—which ironically turned out to be Valentine's Day, 1974. We met at a Chinese restaurant just ten minutes from my house and in University City where she lived.

Probably it was there that I first heard the outline of her life.

3

BECOMING

What had been the shape of Phyllis Strong's life up to the time we had our Valentine's not-a-date lunch in 1974?

Thirty years earlier, the whole St. Louis area, like the rest of the country, was preoccupied with the progress of World War II. With 450,000 Missouri residents serving during the war, everyone knew someone in the military.[1] On January 2, 1944, Allied troops under the command of General Douglas McArthur landed at Saidor in Papua New Guinea, a major steppingstone in a new offensive against the Japanese. At that same time General Dwight Eisenhower was leading preparations for the D-Day invasion in Europe still five-months away. President Franklin Roosevelt, entering his twelfth year in office, was considering whether to run for an unprecedented fourth term.

The city was also preoccupied with the St. Louis Cardinals baseball team. In 1942 they won the World Series over the New York Yankees behind their young new star, Stan "The Man" Musial. Though they lost the 1943 Series to those same Yankees, Musial had had a banner year, leading the majors with a .357 batting average and being named the National League's MVP. St. Louis was hopeful 1944 would be another strong year.

Gabe and Louise Strong were also hopeful about what the year would bring when their second daughter, Phyllis Jeanne, was born on Sunday, January 2, 1944, at 10:40 a.m. at Christian Welfare Hospital in East St. Louis, Illinois. Her sister Judy was five years older, with Diane following two years after Phyllis.

At the time of our lunch, both sisters were married and had three children each. Phyllis loved being an aunt to those kids. Judy and Ward Billingsley lived west of St. Louis, so she was able to see Diane, David, and Donna regularly (Dan coming later). Diane lived in Kalamazoo, Michigan, with her husband, Dick O'Day, and their children, Scott, Chris, and Kim (Keri coming later).

Gabe and Louise lived in Fairview Heights, Illinois, about a half hour east from Phyllis's apartment in University City, Missouri. The two of them had moved there after living for many years in East St. Louis, which, as Phyllis often liked to say, was "that All-American City [having been given that honor in 1959!] where all the gangsters from Chicago migrated to."

All three girls had gone to East St. Louis Senior High. When Judy graduated in 1956, the student body was about ninety percent White and ten percent Black. When Phyllis finished in 1962 it was about two-thirds and one-third. When Diane graduated just two years later, the numbers were about even with the trend continuing at a rapid pace.[2]

As had happened in Chicago and other parts of the country, in the 1950s and 1960s East St. Louis realtors had conspired with lenders in a discriminating practice known as redlining. Realtors mapped out who would live where, determined by race and ethnicity. Lenders helped enforce this by denying loans to minorities who wanted to move into White areas. White and Black people were both hurt financially by this process. Whites often sold their homes at a loss as the rush to get out of a growing Black area gained momentum. Blacks were hurt because of predatory lending practices and an inability to move where they wanted.

The only people who weren't hurt were the realtors and lenders. Realtors made money regardless of who bought or sold a house, and the accelerated pace of houses changing hands during the transition period meant more commissions. Lenders gained for similar reasons.

Gabe and Louise moved out in 1964, either as part of this process or so Louise could be closer to Scott Air Force base where she worked, or both. In any case, the two of them thought it would be great fun to move without telling their youngest daughter, Diane, who was away at college. They didn't sell the Baugh Avenue house but rented it. They could just imagine Diane's shock in coming home to find another family living there. But the plan never came off.

While in Texas Diane had been trying to call her folks many times, but they never answered. In tears she called her sister Judy who explained everything.

Gabe Strong and Louise Sanders had both grown up in and around Shawneetown, Illinois, along the Ohio River, about 150 miles southeast of St. Louis. While Shawneetown is small and nearly forgotten, established in 1800, it was one of the oldest White settlements in Illinois, and home to the state's first bank and second newspaper.[3] Lewis and Clark even visited it in 1803 on their way to Fort Massac.[4]

Shawneetown

Shawneetown was hit by three major floods: in 1898, 1913, and 1937. The last devastated the whole Ohio River Valley from Pittsburgh to Cairo, Illinois, leaving a million people homeless. In Shawneetown, only twenty of four hundred homes remained habitable. As a result, in 1938 the state and federal governments began to move the whole town inland three miles to what is now called Shawneetown. A small community of a few hundred remains at the original site, which is now called Old Shawneetown.[5]

References here to Shawneetown before 1937, then, mean the original community right on the Ohio River. Otherwise, references to Shawneetown after 1937 are to the new inland site. Old Shawneetown refers to the small remnant on the Ohio after 1937.

The Overlooked Boy

Gabriel Bourland Strong was born October 26, 1909, the ninth of eleven children. His father, John Strong, and mother, Dorothy (nee Crabtree), were married on September 6, 1893, in Gallatin, Illinois.

Gabe lived in Junction (five miles from Shawneetown) for some of his early years. When his mother knew she was dying, she asked her unmarried sister, Mary "Barlow" Crabtree, to care for her young sons, Gabe and Harrison. Barlow agreed. Gabe was nine years old when his mother died at age forty-seven. Years later, Gabe's older sister Anita (Aunt Neat) told Phyllis with tears in her eyes, "I don't know how Gabe has turned out to be the man that he is." As Phyllis wrote:

> When the time came for Barlow to take over, everyone knew who her favorite was. In the dead of winter she sent Harrison out with warm coat, hat, scarf, mittens. Gabe wore a light jacket that flapped open. The supply of candy that Barlow gave to Harrison was huge. Gabe had none. When Harrison and [Gabe] visited Barlow as adults, she greeted Harrison enthusiastically and for all practical purposes ignored Gabe.
>
> As I listened to Aunt Neat, I too looked at Gabe, my dad, and thanked God for the man he turned out to be in spite of being an orphan, uneducated, and raised under the dark cloud of blatant favoritism.[6]

Though some of Gabe's gruff nature may have come from such a difficult upbringing, he was largely able to shake off the ongoing ill treatment from Barlow and show his cheerful, gregarious demeanor.

Over the years he held various jobs including being a police officer, but he eventually settled in as a successful, long-time Electrolux Vacuum Cleaner salesman. "I don't make a lot of money," he would joke, "but I do win a lot of prizes." These included dozens of clocks that infested the walls of Gabe's and Louise's home, clocks that were never quite synchronized. As a result, it took about three minutes from the time the first one chimed the hour till the last one finished.

Gabe loved making sales and charming his customers. As part of his in-home sales pitch, he would (to the shock of the homeowner) spread on the carpet some dirt he had brought with him in a paper bag. He would then proceed to thoroughly vacuum the carpet with the customer's own vacuum. After that he re-vacuumed the same area with an Electrolux, showing by means of a paper filter that his machine sucked up dirt the customer's vacuum had missed. That impressed many and sealed the deal.

Once Gabe told me with a sly smile that any vacuum would pick up more dirt after a first vacuuming because you can never get everything out of a carpet. Nonetheless, he was genuinely and thoroughly convinced of the superior quality of Electroluxes.

On one occasion Phyllis had several high school friends over after church. As they sat around eating pizza, one buddy standing in the kitchen and knowing Gabe's enthusiastic opinions, delighted in baiting him by asking, "Mr. Strong, now tell me. Aren't Kirby Vacuums just as good as Electroluxes?" That launched Gabe into a half-hour lecture that everyone at the table had to endure—except for the friend who had asked; he managed to saunter away with a half-smile on his face.

Gabe was a tall, gangly fellow even in his adult years. He could show a brusque exterior (even intimidating some of his grandchildren), but Phyllis and her sisters knew him to be soft inside.

The Judge's Daughter

Phyllis's mom, Anna Louise Sanders, was born on January 20, 1919, in Ridgway, about thirteen miles from Shawneetown. The family's roots in Gallatin County in southern Illinois go back to Louise's great-grandfather, James Sanders, who moved there after serving in the U.S. military during the War of 1812. (James's father had come to the United States before the Revolutionary War, settling in North Carolina.)[7]

James's son Eli, born on Christmas day 1818, continued farming in Gallatin County as his father had done. He and his wife, Nancy Jane McGill, were churchgoing people known for their hospitality and service to many in need in their community. Eli and Nancy also faced the hard reality of living in a time and place with limited medical care and limited knowledge of germs and viruses, for though they had twelve children, only seven survived to adulthood.

One of their sons, Francis N. Sanders, and his wife, Jemima McGee, built a log cabin and began by cultivating just six acres. Eventually that grew to one hundred and forty. They, like Francis's parents, were people of the earth who had eleven children with nine surviving, one of whom was Louise's father, William Solon Sanders (1872–1966).

Solon married Sara "Sadie" Agnes Morgan (1884–1947) and earned a degree from Illinois State in Normal, Illinois, before getting his law degree in St. Louis. He was elected county judge back home in Gallatin County for three terms from 1916 to 1928.

Once during Prohibition, Judge Sanders slapped a big fine on a man caught bootlegging. Since the man couldn't pay the fine, he was thrown in jail. A couple of days later, the man's wife and children came begging for his freedom. Though Judge Sanders had a reputation as being "tougher than a pine knot," he paid the man's fine himself and let him go.

Louise was the fifth of Solon and Sadie's seven children with one being still-born. She was especially partial to her little brother Eugene (Gene). One day she showed her affection by pulling her infant brother off the middle of their mom's bed, taking him and rocking him back to sleep in her own little rocking chair, nearly giving their mom a heart attack when she found them.

Louise and Gene had a mostly loving but often teasing relationship. He delighted in chasing his big sister around the house waving a dead mouse at her. Some years later she showed her affection by locking him in the family outhouse. This may have been due to Gene giving grief to Louise's boyfriends, but in any case, he no doubt deserved it. The only problem was that Louise promptly forgot he was in there! When Gene discovered his predicament, he began yelling, but no one heard him. The only way he could get out was to break the glass window. Louise was even happier because Gene got in trouble for breaking the window while she got off scot-free.

The two of them encountered a true cast of characters growing up in Shawneetown. As Louise wrote Gene on the occasion of his twenty-fifth wedding anniversary in 1971:

Did you ever give any thought to the unique people we were privileged to know in Shawneetown—some of very humble background, like Peg-leg and his son "Wa-Wa"; some very distinguished like Judge Marsh Wiseheart. Remember his eloquent speech which he made every chance he got? I never did learn that dern "Gettysburg Address" Sarah Hannah tried to make me say letter perfect. I kept getting it mixed up with Judge Wisehearts's "from the sunny coasts of Maine." Then there were Soup Frailey, Stutz Calvard, and Ed Stanley—poor boys—they kept walking up over the north levee and couldn't figure out how they got there.

Mary Demon, the old crab—couldn't stand a kid's ball in her yard or a coaster wagon with steel rims on the wheels instead of rubber tires. She had some good traits though—she could tongue-lash Laurie Rowan pretty good. John Rawson, deaf as a dead man, and a hump on his back. Gosh! I wish I hadn't laughed at him. Do you suppose I'll eventually grow a hump, too?

Cratzy Peoples sure was an interesting guy to talk to—or was it listen to? Do you remember Senator Bartley? And his player piano? And his, "Oh, Judge, the house is on fire" at two o'clock in the morning. If he'd called a few minutes earlier I might *not* have wet my bed, but he didn't and I did—every night—and the house was not on fire, not once. Well, at least the senator never woke up over the north levee like Stutz and Soup and Ed—no sir—they were the *common* town drunks. How about Mamie and poor old Tommy Spear? By gosh I'll wager he never started *that* argument again.

Do you realize there were only about 1200 people in our town and so far I've hardly got out of our block. Quaint? Unique? Different??? Ahhh—yes, Eugene, our town was indeed different.

Because Judge Sanders was also a justice of the peace, many weddings were held in the family living room, with Louise as witness. Before each ceremony he would give the couple a brief counseling session. Afterward, he'd always turn to the groom and say, "I officially appoint you head of the house." Then he'd turn to the bride, hand her the marriage certificate, and say, "Now honey, you're the neck that turns the head. If he ever runs off and leaves you, you tell me and we'll go get him."

Phyllis picked up this line from the many times her mom told the story. With a huge smile, she would tell anyone who happened to be around, "Andy may be the head of the house, but I'm the neck that turns the head."

Judge Sanders lost his bid for a fourth term, just as the Great Depression was starting. He had trouble finding work but was finally able to get a job as janitor at the county courthouse—the very building where he had presided as judge for twelve years.

During the Depression Louise, at just twelve years old, had to pitch in to help the family. She began by sweeping, mopping, and doing dishes at Ruby's Barbeque, bringing in three dollars a week for the family. She reluctantly left home at age fifteen to make some money by cooking, cleaning, and serving in the homes of the St. Louis elite. To get the job, she had to lie (totally contrary to her upbringing), saying she was eighteen.

Gabe and Louise

Louise began spending time with Gabe after the devastating Shawneetown flood of 1937. They had known of each other beforehand. But when they met again as adults (when Gabe was twenty-eight and Louise was eighteen), Gabe got up from his chair—and kept going up and up and up. Louise at 5'7" was struck by the lanky 6'5" man she now encountered. All of Gabe's family were tall, with brothers ranging from 6'4" to 6'6". (Ward Billingsley, himself of modest height, who married Gabe and Louise's oldest daughter, Judy, in 1960, referred to Strong family reunions as "walking in the land of the giants.")

Gabe and Louise were married in the home of Louise's parents on January 16, 1938, and soon moved to East St. Louis. Judy was born nine months and five days later on October 21. That was a close one!

Phyllis followed five years later and Diane two years after that. Gabe's and Louise's marriage was, however, filled with contention. Both were strong personalities, and when the girls were young, Louise pushed Gabe's buttons just a bit too often.

Gabe was sitting at the table eating a dish of ice cream and reading the newspaper. Louise thought it would be humorous to give the paper a flip while he was reading it. "You do that again and you'll get a dish of ice cream in your face," Gabe warned.

That was just the incentive Louise needed to flip the newspaper one more time. Gabe took aim with his ice cream, and he didn't miss. Louise walked out of the room furious. Soon she told Judy (who as the oldest could have some understanding of what was going on) the sad news that the four of them would be leaving their Daddy and going to Shawneetown to live with their granddad, Judge Sanders.

Louise wrote to her father about coming to live with them, with explicit instructions not to tell her older brother Frank. Frank was a Presbyterian pastor about fifteen miles north of Shawneetown in

Cottonwood, Illinois, where he founded a youth camp under the auspices of the Cumberland Presbyterian Church.

Years before, Frank had been an alcoholic who came home drunk every night. As a result, the family had given up on him. In 1940, as Phyllis later wrote, "One evening as he walked home with uncertain steps, swaying because of the alcohol in his body, the Holy Spirit came upon him. He knelt, almost falling to his knees, drunk. Miraculously he gave his life to Jesus and stood up sober."[8] He never drank again and decided to give his life to helping young people so they would avoid the misery of his first thirty-five years. He was ordained two years later in 1942.

When Judge Sanders got Louise's letter, not one for being told what to do by a daughter who was planning to leave her husband, he immediately contacted Frank. Within days Gabe and Louise were stunned to find Frank and his wife, Nova, on their doorstep at 1907 Baugh Avenue in East St. Louis. Louise had fond memories of riding the ferry boat Frank operated during the Depression on (what was then) the clear and beautiful Ohio River. But in this circumstance, she was not sure she was glad to see him at all.

The two couples sequestered themselves in the bedroom, away from the three girls, for a long time. When they finally emerged, Gabe had said yes to Christ and yes to staying in the marriage. Louise was not as sure. But later that day, while standing in their kitchen, Louise also gave her life to Christ. She told the girls they would not be leaving their dad.

A few days later Judy wrote her Uncle Frank a thank-you note for all he did for her mom and dad. Frank responded:

Dearest Judy Lou:

Received your very sweet letter today, and I was so happy to have it from you. I wouldn't take any amount of money for it; and am putting it with my other prized keepsakes. And, Honey, I'm just as happy as you are that your Daddy and Mother are going to let God have His Way with their lives. I think they've both wanted to do that for a long time, for all of us have prayed that they would. But as you know, they're both pretty stubborn, and it took even God a long time to bring them to their knees before Him. And I'm sure that God heard your prayers, too, and that perhaps He hurried things up a bit because of your prayers. As for thanking me, Honey, Uncle Frank is just glad he was the one God used in talking with them, and helping them to make the surrender to Him.

Uncle Frank was a hero throughout Phyllis's life (as he was for Judy and Diane), and this often-retold episode was a landmark event for her and the whole family that shaped all that was to come—for generations. Phyllis often said, "God saved my parents, and he saved their marriage." Gabe and Louise realized they had no idea how to be Christian parents. "They decided they had to raise us on their knees," Phyllis said. As a child she often saw the two of them praying regularly in just that way for God's guidance and grace in their lives.

Often Phyllis also looked back with gratitude to her mom's mother, Sadie, a schoolteacher whose fragile health confined her to bed the last year and a half of her life. "For years [my grandmother] had prayed that her children would come to know Jesus," Phyllis wrote. On her deathbed she begged Gene (who was called home from the military to see his dying mother) and Louise to tell her that she would see them again in heaven. But neither could do it. "My mom was too honest of a woman and knew that she would not. She could not comfort her mother with those words."

Although Louise adored her mother, Louise rejected the Lord her mother adored. Grandmother Sadie died in 1947, just a couple years before the episode with Uncle Frank, without seeing her prayers answered. Phyllis, nonetheless, saw the impact of multiple generations in her life. "My spiritual journey," she wrote, "was not only profoundly influenced by my parents but by my grandmother, who prayed fervently."9

Though Gabe and Louise were different people after that critical day with Frank and Nova, their old patterns of relating to each other still popped up from time to time. Louise had a serious hearing loss from the age of nineteen and used strong hearing aids throughout her life. That may have contributed some to the volume of Gabe's conversations with her.

Once during an argument, Louise just sat there calmly taking Gabe's harangue over some issue. When Gabe was done letting her have it, she said, "You know that I'm hard of hearing, and I didn't catch anything you just said." After a moment of stunned silence and looking at his wife's cute grin, Gabe burst out laughing and forgot what he had been so upset about.

Growing

The family began attending St. Paul's Methodist Church in East St. Louis pastored by Reverend Farrell Jenkins. After a few years they switched to Edgemont Bible Church in East St. Louis (now located in Fairview Heights), which was a natural choice since Gabe's brother, Miller, and Miller's family were members there.

Phyllis remembered how even when they were scraping by financially, her parents were conscientious about sacrificing to tithe their income to the church and other ministries. And financial strains were real. When Judy was old enough to babysit, some of the money went to buy groceries for the family.

The little store on the corner allowed them to buy on credit, but at one point it got to be close to $100, a huge sum in those days. Louise laid down a mandate. "No more groceries until that bill is paid." To make do, they ate oatmeal three times a day. Some years later when finances were more secure and oatmeal was again on the table, one of the girls responded in jest, "Are we poor again?" As it turned out, though, Diane couldn't stand oatmeal the rest of her life.

Because they had so little, Gabe tried to earn a bit of extra cash by raising rabbits for sale. Once when Phyllis was quite young, she answered the phone. Afterward her mom asked her who it was.

Phyllis, indignant and in full Elmer Fudd mode, said, "It wath a wong number. The lady asked if it wath the place that had chickens, and I told her, no, it ith the place that has wabbits, and she hung up on me!"

The house on Baugh Avenue was just down the street a few houses from a corn feed mill. Little Phyllis got to know the guys working there because even at an early age she regularly practiced her extrovert's magic to charm chewing gum from them.

Diane was not so charmed by her sister's sleeping habits. They shared a bed when they were young, and Phyllis was often an active sleeper. One time she had spread out so much on the bed that Diane only had one corner left to herself. As she sat there groggily trying to figure out what to do about her sound-asleep sister, Phyllis flipped one more time and knocked Diane onto the floor. Years later Phyllis would say of the two of them, "My parents used to call us Moose and Mouse." Sheepishly she would add, "Guess who was Moose?"

Doctrinal disputes were not unknown on the block. At a tender age Phyllis learned an important lesson in interfaith discord, a lesson that stuck with her and had an impact even into adulthood.

> I remember an argument between the Catholic and Protestant kids in the neighborhood about who would go to heaven. The conflict heated to a degree only possible when six-year-old theologians do battle. I feared not only the rapidly approaching impasse but began to wonder if any of us would come out of this one alive! The day was saved by one Catholic friend who announced that no matter who is right and wrong, she was sure Jesus would not want us to fight about it. We all agreed and went back to play in the sandbox.[10]

The family's limited finances also meant getting a television was out of the question. The three sisters found ways to play and have fun with each other, neighbors, and cousins without the "boob tube" to entertain them. But when Phyllis was about ten someone took mercy on them and had a small, black and white TV delivered anonymously. Louise thought Uncle Charlie had sent it, but they didn't know for sure.

They were soon watching the popular variety shows of the day hosted by such stars as Dinah Shore, Perry Como, and Milton Berle. Westerns were also all the rage. Even though the "Wild West" only lasted twenty years from 1870-1890, it had had a profound impact on the American psyche. Television picked up where the movies of the previous decades had left off. Phyllis loved dressing up as a cowgirl and watching *The Gene Autry Show, Hopalong Cassidy, The Lone Ranger,* and *The Roy Rogers Show.*

Despite their circumstances, Phyllis was especially delighted with one Christmas morning. Though they could not afford a lot of expensive toys, her parents bought a stack of board games. The whole day the family had tremendous fun playing them all.

Phyllis's passion for board games and card games marked her whole life. She may have seemed competitive, but what she really loved was the trash talking and the thrill of taking a big risk to win a game. The next day she would hardly remember if she had won or not.

Even if her parents were now redeemed, Phyllis apparently was not yet entirely sanctified. Once her mom told the three of them to pick up all the toys, clothes, books, and games that were strewn around the house. Judy and Diane got right to it, but Phyllis continued to lie on the couch sucking her thumb.

"Phyllis, why aren't you helping your sisters pick up?" her mom asked.

Phyllis took her thumb out of her mouth long enough to say contentedly, "Judy and Diane are already doing it, Mom."

Louise promptly excused Judy and Diane from pick-up duties, and Phyllis had to do the rest on her own.

Her parents' values and commitments came through in the way they were disciplined. When Diane was five or six, she decided it would be great fun to break some sheets of cork her dad had in the back of the car. When he found the pile, he asked Diane if she had broken them. She told him no. But before she could run away, he asked Phyllis, who promptly ratted out her sister! "I didn't do it. Diane did." (As Diane said cheerfully decades later, "Phyllis had a dark side. Who knew!")

Gabe proceeded to tell Diane that he was not spanking her because of the damage but because she had lied to him. He swatted her once (which according to Diane didn't really hurt that much). But that night when her mom got Diane out of the tub, she called Gabe in and calmly showed him a red mark on Diane's backside—just the size of his hand. He was shocked. He clearly did not have a sense of his own size and strength. He vowed never to lay a hand on any of the girls after that, and he never did.

Their dad, however, continued to emphasize the importance of telling the truth. If it was a missing cookie, a broken flowerpot, or a bent fender, he always required the truth. "Tell me the truth, and you won't get punished," he would say. This made such an impression on Phyllis that it carried through into her own parenting decades later.

How to appropriately punish indiscretions is a quandary every parent faces. One time a sixteen-year-old Phyllis and a boy from youth group ended up running through the yard and into the house throwing clumps of grass at each other. As they careened through the dining room, they accidentally knocked a chair into the curved glass side of her mom's cherished china closet. (This was the same china closet that Phyllis inherited after her mom moved out of the Fairview Heights house, and the same china closet that Phyllis's grandson Gabe crashed into fifty years later, also breaking the curved glass. That episode likewise involved a chase with his brother, Luke, pursuing Gabe through the house.)

Phyllis dreaded having her mom find the damage. After Louise came home, she calmly walked into Phyllis's bedroom and said, "Hand over your driver's license. You're not driving for the next three months." Since Phyllis loved to drive, this was about as painful a punishment as her mother could have devised. Her dad had to take her everywhere now.

About a month later, however, Gabe said to Louise, "Would you quit punishing me and give that girl her license back?" And so it was that Phyllis's sentence was reduced to time served.

Extended family was never far away. Uncle Gene and Aunt Dot lived nearby with their son and daughter, Dale and Daryl Jean. Gene had met Dot in 1946 after he returned from the war, which included service at the Battle of the Bulge. Dot was going to have dinner at a restaurant with friends when Gene happened to enter at the same time. He did a double take, sat down with them, and decided immediately he wanted to get to know Dorothy better. After dating a couple of weeks, he introduced her to his big sister, Louise.

When he did, Dot looked at Louise and after a moment said, "I know you. I'm a nurse at Christian Welfare Hospital and took care of your baby in the nursery when she was born two years ago. Phyllis was my favorite!" Gene and Dot were married just four weeks after that.

The two of them lived in a small apartment that was part of Gabe's and Louise's house on Baugh Avenue. They were close enough, though, that Louise could yell through the heating vent, "Coffee's on," and the two would come over. When their oldest, Dale, was born, three-year-old Diane let everyone know, "He can be the Dale, but I'm still the baby!"

The three girls were especially close to the family of Gabe's brother, Miller, who had three boys, John, Bob, and Gary (later calling himself by his middle name Michael). They were near the same ages as Phyllis and her sisters. The six children spent so much time together growing up that they were like brothers and sisters.

Louise could crack wise with the best of them and often did. She was well known for her humor which could be barbed at times. As I wrote elsewhere:

Louise Strong, my mother-in-law, was a blunt-spoken, hard-smokin' woman from southern Illinois who died several years ago at age ninety-one. If she had an opinion, which she often did, she was not afraid to share it.

She grew up with five siblings, including her sister Bertha. The two of them were regularly at odds. While Bertha helped Louise get a job at the local Air Force base, she was anything but pleased that Louise kept getting promoted while Bertha did not. In turn, Louise didn't look very kindly on Bertha wearing the same color dress as she did to the wedding of Louise's oldest daughter.

Then there was Bertha's ability to make sure those in the family knew the indiscretions of everyone else in the family. Even some time after Bertha died, Louise still held a distinctively acerbic perspective on her sister. "Why, Bertha," she told me, "had a tongue that could sit on the front porch and pick grapes in the back yard!"[11]

When it came to politics, Louise always said she was not a Republican or a Democrat. She was an independent. She simply voted for the best man. "It just turned out," she'd say with a wry smile, "that the best man was always a Republican."

When recounting how the little boy of their neighbor Ethel kept taking the toy truck of Louise's little brother Gene, Louise said, "Every time mom had to retrieve that truck, she gave Ethel a piece of her mind. It's a wonder she had any mind left."

One year Phyllis and I brought our pre-teen children to Fairview Heights for Thanksgiving. Judy and Ward also brought their kids as did Dick and Diane. Everyone pitched in to help feed the crowd. Afterward Louise sat in her favorite chair to take a break and a smoke while others did all the cleanup. Amid the noise and chaos that still swirled around the house, she looked at me deadpan, cigarette in hand, surveying the aftermath of hosting the extended family for the meal, and said, "Well, Andy, the only thing worse than having it is not having it."

A few years later when our son Phil was a young teenager, he asked Louise, "Did you ever wish you had any boys, Granny?"

"Yes," came the immediate reply. "Three times!"

Despite the façade she would sometimes put on, she was clearly a devoted mother, committed to helping meet the needs of the family. To pay for an eye operation for their youngest, Diane, Louise went to work at a department store, W. T. Grant.

In 1957 (with the help of Bertha, as mentioned) she became a key-punch operator at Scott Air Force Base near Belleville, Illinois, about twenty miles southeast of their home. In the early days of computing, processors filled whole rooms. Data was input by cards about twice the size of a smart phone. The information was encoded via a series of holes that were punched into the cards. The computers read these and stored the information on large reels of electronic tape since hard memory was very expensive. Though she lacked a college education, Louise became responsible for organizing the tape library because data was being lost and tapes were inadvertently being copied over.

During the years Phyllis went to Longfellow Elementary School and East St. Louis Senior High, the family continued to attend Edgemont Bible Church which was associated with the Independent Fundamental Churches of America. Later Phyllis would joke that because of the group's separatist ways, IFCA stood for "I Fight Christians Anywhere" or "I Fellowship Completely Alone."

Even as a high school student, Phyllis knew that refusing to associate with other Christian groups was the wrong choice. One year the church held a weekend conference on the theme "Separation from the World." She saw that "separation from the world was not the issue. Rather, the speakers were advocating separation from brothers and sisters in Christ. The list of other Christian groups to avoid was long. They did not cross their doctrinal *t*'s or dot their *i*'s quite like my particular church. So instead of fighting the enemy, they were fighting each other."[12]

Not only would such churches refuse to relate with those who disagreed on various points of doctrine, they practiced "double separation." They wouldn't associate with those who did associate with such groups. So even though they had much in common doctrinally with Billy Graham, they condemned him because he included Catholics in his evangelistic events. As was said, "They disagreed so strongly with him that they wouldn't even eat Graham crackers!"

Nonetheless, the church had a strong influence on her. She heard many missionaries who came to preach at Edgemont when she was growing up. She was particularly struck by one missionary at her church who told of the heartbreak he felt leaving his young daughter behind to go overseas. At the time she wished she could have such spiritual courage and strength. Though working full-time for the gospel was always an aspiration, she later realized that forsaking one's children was not the way to go about it.

When Jim Elliot and four other missionaries were killed in 1956 trying to reach a remote tribe in Ecuador, the Christian community and much of the world were stunned.[13] The missionaries had been attempting first contact by Westerners with the Huaorani people, a violent, fiercely isolated group. The news hit twelve-year-old Phyllis and her home church with force. Martyrdom was not just something the early church faced. The call to sacrificial commitment was a twentieth-century reality.

Phyllis also grew as a leader. Though the church believed that only men should preach or be deacons, Phyllis never felt like she was unable to do whatever she wanted for and with the church. She was active in the high school youth group and was even the president of the group her senior year. She was such a force to be reckoned with at church that a family adage was, "If God and Phyllis can't do it, . . . Phyllis can!"

Five years later the church even gave financial support to Phyllis out of their missionary budget when she started working for Nurses

Christian Fellowship. While fundamentalist churches would often give support to missionary couples, it was not standard practice to support single women in the same way. Perhaps she got a pass because she would be working with nurses who were exclusively women in that era. Sometimes single missionary women were also given more latitude to engage in ministry. Perhaps because she had grown up in the church, they simply knew, loved, and trusted Phyllis for her strong commitments and engaging personality. Perhaps Phyllis was fortunate enough to grow up in an era before women in ministry became such a hot-button issue among conservative Christians. Beginning in the 1980s the complementarian movement arose and limits were more consistently imposed.

During her middle teen years, Phyllis volunteered several summers at Cedine Bible Camp in Tennessee which had been founded in 1946 as a ministry to African American children. She served the children in the cafeteria, in camp games and activities, and by teaching about Jesus through stories and Scripture memorization. Horseback riding, swimming, canoeing, archery, softball, crafts and more kept everyone busy and entertained. The ministry also ran summer Family Bible Conferences and year-round adult retreats.

Phyllis also threw herself into Bible quizzing, an activity Youth for Christ began among high school students in the 1940s. To prepare, quizzers would memorize whole books of the Bible, often in the King James Version. They would then compete in teams at local, regional, and national levels answering various questions.

The books assigned for quizzing in the fall of 1960 were the Gospel of John and two of Paul's letters, First and Second Thessalonians. Over 18,000 students in the United States and Canada participated, culminating with Phyllis's all-star team from St. Louis making it to the national finals. Ron Hutchcraft (who later became a regional Youth For Christ leader, radio host, and founder of his own intercultural ministry to teens) captained the team of five.

After competing head-to-head for two days at Winona Lake, Indiana, with the other finalist from Long Beach, in front of hundreds of people, the score was tied. The emcee of the event began to read the final question which would determine the winner. The first team to answer correctly would win the championship. He began, "From where . . . ?"

Immediately one of Phyllis's teammates, Linda Fletcher, stood up to answer, and the emcee stopped. According to the rules of the competition, if a quizzer stood to answer before the question was completed, he or she had to finish the question accurately *and* give the correct answer to be awarded any points. Otherwise points were deducted.

Silence engulfed the room as both teams and the crowd waited to see what Linda would say. She looked off into the distance and after a moment said, "From where . . . ? From where . . . ?" Finally she went on, "From where shall the Lord return? From heaven." Miraculously, she was right. The team won. They and the crowd exploded in cheers. Phyllis was stunned that her teammate could pluck the correct question, seemingly from nowhere, and answer with such calm assurance.

Phyllis graduated a semester early, in January 1962, as a member of the National Honor Society, but not before she joined the cast of the East St. Louis Senior High theater production of *Shangri-La*. The story, based on the 1933 novel *Lost Horizon* by James Hilton, is about a group of westerners whose plane crashes high in the Himalayas of Tibet. They survive by stumbling into a secluded idyllic paradise centered around a monastery headed by a High Lama.

Phyllis seemed to be typecast as one of the survivors, Miss Roberta Brinklow: a prim, proper, and unmarried missionary who believes Providence has brought her to this valley to preach Christianity. Regardless, Phyllis threw herself into the role. She enthusiastically uttered her favorite line in a high-pitched vibrato: "I've never had a territory of my own, and such a *viiiiirgin* territory, as you might say." The crowd loved it.

While everyone enjoyed Phyllis, her energy, and her humor, she was not as successful in the dating world as her younger sister Diane. "She was dating the neat guys in youth group. I was not. I cringe even now when I think of the way I treated her. The sharp words. The hatefulness."[14] In frustration she accused Diane of "stealing all my boyfriends," which was untrue. Phyllis barely had any boyfriends. But it created a barrier between the two of them that lasted until Phyllis's mom told her that she needed to straighten out her relationship with her sister and ask God to forgive her.

Phyllis began to see that she was unjustified in treating Diane so poorly. She asked her sister for forgiveness. Phyllis learned the destructive power of jealousy, and she learned from Diane what it meant to be readily and fully forgiven.

That was not the only sibling tension in the family. Once Phyllis was so mad at her mom about something that she unfairly lashed out, "You always favor Judy." She wanted to hurt her mom, and she succeeded. As with Diane, Phyllis came back later to ask for forgiveness.

While Phyllis had typical rivalries with her sisters, rambunctiousness was about as rebellious as she got during her teen years. She never went through the dark, moody, or defiant phases so many teenagers do, which may have been one reason she had difficulty understanding her own children at that age.

Becoming Phyllis

Many people, factors, and experiences shaped Phyllis into the person I saw (but did not fully know) who sat across the table from me at that Chinese restaurant in University City on Valentine's Day 1974. The strong personalities of her southern Illinois, small-town parents; living in a racially mixed community and working with Black youth and adults in her summers; the minimal economic resources she grew up with; and her strong Bible-centered upbringing. All those combined with her own highly energetic, open-hearted, fun-loving, extroverted personality that thrived on getting things done—making her a person who welcomed, affirmed, and loved others.

Growing up in just one town and one house until she went to college, with parents who consistently loved her contributed to her remarkably secure personality. That geographic and familial rootedness were key to her emotional and psychological stability. She entered the world and relationships with a solid sense of self, expecting that she would like the people she met and that people would like her. And that consistently proved to be the case.

Where else might that extroverted love for everyone she met have come from? Family lore said it came from Gabe's older sister, Aunt "Polly" Pauline, who had the same effect on people that Phyllis was known for. Polly's outgoing, bubbly, talkative nature made everyone she met feel just a little bit better about themselves. Phyllis also admired the care and wisdom Aunt Polly showed as a schoolteacher to her sometimes-boisterous students.

A tendency toward black-and-white thinking was also part of her makeup that came from those early years. Not a lot of gray was found in her world. Her fundamentalist upbringing meant there was right and wrong, truth and falsehood. The Bible was true. The world was wrong.

Yet that was not how she saw people. Phyllis viewed people through a lens of grace. She was not one to fall prey to a common misunderstanding of Calvin's doctrine of total depravity. Both fundamentalists and others often mistakenly believe this means that every human being is completely sinful and evil. Instead, the doctrine holds that every aspect of a person (mind, heart, soul, strength, will, emotions, and so forth) is at least tainted by (but not totally corrupted by) sin. God puts value and worth and grace in each person's life, which is not eliminated by sin. That's how Phyllis saw everyone she met. Here was another person God made to enjoy and to love.

She treated everyone with care, respect, and intense interest. Phyllis was conscious that there were no perfect people—and no perfectly bad people. "Everybody has a backstory. No one is immune from hard things in life," she would say with compassion. Life happened to everyone, affecting who each of us was. She was so upbeat about life that she may have seemed Pollyannish, but she also knew that sometimes each of us needs to ask for and be granted forgiveness.

She firmly believed no one was beyond redemption. If we believe the gospel, she thought, we have to believe that people can change, that reconciliation is possible. Uncle Frank's own dramatic conversion story from alcoholic to pastor loomed large in how she saw the world. She was energized by the desire to see that kind of change in people, and thus loved talking to people about Jesus and the good news. She never tried to force people to make a decision for Christ. But she delighted in seeking to encourage them along that path.

Like most people, Phyllis was shaped deeply by the family she grew up in. How did this happen? By her experiences, certainly. But also by the stories her family told. In *The Good and Beautiful God*, James Bryan Smith puts it this way, "Our parents impart to us their worldview and their ethical system through stories. Key questions such as Who am I? Why am I here? Am I valuable? are answered early on in the form of narrative."[15]

Decades after she left East St. Louis, Phyllis was studying Smith's book with a group of women she was discipling. After reading Smith's comment on family narratives, she listed in her journal the following stories that formed her:

- My grandmothers praying

- My parents' conversions

- People always welcomed in our house

- "Tell the truth and I won't punish you"

- My dad crying because [of a] bruise on Diane when he spanked her. "I will never touch one of them again." Diane— "It really did not hurt."
- Sex is great in its rightful place
- Jealousy— "You need to get on your knees."
- Not comparing sisters
- I hurt my mom by saying she favored Judy. I knew she did not.[16]

Phyllis was grateful for all these, even the hard lessons, but perhaps most for how God saved their home through Uncle Frank's intervention, and how her parents responded and changed in many ways. Phyllis highly valued relationships, good relationships, healthy relationships. She wrote:

In most areas of life, I think I am pretty realistic. When it comes to conflict among believers, however, I tend to be an idealist. I believe that unity is something that God requires of us. Believers should be able to talk, pray and work through conflict—just the way it was worked through by the church in Jerusalem [as seen in Acts 15].

That desire for unity and reconciliation remained with her throughout her life. Life experiences did eventually temper her perspective. She went on:

However, I am becoming a little more realistic about this. I have experienced several situations in which I felt like I did everything within my power to bring about reconciliation—but failed. The late Kenneth Strachan of the Latin America Mission said, "We all need to live and serve in the constant recognition of our own humanity."[17]

Working through conflict was always a priority for her in our marriage. She often said to me when we heard of other marriages that were on the rocks, "If our marriage ever starts to get in trouble, we are going to get help. No questions asked. We will find someone to help us work it through." Perhaps her urgency was heightened because of the lasting impact of the near divorce her parents experienced.

Despite Gabe's and Louise's dramatic and wonderful about-face and reconciliation, Phyllis also told me often that she never wanted a relationship like her folks had. The carping and bickering that continued to pepper their life together was not a model for her in marriage. Certainly Gabe and Louise loved each other in their way, but Phyllis was looking for a deeper unity and common commitment to ministry in a spouse. She was interested in dating, but she didn't want to settle for good. She was willing to wait for something better. Somehow she eventually thought I was that something better. But as I look back, I am incredibly grateful that I got the best.

EDUCATING

While growing up, Phyllis and her sisters spent plenty of time with Uncle Gene, Aunt Dot, and their kids. She loved her Baptist preacher uncle, but Dot may have had the greater influence. Not only did Dot care for Phyllis in the hospital when she was born (two years before Dot met Uncle Gene), Phyllis was also deeply impressed by Dot's work as a hospital nurse, inspiring Phyllis to pursue a similar career.

As she entered her senior year of high school, Phyllis began to focus on what was next. She soon zeroed in on the three-year program at St. Luke's Hospital School of Nursing on Delmar Boulevard in St. Louis. The school, established in 1889, had a strong reputation as the oldest institution of its kind west of the Mississippi.

The hospital itself opened its doors in 1866 and quickly faced its first challenge—a cholera epidemic that brought in seven thousand patients during its first twelve years. Though the nursing school would close in 1988, just shy of a hundred years old, the hospital still has thirty locations in and around St. Louis.

Nursing students in the early 1960s, like all young women of that era, were not as independent as many high school graduates are now. They would need their fathers to sign if they wanted to open a checking account or rent an apartment.

This generation, however, was becoming aware that the world

was changing. The Civil Rights movement was bubbling, and Elvis Presley was gyrating. Chubby Checkers, Jerry Lee Lewis, the Everly Brothers—all these famous stars were part of the cultural landscape for Phyllis's peers, but not for Phyllis. She had been raised without the influence of popular music or movie theaters, things she didn't really miss much then or later. She managed to have great fun in life without them.

Phyllis and her classmates who arrived at St. Luke's School of Nursing in 1962 were part of the Silent Generation squeezed between two other major groups—the Greatest Generation which survived the Depression and won World War II, and the Boomer generation whose size and sense of entitlement dominated American culture for decades. The irony was that there was almost nothing silent about Phyllis. She brought her outgoing, talkative, joyful personality wherever she went.

When she arrived as a first-year student, a way had been prepared for her and the other seventy-seven women of the incoming class. In the spring and summer beforehand, many members of the Class of 1963 had come together with a commitment to pray for those, like Phyllis, who would be in the Class of 1965. They prayed by name for the new students, that they would feel welcome, would be successful, would grow in their walk with God, and that those who weren't yet believers would become committed followers of Jesus.[1]

When the new students arrived that fall, the upperclassmen helped them move into the dorm and befriended them. They led Bible studies and prayer meetings for their fellow student nurses and told stories of God's work in their lives. Phyllis credited those seniors with having a profound effect on her and her classmates, many of whom became Christians.

Nurses Christian Fellowship (NCF) was active at St. Luke's and other nursing schools in the St. Louis area. The organization emerged in the 1940s to encourage nurses and student nurses across the country in their spiritual lives. In 1948 NCF joined InterVarsity

Christian Fellowship as its nurses' branch due to their similar goals.

The NCF chapter at St. Luke's met twice monthly, with speakers who included professional nurses, missionaries, doctors, and NCF staff. They held Bible studies during the week in the residence halls and sponsored an annual weekend fall conference at Whispering Winds Bible Camp, a hundred miles southwest of St. Louis. One year the speaker there was Jim Nyquist, an InterVarsity regional director Phyllis would cross paths with again ten years later.

Being a cheerful evangelist was natural for Phyllis in nursing school. Her room on the seventh floor of the dorm became the gathering place for talking about faith or just hanging out.

She happily led a weekly Bible study, knocking on dorm-room doors before each meeting to invite her classmates. Sandy Dowdy (Links) was one who declined each time Phyllis came by. She and her roommate, Linda Billingsly (Niedringhaus), quickly figured out what that knock meant on Sunday afternoons. Each week as they heard the door knocking making its way down the hall, they began a ritual of locking their door, turning off the lights, and staying quiet so Phyllis would think they weren't there. For two years Phyllis knocked regularly on the door of room 704, not knowing the truth.

Then one Sunday evening, Sandy and Linda came bursting into Phyllis's room. They had been at a weekend Christian conference for college students. Their faces beamed as they said they had both become Christians. Only after that did the two roommates confess to Phyllis that they had hidden from her every Sunday. Perhaps Phyllis's faithful knocking had something to do with their new life in Christ. And Sandy's daughters and grandchildren would know of Phyllis as the "door knocker," but during those two years, Sandy and Linda had her completely fooled.

Judy, one of many classmates drawn to Phyllis, said, "She was so charismatic, everyone wanted to be with her and near her." After all, Phyllis was often the ringleader of various class shenanigans. Whenever a fellow student had a birthday, Phyllis and her accomplices would grab the honoree and plunge her fully clothed into a bathtub full of water.

Once Phyllis's good friend Jane Hutchinson went home for a weekend and came back to the dorm only to find her bed and bedside table out in the hallway. Phyllis didn't admit to it, but Jane never had a doubt who was behind the prank.

Another time Jane was to give a speech before the Student Council. As she got up to the podium, she looked at a dozen of her classmates in the front row. One of them seemed to be wearing a familiar blazer and another had on a scarf like hers. Was a third wearing one of her blouses? It finally dawned on Jane—all twelve had raided her closet and were wearing her clothes! Already nervous, she was so distracted that the speech did not come off nearly as smoothly as planned, much to the delight of the conspirators.

One time Phyllis invited a half dozen nursing friends to her home for dinner. When her mom was out of the room for a moment, Phyllis said, "When I give you the signal, just mouth words like you're having a conversation but don't say anything aloud." Louise, who was deaf without the use of very powerful hearing aids, returned, and the silent discussions began. She adjusted her hearing aid, she twisted it, and then she started pounding her ear, thinking her hearing aid had gone bad. When everyone burst out laughing, Louise had no trouble hearing that!

Phyllis recounted their best-known escapade years afterward:

In our senior year . . . we dressed in our class colors of red and white, hung streamers of the same colors on our cars and kidnapped the faculty. To their horror we took them to the home of Harry Piper who was director and chief of St. Luke's Hospital.

We sang Christmas carols in his front yard—the faculty's boss! Never mind that it was the middle of August. And he was not known as one who walked through the halls greeting people with a smile. He was the serious type.

But Mr. and Mrs. Piper graciously invited us into their living room for lemonade. And everything was fine until a young son of one of the faculty peed on the Pipers' beautiful new white carpet. But all is well that ends well. After our visit Mr. Piper smiled and waved whenever he passed any of us in the hall. He enjoyed our visit.[2]

Phyllis likely had a hand in other capers. Once some students managed to tie up Miss Bradshaw, the school's number two administrator, in her desk chair, roll her onto the elevator, punch the buttons for all seven floors, and then left her alone so everyone would see her predicament as the doors opened one-by-one on each floor. The students loved Miss Bradshaw and admired her as a good and demanding teacher. Apparently, they thought this would be the best way to show their affection.

Their second year, the students managed to write a long Christmas message to Mrs. Sherk, the director of nursing education, on a roll of toilet paper. They had great fun watching her unravel the entire roll to find out what was on their minds. Another roll was signed for her by all the students at graduation, a memento she kept for years from one of the most memorable classes in Mrs. Sherk's whole career.

Besides being part of the student council her first year, Phyllis also played on the basketball team which won the league championship her second year. She often joked that she went to nursing school on a basketball scholarship.

Humor was also part of the spiritual influence she offered. Linda Sauer (Floyd) thought Phyllis was a joy, but not always. Once Linda told Phyllis she wanted God to give her patience right away and was annoyed when Phyllis told her she couldn't have patience just by asking for it. Patience, by definition, had to be a process. Phyllis also recruited Linda to attend the InterVarsity Urbana Missions Convention held at the end of December 1964 on the campus of the University of Illinois.

ℙ ℙ ℙ

Student life was not just one of showing up for classes. The school took its role seriously as *in loco parentis,* something colleges across the country almost entirely abandoned within just ten years due to the campus upheavals of the sixties. In the dorms students had to sign in and sign out. The school conducted inspections of the rooms, and demerits could be issued if things were substandard. Dresses, even if they were not school uniforms, had to be at least one inch below the knee. Teasingly the students said that during those nursing school years, "We went into the convent."

Student nursing uniforms were laundered regularly at the school. Each uniform had about ten mother-of-pearl studs that were used as buttons and had to be removed before they were washed. The collar of the dress was also removeable. It was starched so stiffly that students had to rub white ivory soap thickly on it before it was attached so they wouldn't get raw skin. Garter belts held up their hose, which lacked elastic and had thick seams up the back. Fortunately, each student had several white aprons which meant the uniform itself didn't have to be laundered as often.

Since assembling all this took time in the morning, students would put in the studs and do as much as possible the night before to get ready for the next day. Though the dorm on Delmar Boulevard near DeBaliviere Avenue opened only a few years before, it only had four showers and one tub for thirty-six women which also meant that planning ahead was a priority.

The schedule for the three-year program only allowed for a few weeks off each year. After the first nine months of classes, students alternated between three-month "rotations" and three months of classes. Rotations were in cohorts and involved on-the-job training at, for example, the state sanitarium on a psych ward or at Barnes Children's Hospital. They also worked at a lower income unit run by St. Luke's that had a men's ward and a women's ward with four to six beds per room. Phyllis roomed with Linda Sauer (Floyd) during these months.

Students were also called on to participate in clinical conferences in which various medical personnel would gather to discuss issues and share cases. Jane Hutchinson was a classmate notorious for having a serious case of spoonerism—unintentionally switching syllables around. Once at a clinical conference she introduced a case to the class by saying, "Mr. H. was admitted to the hospital for a hiptured frac."

The whole room erupted in laughter, though Jane couldn't figure out why. When things finally died down, she continued, "He hipped his frac when the garage door came down on him."

Jane was also a huge, lifelong St. Louis Cardinal fan! She especially loved Stan "The Man" Musial who had starred for the Cards for twenty years. But even when they were still winning the World Series in the sixties after Musial retired, she said, "They are still not as good as the days of Man the Stan."

Once at Children's Hospital Jane was working in the cardiac clinic. Over the speaker nurses would direct parents sitting in the waiting room to bring their children to the blue door and turn right. When it was Jane's turn to call in a patient, she enthusiastically announced, "Mrs. Jones, please bring Susie to the right door and turn blue."

The cardiologist burst in and asked, "Who is telling my patients to turn blue?!"

Outside of school Phyllis stayed connected to Edgemont, her home church, but she began spending more time at Hanley Road Baptist Church in Clayton, Missouri. A lot of nursing students went there because the church paid for taxis to pick them up on Sundays and because they served a hot meal when only cold leftovers were available on Sunday nights at St. Luke's. The church had various youth revivals, and Phyllis was right in the middle of it all, sometimes singing solos.

August 1965 was bittersweet. The class was extremely close to each other and to the faculty. They were proud of the school and of what they had achieved. They were also sad that with their three years finished they would be going different directions. However, the class stayed tightly connected with a newsletter and well-attended reunions even sixty years later.

Not only was theirs a close-knit class, the students were bright and accomplished. Nearly all graduated, most with honors. Several later obtained Ph.Ds. in nursing, with one becoming the head of nursing education at Northwestern University and another at the University of Virginia.

While most educational institutions had a graduation, the nursing school had a traditional capping ceremony to recognize the students' hard work, discipline, and the successful conclusion of the program. The nurses recited the Florence Nightingale Pledge, similar to the Hippocratic Oath. Instructors offered their reflections and encouragement for the future. The ceremony concluded with each student having a traditional nursing cap pinned on by a faculty member. While the cap has disappeared from standard nursing uniforms, Phyllis and the rest continued to vividly remember that day and the school.

That summer saw another landmark event for Phyllis. The movie *The Sound of Music* starring Julie Andrews was released in the spring to rave reviews, becoming the number one box office hit of 1965. Many friends invited Phyllis to see it that summer. But she and her church were committed to not seeing movies in the theater. They didn't want to support the questionable influence and morals of Hollywood. As she and her church friends would say in those days, "We don't drink, smoke or chew, or go with boys who do."

Phyllis was shocked then to learn that her younger sister Diane, who was herself attending the conservative LeTourneau College (now LeTourneau University) in Texas, went to see *The Sound of Music* with cousin Daryl Jean Sanders. She reported back enthusiastically to her sister, "Phyllis, the scenery and music were beautiful. It blessed my heart!"

That was enough to put a crack in her resolve. Phyllis went to see it with Diane and Daryl Jean who pranked Phyllis at intermission by saying that the movie was over after the first half closed with the magnificent wedding scene. She was at first disappointed but quickly caught on.

Phyllis especially loved the scene toward the end when German soldiers are futilely trying to start their cars so they can pursue the escaping von Trapp family. A trio of nuns is watching as the engines grind away but never start when one says, "Reverend Mother, I have sinned."

The other adds, "I, too, Reverend Mother."

Their superior then asks, "What is this sin, my children?"

The two look at each other guiltily and then reluctantly pull out from underneath their habits engine parts they had removed from the Nazi vehicles.

The movie was a lifelong favorite.

5

NURSING

After graduating, Phyllis took a full-time nursing job working the night shift across the river in Illinois. She got off duty at 7 a.m. and then traveled back to St. Louis for her next job at St. Luke's Hospital, beginning the evening shift at 3 p.m. On such days, she needed a place to crash between jobs, and Sandy Dowdy (Links) let her sleep in her apartment across the street from St. Luke's.

As a nurse Phyllis had lots of hands-on experience dealing with the physical concerns of patients. She also took her compassionate instincts into her hospital work. Her nursing was wholistic, doing all she could for patients physically, emotionally, and spiritually. One episode was typical.

> I was back at work after several days off. I received the report about the patients on the unit and was scurrying around setting up medications. Before I made my first rounds, I was startled by a crash that came from down the hall out of one of our isolation rooms.
>
> I rushed down to the room. Kathy was sitting on the side of her bed crying. I glanced at the chair that she had thrown against the wall. The telephone was off the hook hanging over her bedside table.
>
> When I sat down beside her and took her hand, she cried out, "I hate my father!" She had been talking to him on the phone and ended the conversation abruptly by hanging up on him.

Kathy was in the hospital with hepatitis caused from taking drugs with contaminated needles. The father that she hated was an alcoholic. Her parents were divorced and her mother was remarried. She had had sexual relationships with several young men. She was nineteen years old and was not in school or able to keep a job.

In the midst of great physical and emotional needs her spiritual needs were evident too. Because she had never known the love of an earthly father, God's love was foreign to her. Yet her sexual life and hatred for her father revealed her craving for love. She had never known what it was to be forgiven. Using drugs and her directionlessness were symptoms of the absence of meaning and purpose in her life.[1]

Phyllis spoke to Kathy about God's love. Sometimes Kathy was responsive. Sometimes she was defensive. Eventually Kathy's deep need for God was met when she came to know Jesus. Her life changed. She got off drugs. She became involved with a group of Christians. She prayed. She worked to heal her relationship with her parents. Later she married and established a Christian home. Her life was not perfect. There were still scars, but she grew toward wholeness because Phyllis was willing to ask risky questions, motivated by love for someone in need.

Phyllis wrote about another patient during this same time:

I met Mr. Lemont while making rounds on the nursing unit. He had just been admitted that afternoon and was scheduled for surgery the next morning. When I walked into his room, he had the curtains pulled around his bed and was sitting quietly in his chair in a dark corner. He didn't say anything. He clasped his hands tightly. His eyes were full of anxiety. I asked him the normal get-acquainted questions like, "Where do you live?" "How many children do you have?" "Grandchildren?"

Though she had just met the man, she felt that she should ask:

"Mr. Lemont, are you afraid?" He readily answered yes and seemed relieved to be asked. "What are you afraid of?"

"I'm afraid I will not make it through surgery," he replied as his tears came to his eyes.

I took his hand and said, "May I pray for you?"

He squeezed my hand tightly and eagerly said yes.

I thanked God that he was a loving heavenly father and the Good Shepherd. I thanked him that he loved Mr. Lemont very much and that he understood his apprehension and promised to go through the surgery with him. I prayed for the doctor and the anesthetist. I asked God to use this situation to draw Mr. Lemont closer to himself.

After we prayed, it was like the clouds opened and the sun came out. Mr. Lemont opened his curtain and began interacting with his roommate. He smiled and the smile was real. He was relaxed. He had had an encounter with God.[2]

Consistently, throughout her life, Phyllis loved God and others. In a hospital, people often find themselves in crisis, at a point in life beyond their competence or strength. Their limits are exposed; their sense of control is gone. Instinctively Phyllis knew that when people were gruff or angry, they were often covering their fears and vulnerability. She wrote:

It was difficult to care for Jane. To be quite frank, many nurses did not go into her room because of her unreasonable demands. One day after making her comfortable, I took her hand. Her voice was anxious. She said, "Please don't leave me!"

I responded, "Jane, I will have to leave you. But I know someone who loves you very much and will never leave you." That day her deepest need, a spiritual need, began to be met by the one who came to call sinners to repentance.[3]

Because Phyllis loved laughing and loved laughing at herself, she often told about one morning after a shift at the hospital. She and her roommates were driving back to their apartment without having changed out of their late-1960s standard-issue nursing uniforms and caps. On the way Phyllis was stopped by a police officer for some unspecified infraction.

When he approached the car, he looked at the three of them and said, "What hospital are you nurses coming from?"

In shock Phyllis demanded, "How did you know we were nurses?"

With a flat expression and through narrowed eyes he said to her, "Ma'am, how did you know I was a police officer?"

Eventually Phyllis and Sandy became full-time roommates. But they shared something more important than just an apartment in St. Louis. As Phyllis put it:

> We were both in love with a man . . . *not* the same man. Different men. And we both knew we would marry the man in our life if they asked. But neither of the men could make up their minds about what they wanted. . . . I predicted that by Christmas one of our relationships would be moving toward marriage and the other relationship would be over! Guess who came back to our apartment that Christmas evening with an engagement ring? It was not me.[4]

Sandy became engaged to Herb Links, and Phyllis broke up with Walter. She had worked with Walter in youth ministry for several years. They had been seeing each other for some time, and things seemed serious.

Then, without warning, Phyllis found out through mutual friends that Walter was engaged to Phyllis—a different Phyllis! Some people even thought at first it was her who Walter was engaged to, not to another woman with the same name. Walter didn't even talk to her about it.

She was crushed, but even in the midst of her sorrow, in true Phyllis fashion, she believed that God had something better in mind for her. After all, it was probably best not to marry someone who would behave in such a way.

❧ ❧ ❧

Like the rest of the country, Phyllis was shocked on Thursday, April 4, 1968, by the assassination of Dr. Martin Luther King, Jr. King had been the country's most prominent voice for Civil Rights, advocating for the rights of all, but particularly for Black Americans. His "I Have a Dream" speech culminating the March on Washington on August 28, 1963, is still considered one of the great moments in American history.

Six months later King delivered a sermon in St. Louis at the Episcopal Christ Church Cathedral. On October 14, 1964, he won the Nobel Peace Prize in recognition of his work on behalf of racial equality through nonviolent means. His support was instrumental in successfully advocating for the Civil Rights Act of 1964 and the Voting Rights Act of 1965.

When King was killed, much of the country erupted in violence. St. Louis avoided that due to the skilled leadership of local civil rights leaders who instead planned a peaceful protest march in response.[5]

Phyllis had several friends in the St. Louis Black community and knew they were hurting deeply. One had the additional grief of just having lost her mother. In fact, the day of King's death was the day she and Jane Hutchinson had planned to go to the funeral in north St. Louis. Despite the tensions of that moment, the two of them attended. The only White faces in a completely full Black church, they were very warmly welcomed.

The service began at 8 p.m. and was full of gospel songs like "Shady Green Pastures" as well as much energetic preaching. Four hours later the service was still in full swing as the entire congregation marched and stomped around the church singing, "When We All Get to Heaven." At that point Phyllis and Jane made a discreet exit as they stomped by the main door.

Phyllis's natural impulse was for people to come together. She appreciated her opportunity to work with Black children at Cedine Bible Camp in Tennessee during the summers, but thought it was strange that the leadership of a ministry to Blacks was primarily White. And when her home church of Edgemont wanted to leave East St. Louis and move to Fairview Heights, Illinois, she knew intuitively that they shouldn't and said so. But she was a lone voice among many for whom it seemed like the commonsense thing to do.

Phyllis had a wide range of nursing experiences at school and in the following six years, including work in an emergency room and one year as a pediatric nurse at Christian Welfare Hospital—the very place where she had been born.

But her favorite was working on a surgical floor. Patients were often nervous beforehand as they faced the unknown, especially if the surgery was serious. Phyllis was there ready to offer all she could.

Phyllis's own spiritual life in those days focused on prayer, Bible study, worship, and evangelism. But an important spiritual practice focused on the time she spent singing and meditating on traditional hymns. Gospel songs like "Amazing Grace," "What a Friend We Have in Jesus," and "Blessed Assurance" were part of her regular diet.

In 1966 she got a copy of InterVarsity's collection *Hymns*, a small volume that contained just 164 pieces. These had quality music as well as lyrics that were theologically rich and spiritually deep. The book became a kind of journal for her. She wrote down dates next to hymns that were significant to her.

She listed 10/25/67, 9/3/74 and March 1975 next to "Be Still, My Soul." Sometimes she added a brief note regarding the occasion. For example, she sang "Here, O My Lord, I See Thee Face to Face" on August 23, 1973, at the communion service at InterVarsity's month-long Student Leadership Training conference at Bear Trap, the one at which we had first met.

At one such conference she gave a book plug for the hymnal, noting that if she could only take three books to a desert island, they would be the Bible, the pamphlet *Quiet Time* and *Hymns*.

Afterward the students immediately bought all that were available. Phyllis used her copy so much that it fell apart and ten years later a friend had it rebound for her.

Camps and conferences were also key to her walk with God. Her St. Luke's connection to NCF was strengthened when, beginning in 1966, she attended NCF's annual national conference at Camp Li-Lo-Li (Life, Love, Light) in western New York state. The spiritual content was rich as were the stories of encountering snakes, of braving flood waters, or even of mice giving birth in suitcases.[6] She attended Li-Lo-Li several times over the coming decade. Influential speakers included J. Dudley Woodberry, who had a ministry with international students at Harvard before working with the United Presbyterian Church in Pakistan, Afghanistan, and Saudi Arabia.

Phyllis sometimes led music at the camp. She didn't just announce which hymns they would sing but drew the group's attention to the content of the words, helping the nurses focus on their meaning and significance. One person influenced by the way Phyllis and others pointed to Jesus was Carol Lankes. She joined NCF staff herself and later served as a Lutheran pastor in Elma, New York, for a quarter century.

In the summer of 1970 at Li-Lo-Li, Phyllis met a blond nurse who matched Phyllis in wit and humor, if not in height. Rita Smith (Tower) joined NCF staff the next year in Chicago. Phyllis joined staff the year after in 1972.

That summer of 1970 the medical profession was being profoundly influenced by Elisabeth Kübler-Ross's book *On Death and Dying*, published in 1969. The bestseller introduced the theory of the five stages of grief—denial, anger, bargaining, depression, and acceptance. While the academic underpinnings of the framework have since been questioned, at the time it had everyone discussing it.[7] Nurses were suddenly encouraged to talk openly with patients about death, which had previously been discouraged.

In response, Bonnie Miller spearheaded the development of the

Love That Heals seminar that NCF used with nurses and in churches so they could better minister to people who were sick. One exercise was to think and journal about your own death so you could be better prepared to discuss the topic with patients. Two assignments were to write your own obituary and to plan your funeral.

Most people had few ideas about a funeral, but Phyllis had a specific and elaborate outline. It was obvious she had given this a lot of thought. When she shared about her funeral her mother, Louise said, "Phyllis, you plan your funeral the way most girls plan their wedding."

With sparkling eyes she responded, "Yeah, well, Mom, I know I'm going to die; I'm not sure if I'll ever get married."

Once when talking with Rita about all this, Phyllis confessed she thought she would die young. Rita dryly responded with a dose of reality: "Phyllis, it's too late!"

＠ ＠ ＠

Phyllis continued her connection to InterVarsity and explored missionary work by going to Costa Rica for InterVarsity's first Overseas Training Camp in 1970 (which later multiplied into dozens of opportunities around the world each year under the name Global Projects). David Howard (who would later direct InterVarsity's Urbana Missions Conventions in 1973 and 1976) spearheaded the event. He led a few dozen students and staff in what was at the time an innovative short-term mission experience.

Issues of life and eternal life came to the fore when one of the students was caught in a rip tide in the ocean one afternoon. Another student swam out to rescue his friend, but a wave crashed into him and broke the grip he had. He never saw his friend again. Once more, the ultimate cost of the gospel became very real to Phyllis.

Though a three-year nursing degree was standard in those days, the medical field was beginning to change, encouraging nurses to obtain bachelor's degrees. Phyllis therefore enrolled at St. Louis University to finish out the credits she needed, graduating in July 1970. This also qualified her to take on a role as a much-appreciated teacher with student nurses at St. Luke's, adding that to her already busy schedule.

One night during these years when she lived in St. Louis, Phyllis was walking to her apartment and was nearly home when a man approached her. He pointed a gun at her chest and said, "Don't make a sound."

Obviously, the man didn't know who he was dealing with. "Of course, I screamed immediately," Phyllis reported. He then hit her on the head with the gun, knocking her down, grabbed her purse, and ran off. She didn't suffer any serious injury. He just left her with a dramatic story she loved to tell, with herself as the punchline.

Even so, in that situation, the reality of the spiritual world was once again not far from her. "I thought he would kill me. The thought that flashed vividly through my mind was, 'To be absent from the body is to be present with the Lord.'"[8]

After the incident one of her roommates, Jane Hutchinson, took to keeping a knife under her pillow at night. Skeptical of this precaution, Phyllis asked, "And Jane, just what are you going to do with that knife if someone breaks in?"

"Oh," Jane said, "I'll tell him, 'You take one step closer and I'll kill myself!'"

Although she loved her career as a nurse, Phyllis was drawn toward the work of Nurses Christian Fellowship. Not only did she love nursing, she loved encouraging others in their spiritual lives and helping them share their faith as she did so naturally. She deeply admired the NCF leader Helen McMurtry in particular. In the fall of 1972 Phyllis began with NCF full time. She not only worked with NCF student and professional groups in St. Louis but also traveled to Kansas and Nebraska.

While NCF was a division of InterVarsity Christian Fellowship (IVCF), often there was little interaction or coordination between the two. At that time, nursing schools were mostly stand-alone institutions, not part of larger colleges or universities. NCF and IVCF followed that arrangement and so tended to operate independently.

Paul Woodard, the InterVarsity area director for Missouri, Kansas, and Nebraska, apparently never got the memo. He invited Phyllis to participate in InterVarsity staff meetings for the area even though she didn't report to him. She was glad to be part of that larger team. She found encouragement and support from those doing similar work with students in other settings.

From her first staff meeting, she added fun and merriment to all they did. An earlier area supervisor, Bill McConnell, in one of his poems described those early days as "sharing uproarious laughter with colleagues at down-to-earth roadside cafes." Phyllis was often the instigator.

Like all InterVarsity staff, she had to raise her own support, which meant finding individuals and groups who would donate money to InterVarsity to allow her to work full-time with students. Her home church and other churches in the St. Louis area where she had attended were among her major contributors. As always, she loved them and they loved her.

But in the early 1970s, the fundamentalist tendency to place a high priority on doctrinal purity raised its head regarding the charismatic movement. Some Christians were beginning to experience dramatic gifts of the Spirit like speaking in tongues, prophecy, and healing.[9] Fundamentalists were sure that such miraculous experiences had ended with the apostles. This became a flash point of controversy. One of Phyllis's supporting churches decided to cancel funding for any missionaries who disagreed with the church on this issue.

What would she do? First, she knew she hadn't given the issue much serious thought. So she read and studied and produced a position paper. She argued that the Bible didn't teach that such gifts of the Spirit were only part of the past. She knew this might end her funding, but she wasn't going to fudge just to keep getting support.

But another issue continued rumbling under the surface. Even as early as her high school days, she sensed that many in her home church were on the wrong track when they advocated staying separate from other believers who didn't cross their theological *t*'s and dot their ecclesiastical *i*'s just so. She grieved when Christians insisted on dividing over secondary issues. What she saw in the Gospels was a Messiah who did not look for ways to exclude people but who was instead looking for ways to include those on the outside. That's who she followed.

6

COURTING

After that February 1974 not-a-date lunch, Phyllis and I continued to have contact off and on at InterVarsity meetings. In May we ended up driving together to the area spring staff planning retreat with another member of the team. A canoe was strapped to the top of the car, overhanging the hood. Somehow this inspired us to imagine ourselves flying an airplane to the meetings as pilot and copilot. We laughed and joked. Such good fun.

The canoe played another role. After arriving I asked the team if anyone wanted to paddle out half a mile to a small island on the lake for a pre-breakfast quiet time. Phyllis readily volunteered. The next day we went to that beautiful setting. An hour later we saw the fog start to roll in and decided to head back. But immediately we lost all visibility.

I set a course but inadvertently drifted to port, missing the inlet the house was on. Unknowingly we moved out into the main body of the lake and were soon completely disoriented. Before the day of cell phones and GPS, and with no map, we stopped at a couple of houses on the lake to get directions. Shortly before lunch we got back, with the team barely concerned. They had seen the fog and guessed what happened.

Afterward Phyllis laughed when her mother responded to the story with her wry humor: "You're the only woman who could be lost on a lake for four hours with a man and not get him to propose."

The summer took us in different directions, however. The main one for me was staffing a month-long leadership camp at Bear Trap, like the one I had attended as a student three years before. I also spent time in Minnesota seeing my parents and friends.

When I got back to St. Louis in August, I called Phyllis just to see how her summer was. No answer. A week later I called again. No answer. Apparently even her roommate wasn't home. Because these were the days before answering machines, I had few options. I may have written a note asking her to get in touch or even stopped by her house. Eventually I saw her at some InterVarsity event and got a little bit of an update, but I went on with my campus work and she went on with hers.

In October we both attended a meeting of the InterVarsity Local Committee, which was a group of about a dozen people committed to helping staff with their fundraising. I arrived after most others did and took one of the few empty seats, which was next to Phyllis. During the meeting I put a scrap of paper in front of her saying, "Could we talk after the meeting is over?" I had some issue (now forgotten) to talk about with her. I respected her opinion and thought she'd have some helpful input. She agreed to meet.

We decided to go to her place for coffee. We talked and inevitably took time to pray about it. As we held hands for prayer I thought, "I'm holding her hands to pray. I think she's holding my hands for a different purpose." Something was going on, or so it seemed.

Afterward I just wasn't quite sure what to do with this. A couple of weeks later she invited me over for breakfast, as she did from time to time with all the staff on our team. During the meal I said lightheartedly, "So I hear you are seeing other men."

She played right along, pretending we had been in some kind of relationship, "Oh, Andy, I'm so sorry you had to hear about it from someone else." In fact she had had a single date with someone, which she mentioned.

I realized that such an approach was not going to work, so I plunged in and asked directly, "Is there something going on between us?"

She responded, "I'll be happy to answer that, but first, have I done anything to make you feel uncomfortable?" I answered that nothing like that had happened.

Phyllis then told me her whole story. As the previous spring had unfolded, she began to realize that the nerve Patti Strong had touched the fall before at the Love That Heals seminar was real. She began to admit to herself that her feelings for me were growing. But she thought, possibly because of the age difference, that it was ridiculous. Yet she enjoyed our time going to and attending the spring staff conference. "I wasn't interested in playing *Risk* in the evenings with the group. I was interested in being with you," she admitted. That summer, however, she purposely avoided my calls. The tension was too much for her, and she (quite uncharacteristically) isolated herself.

During this period, as she traveled to help nursing groups in Kansas and Nebraska, she came across an article about singleness and dating that struck her deeply. It convinced her that she needed to turn the relationship completely over to God. Even if our friendship meant helping me get ready to marry someone else, she was willing to do that. She got down on her knees to make that commitment and got up with a sense of peace.

When I sat next to her that October at the Local Committee meeting, she was greatly relieved because it felt so normal.

"That's the whole story," she concluded.

I said I was completely unaware of this. I had no idea any of it was going on.

"Why did you ask, then?"

I told her about my impression when we prayed together at her place after the previous meeting.

"Oh," she said, "I think I was just feeling relief that our friendship was back to normal."

I definitely enjoyed Phyllis. Everyone did. She was always fun and great to be around. She was a good friend. But I said, "I think you should know I will probably fight this." I was trying to be honest since that had been my response previously when I was receiving unwanted attention from women. I didn't want to get her hopes up when something could be unlikely to develop.

Phyllis (in her typical way of taking everything positively) thought that was an encouraging response. *At least,* she thought, *there's something inside him that he's trying to resist.*

I also mentioned that the age difference seemed a bit of an issue to me. I mentioned the thirteen-year age gap between my mom and dad, with my mom beginning to care for my dad whose health was failing. But I also said that I realized that in a relationship, sometimes you would need a friend, sometimes an advisor, sometimes a lover, sometimes someone to take care of you. A good relationship is not going to be one-dimensional.

Again she thought, *Wow, he's really been thinking about this. That is encouraging!*

Later she talked to a friend about our relationship who said to her, "Oh, a man's head is often way ahead of his heart." Once again, Phyllis was hopeful.

Afterward I kept thinking about Phyllis and our conversation. But I was not thinking about ways to resist the relationship. I heard some friends were organizing a group outing to the St. Louis Symphony in December for a performance of Handel's *Messiah*. I asked Phyllis if she'd like to go with me and the group. She said yes immediately and thought, *I like the way this guy is fighting it!*

She was nervous about what to wear, whether she should let me open the car door for her, and so on. But once I came to pick her up, she relaxed. The *St. Louis Post-Dispatch* called the performance, with Leonard Slatkin conducting, "buoyant." I had listened to recordings of *Messiah* many times over the years, but I had never heard "All We Like Sheep" as Slatkin directed it. The choir sang with a marked lightness and frivolity. The sheep were having fun going astray, getting lost.

Then came the contrasting tone and tempo of doom as they sang, "And the Lord laid on him the iniquity of us all." We sheep had no idea of the consequences of our waywardness. The cost was cosmic.

After we were married, people would sometimes ask, how long we dated before we got engaged. With wry smiles we would say, "We had one date. We went to the *Messiah*." That was essentially true. We spent a good deal of time together in the next months, but never on any other formal dates.

A few days after the *Messiah* we both received letters with our assignments for the winter camp at Bear Trap we would be staffing between Christmas and New Years. Among other duties, we were assigned to colead a small group. I told Phyllis I thought she had set that up, emphasizing that it was quite okay with me. She denied it emphatically (and was probably a bit insulted that I suggested it). I still thought she had until the conference director explained that he just thought it made sense—we knew each other from the same team and also made a good male-female pair, as most coleaders were. Clearly my arrogance had gotten the better of me, and I apologized to Phyllis.

Another assignment Phyllis had was as the camp nurse. In my free time, then, I would hang out with her at the nurse's station under Pooh Bear, a cabin across the triangle from the cookhouse and dining hall. Since she wasn't too busy during her assigned hours, mostly handing out cold medicine and band-aids, we had extra time together. One night I told her that the age difference no longer bothered me. In keeping with the "fighting it" theme of our talk six weeks earlier, I told her, "I think I may be losing the battle."

"Oh, Andy," she said, "there's no battle in your life I will ever want you to lose . . . except this one!" Not only was Bear Trap where we first met a year and a half earlier, it was also where we first kissed.

Right after the camp at Bear Trap we went to Horn Creek Ranch in Westcliffe, Colorado, a two-hour drive away. For five days in early January 1975, we joined about a hundred other InterVarsity staff for the Regional Staff Conference. At the time, we were trying to keep our relationship under wraps. I didn't want to be under the spotlight. I wanted to have the freedom to develop our relationship without the burden of having to deal with the expectations of others. We didn't hang out a lot as a result, though we did manage to get in several rounds of bumper pool.

After we both got back to St. Louis, on January 12, I took her to meet my sister, Mary, her husband Kirby, and their two-year- and three-month-old girls, Kim and Rachel, who lived nearby. I got my first introduction to some of her family a few days later.

We had Sunday lunch with her sister Judy and her husband, Ward Billingsley, along with their three children—Diana, David, and Donna. Gabe and Louise were also there. Phyllis had told me about everyone, but I was still scrambling to figure out the history and dynamics of this group as they also sized me up. Clearly, everyone knew Phyllis was introducing someone special to the family.

The mood of the gathering was cheerful with lots of inside jokes I didn't quite get. I learned that Diana, the first of Gabe's and Louise's twelve grandchildren, was special to Phyllis as the one who had made her an aunt. I heard about the many accomplishments of David, who was just turning eleven.

Donna was seven at the time. Years later she told me she was not too happy about this interloper who looked like he might be taking away her special aunt. As with all things, Phyllis had thrown herself into being the fun, engaging, game-playing aunt with all three Billingsley children. They loved her in return.

Phyllis then got ready for a six-week trip for NCF to work with nursing groups in Kansas and Texas. On January 20, I took her to the airport and said a reluctant good-bye. I couldn't stop thinking about her, and within three days I knew I was a goner.

Six years later we both thoroughly enjoyed *Chariots of Fire*, a movie about the Olympic runners Eric Liddell and Harold Abrahams. One of Phyllis's favorite lines comes when a group of Cambridge friends go to see Gilbert and Sullivan's *The Mikado*. Abrahams is quite taken with Sybil Gordon, the female lead of the musical. During the intermission, Abrahams goes backstage to ask her out to dinner. Harold's friends are amazed as they discuss this in the lobby, and one of them says, "Abrahams is smitten, you say? Smitten? He's decapitated."

That described me in late January 1975. I was decapitated.

While Phyllis was traveling, my parents drove through St. Louis on their way to a month's vacation in Florida, as they had done for several years. I told Mom I was seeing a woman who also worked for InterVarsity. Mom guessed Phyllis was Protestant, but I also knew I had to let her know Phyllis was older. When I said she was thirty, Mom gasped.

"Andy, she's older than your sister!" I assured her Phyllis was quite young at heart, but that was a lot for my mom to take in.

Such age gaps were not unusual in my family. My dad was thirteen years older than my mom. Her father, John Stutz, was ten years older than her mother, Lucy. Also Gabe was ten years older than Louise, and her dad, Judge Sanders, was twelve years older than Louise's mother. What was different, of course, was that in our case, the woman was older. (Phyllis and I ended up paving the way for my brother, John, who a year later became engaged to Nancy Sisty, who was also eight years older than he was—with absolutely none of the family drama that accompanied Phyllis and me!)

During those days, Phyllis confided to her nursing school friend, Delores Moore, about her concerns regarding our age difference. Delores responded, "So what? What difference will it make? When you are 108 and Andy is 100, he still won't be able to keep up with you . . . even if you have one foot nailed to the floor!"

Phyllis and I set Monday, March 3, to talk about (as I jokingly said) "marriage in generalities." I had profoundly mixed feelings, still trying to get used to what seemed like a monumental idea. One topic would be the book *Sacrifice* by Howard Guinness, a book on discipleship that included a chapter on love. I had mailed it to Phyllis during her travels.

Guinness outlined half a dozen common sense questions a couple should work through before deciding to marry. How long have you known each other? Have you been with each other in ordinary life and not just for special occasions? What do you miss most when separated? What common interests and common values do you share? How much do you trust each other? Do you admire and respect each other's character?

Phyllis wrote me back right away: "Andy, I got all the answers right!"

We met at my house and talked all morning about what marriage would mean for us, the questions and dreams we had, and how we might decide if it was right. We both took it so seriously that our approach was to consider reasons we should not get married. Neither of us had made a decision like this before, and we just weren't sure how to go about it. We concluded we should get the advice of Paul and Kathy Woodard, who both knew us and whom we both respected.

Phyllis already had a date set that week with Kathy to take the Woodards' two daughters, Kim and Kelly, out for ice cream. She could ask Kathy then about scheduling time for the four of us to talk. When Phyllis arrived at Kathy's house, she told her, "There is a man in my life." Since we had continued to keep our relationship quiet except with family, Kathy was totally surprised.

"Who is it?"

"Why don't you guess?" Phyllis suggested mischievously.

Kathy proceeded to name various people Phyllis had already dated. No, none of those. "Is it someone in InterVarsity?"

"Yes."

Kathy then guessed all the staff in Kansas and Texas and several elsewhere. When Phyllis said it was none of those but that it was someone in the area, Kathy paused and looked totally perplexed.

Finally, Phyllis said, "Kathy, it's not Kathy Schulz and it's not your husband," the only remaining options, save one.

Kathy gaped, and she finally said in shock, "Aaaaandy?"

Phyllis said, "Kathy, you just let that sink in a moment while I take the girls for ice cream, and we'll talk about it more when I get back." When she returned, they set a date for that Saturday evening, March 8.

As the four of us talked, Paul and Kathy asked how our relationship had developed and come to the point of thinking about marriage. They asked good questions and listened carefully. We said we wanted to ask both sets of parents for permission and were tentatively thinking about a date a year later, in the summer of 1976, because InterVarsity generally recommended not marrying in the middle of a school year, and we didn't think we'd be able to get together with my parents soon enough for a wedding by next September.

After an hour and a half of conversation, Paul said, "Well, I just have one question." I thought in my nervousness and uncertainty, *Great, this is it. He knows the one thing we haven't thought of for why we shouldn't get married.*

Paul continued, "Why do you two want to wait so long to get married?"

I was shocked. He was assuming we *should* and *would* get married. There was no question or barrier left. I had no more obstacles. We were done processing. It was time to move ahead.

We mentioned again the problems with schedule and my parents, but Paul would have none of it. "Just tell them you want to get together. This is important enough. They'll do it."

That night we went back to Phyllis's place, both of us a bit stunned. We sat on her couch and talked for another hour. The reality sunk in.

Some men come up with wonderful plans for proposing—like a beautiful, rooftop, candlelight dinner, and her pet dog suddenly showing up with a small box strapped to his neck; or a gorgeous sunrise walk on the beach with that small, precious ring tucked in a brown paper lunch bag, just the way his dad had done it with his mom.

I had no plan and no ring. All I knew was that I was deeply in love with this funny, substantive, outgoing woman who filled every room she walked into with life and laughter. Though I was daunted by the size of the decision, I sensed God at work in us.

Seeing only one path to take, I got down on one knee, held her hand in mine, and said something that was no doubt profound and eloquent which I do not recall at all now. I then said, "Will you marry me?" and concluded the "fighting it" theme by adding, "I declare unconditional surrender."

Phyllis smiled gently and paused. And paused.

And paused.

Oh, I thought, *she's just letting it sink in.* But the silence continued to go on . . . and on. I was not used to this. In an uncharacteristic break from the norm, Phyllis was silent! Finally, I had to ask, "Are you going to say something?"

"Oh," she said, "I'm going to say yes. I'm just savoring the moment."

"In that case," I said, "take all the time you want!"

ENGAGING

The day after I proposed, Phyllis called her folks about the four of us getting together. I also wrote my parents (who were still on a month's vacation in Florida) about coming through St. Louis on their way back to Minnesota so they could meet Phyllis "and her parents"! My dad, Phil, was reluctant to take the detour on their way back. He was seventy-six and not in the best of health. Besides, they had driven through St. Louis on their way to Florida. My mom, Dorothy, had other ideas. "Well, you may not be going to St. Louis, but I am." A couple of weeks later, they both arrived.

March, a month of monumental moments for the two of us, didn't stop there. On March 12, two weeks before my parents arrived, I received a phone call from Jim Sire, editor of InterVarsity Press in Downers Grove, Illinois. A few months earlier I had read about two job openings there and wrote to say I was interested. Jim was calling to see if I could come for an interview right away and I agreed. We set a date for March 17.

I immediately called Phyllis with the good news and was met with shocked confusion. Though we thought we had talked and talked about everything possible about our future, somehow I completely forgot to mention my interest in publishing or that I had written to IVP. Phyllis had imagined our life together would be one of joint ministry to students on campuses in St. Louis, not one of me editing in Chicago. Here was something quite different.

I once again found myself apologizing profusely to Phyllis. Why I hadn't mentioned it to her before is still a mystery to me. Phyllis was amazingly gracious and forgiving as she tried to absorb this dramatic turn of events.

To add to the shock, when I called, Phyllis was meeting for several days with three nurses from Kansas who were about to graduate. Jane, Cathy, and Joleen planned to spend their first year on the job in community, being discipled by Phyllis in St. Louis. That morning they were making plans about which hospitals to apply to and what shape the discipleship program would take. Just before my phone call she told them, "I don't know for sure if Andy and I will be married next fall, but I do know we'll have this discipleship program in St. Louis."

After our call, Phyllis went back to the group. Rather stunned, she told them the news that she and I might be living in Chicago next fall. The women didn't miss a beat. "Hey, we're leaving Kansas anyway. It doesn't matter to us too much if it is in St. Louis or Chicago as long as we're with you. Besides, didn't we just finish a Bible study about Abraham trusting God to lead him to a land he would show him, that he didn't know anything about?"

Two days later we got together with Gabe and Louise to ask their permission. I was nervous, but they had no problems. Maybe they were just a bit glad that their middle daughter was finally getting married.

Louise did ask one question: "How many children do kids want?" In the same breath Phyllis said, "Twelve," and I said, "Three."

In her flat sardonic tone, Louise responded, "Well, I guess you two have something to talk about."

Three days after that I flew to Chicago and was interviewed by Jim Sire, assistant editor Linda Doll, and IVP Director Jim Nyquist. A few days later I had a job offer.

Back in St. Louis, Phyllis and I discussed it. I was excited about something I had thought of as a dream job for years. But as we talked, I realized that she was a bit distressed. Moving wasn't her concern but how important the job might be to me. I then said to her, "My job will never be more important to me than you." She remembered those words our whole marriage. They gave her a sense of peace knowing that she was number one for me.

I called Jim Sire, said yes to the job, and together we settled on a starting date at the end of May, after I finished my assignment staffing a camp for student leaders in Colorado.

The packed calendar had no let up. Weeks before all this, Phyllis had agreed to speak on Friday, March 21, at the InterVarsity chapter meeting at Washington University. The topic? "Sexuality and Singleness," of course. They had asked her as someone who had lived a full and satisfying unmarried life. The irony was not lost on either of us, though it was on the students who attended since we had still not gone public with our relationship. Though she felt a bit awkward, she told me that she firmly believed everything she said about how we can be fulfilled as single people.

My parents arrived the next week. We planned three evenings in a row together. The first was Wednesday, March 26, at Mary's and Kirby's house along with their daughters, Kim and Rachel. Phyllis (again uncharacteristically) was nervous and quiet. My dad, though an introvert himself, had an instinct for finding the most uncomfortable person in a room and making him or her feel welcome and at ease. He sat next to Phyllis and engaged her in relaxed conversation.

The next night the six adults went out to a nice restaurant. Phyllis was still quiet, but Kirby's sociable chatter helped make for a pleasant evening. The third night the four of us met at Phyllis's for dinner.

As it came time to discuss what we all knew was the topic of the evening, my mom was clearly tense. My dad opened, "As I see it you have three issues you need to work out. First, the age difference.

Second, the religion difference. Third, your financial situation. I see the last one as most important, but if you can figure those out, you've got my blessing."

Finances in marriage was a big issue for my dad. He had told me and my siblings years before that he had decided he would never get married because he had never seen a happily married couple—and the reason for the unhappiness was always money. When he was himself smitten by my mom, he decided that money would never be an issue between them: first, because he was determined to make enough that it wouldn't matter; and second, because he decided to never fight with her about how to spend it. And he lived that out.

I had often heard the story from my parents about the time they were at a department store, and my mom was shopping for a new purse. She couldn't decide between two, one a bit more expensive than the other. She showed them to my dad and asked, "Which should I get, Phil?"

He immediately answered, "Get both."

Phyllis and I then responded to the three areas of concern dad had. We gave our thoughts about age, about how we planned to work out the Catholic and Protestant question, and that we both intended to work after marriage, me with IVP and she as a nurse. We would live within our means. We might not have a lot of money, but we would have enough.

My dad was satisfied and, being tired, said he was ready to go home. I was relieved.

But my relief didn't last long. My mom interjected immediately, "I'm not ready to go yet. I have more questions about religion." She was seriously concerned about me potentially leaving the Catholic Church. Catholic mothers often feel they have one job—raise Catholic children. She was upset. She wasn't ready to let us "just decide." She wanted us to go to a priest and get some serious counsel.

"And Phyllis," she added, "you can't just become Catholic because

Andy is. You have to do so because you believe in it yourself and feel called that way."

We promised we would do as she asked, and my parents left with some resolution among us but also some uncertainty.

Our week with my parents wasn't over, however. The next day we were to have lunch with my parents and Phyllis's parents. We would arrive separately at a restaurant on the Illinois side of the river, near Gabe's and Louise's house.

As it turned out, Phyllis and I were late and the other four were early. The two couples were able to identify each other and started chatting.

Louise thought they might as well get to it and asked, "Well, what do you think about the kids getting together?"

"Phyllis is very nice, but isn't Andy kind of young?" Dorothy asked.

"Oh, he seems like quite a mature man to me," Louise responded.

On they chatted. Eventually we arrived and realized they'd already been talking. Though we were kicking ourselves for being late and were nervous about the four of them meeting without us to smooth the way, it was for the good. The four could talk more openly on their own. My parents were helped by seeing that Gabe and Louise were comfortable with the marriage.

They all then asked what date we had set. They couldn't believe it when we told them we hadn't done so yet. We genuinely wanted their blessing before moving ahead. The six of us finally settled on a date six months later—September 6, 1975. Gabe and Louise said that was the day Gabe's folks had gotten married eighty-two years before. I was encouraged that they took this as a good sign.

℘ ℘ ℘

Over the spring and summer we worked on invitations and finding a place for the wedding and reception. We also continued to work through the Catholic-Protestant question as my mother had requested. She wasn't the only family member, however, with such questions. Louise's sister, Aunt Bert, was somewhat scandalized that her niece would even consider marrying a Catholic. Clearly, I was suspect.

Fortunately, I had met their brother, Phyllis's Uncle Gene, even before I met her mom. He was a Baptist pastor who had come to have lunch with some InterVarsity students and me at Washington University. I don't recall exactly the reason for the visit, but it certainly made a difference when Phyllis and I got engaged. When Aunt Bert voiced her strong objections about me to Uncle Gene, he said, "Why, I met him. He is a fine Christian man." Bert was thoroughly dismayed, but she knew she had no basis to argue since Gene was the religious authority in the family.

Phyllis and I thought a co-officiated service would be the way to go since that would give us plenty of the time after the wedding to more thoroughly investigate things, especially for Phyllis who had limited exposure to the Catholic Church. Phyllis knew a Father Richard "Dick" Pendergast from St. Louis University, and we set April 20 to meet with him.

Father Pendergast was a courteous and friendly Jesuit who welcomed us cordially. Certainly a co-officiated service was possible. All we had to do was sign a Church document agreeing to raise the children Catholic. Though I was a lifelong Catholic, this was new to me because nothing like that was ever required when two Catholics married. I just didn't have experience with mixed marriages. It was certainly new to Phyllis.

"We would like to have more time to decide. Why can't we wait till after the wedding to figure out which church we should be part of?" we asked.

"It is the wisdom of the Church," he said, "that these issues should be settled before the wedding so that they do not disturb the marriage later."

Though I was a bit frustrated, that did sound like wisdom to me.

As we continued to talk, sharing our stories and desires, he also said something that nearly had prophetic qualities to it. "I see the two of you being bridge people throughout your lives between Catholics and Protestants, between these two branches of the Christian family. That could be a wonderful calling on your spiritual journey."

As much as we appreciated Father Pendergast, we were still left with a dilemma. Our Protestant acquaintances thought we couldn't sign such a document because it absolutely committed us to a certain direction with no room for change. Our Catholic friends were much more relaxed, saying something like, "Don't worry about the details. Go ahead and sign it! It just means you will raise your kids as Christians, following your conscience as God leads you. And if he leads you to a different church later, no problem."[1]

As Different As We Think

For years I reflected on the differences between the answers given by our Catholic and Protestant friends about the document on raising our children Catholic. The answers seemed to reveal more than just differences in doctrine and church practice. The two groups had markedly different mental frameworks, two different ways of understanding how the world works and how we should live in it. I finally put these thoughts together in an article published in *Books & Culture*. The essence was this:

> Evangelicals tend to think in either/or terms. If one thing is right, its opposite is wrong. Either Scripture or the pope is the supreme authority. It can't be both. There is a yearning for consistency of faith and practice. Knowing that we have flawed natures, evangelicals warn against error and in the prophetic tradition call God's people back to his truth and purity.

> Catholics, by contrast, are very happy to think in terms of both/and. John Paul II was highly revered by Catholics, yet large majorities of Catholics (particularly in North America) felt perfectly at peace disagreeing with him on birth control, priestly celibacy and stem cell research. The inconsistency bothers them little.[2]
>
> This explains why Protestants prioritize truth while Catholics prioritize community and grace. And it undergirds the evangelical emphasis on crisis moments of decision in our spiritual lives while Catholics primarily see our spiritual life as an ongoing journey. The truth is that we need both ways of thinking and living.

That summer I wrote a detailed four-page summary of our problem, weighing several factors. But two issues guided our final decision. First, though our spiritual lives would grow and change over the years, at that time our evangelical either/or way of thinking overrode our Catholic sensibilities. Second, though Phyllis was genuinely open to exploring the Catholic faith, I was much more familiar with the Protestant world than she was with Catholicism. With only five months till the wedding, we didn't feel like she had the time for a thorough study. She would have to travel a great distance to make a change while I would not. As a result, I felt we should go her direction.

This decision was extremely difficult for my mom. Yet she was very gracious. In August Phyllis, being Phyllis, wrote my parents:

Thank you for standing with us concerning the decision on the church. I want you to know I do not take it lightly. As Andy said, we read and prayed and talked and struggled before coming to a decision. I know it is hard for you and my heart hurts because of that. I really care about what you feel and think. I do love you both.[3]

On April 21, we drove to Downers Grove for a brief visit at IVP and to begin looking for housing. We then went on for a week in the Twin Cities to visit my parents and other friends. One night we went for dinner and an evening of playing cards with my high-school friend Mike and his wife Kathleen. It was Phyllis's first time meeting Mike, and she wanted to make a good impression. We all enjoyed a good meal, and then we turned to playing Hearts.

After a rousing game, Phyllis and I said our good-byes and got in our car. As soon as we closed the doors, Phyllis burst into tears. I was shocked. What happened? Where did this come from? "What's the matter?" I asked.

She told me how inadequate and stupid she felt. When we played Hearts, she had no idea what was going on in the game she'd never played before.

"But you won!" I said in surprise.

"Yes, but that's only because you and Mike were going after each other. Please, let's just drive."

We did, but later that evening we went for a long walk. Eventually Phyllis said she wasn't sure if she was going to be good for me. She couldn't keep up intellectually and wondered if she'd hold me back. I could hardly believe what I was hearing. Somehow being with me made her feel bad about herself—and this from someone who was typically so at ease with herself.

I stopped in the middle of our walk and stomped my feet over and over in frustration. "Being smart is fine, but you have so many qualities and skills in life that I don't have," I told her. "I'm the one who should feel inferior. And if my presence in your life is going to make you feel worse about yourself instead of better, maybe we shouldn't get married. I love you and respect you just the way you are, and at the same time I want you to be free to grow and flourish in any way you want. I wanted our marriage to be one that will lead you to feel good about yourself and grow in all kinds of ways. You have so much to offer me. If we don't help each other and build each other up, what's the point?"

That was a turning point. Somehow, inside, Phyllis had reached a new level of assurance that I accepted and respected and loved her just the way she was.

On May 8 we went ring shopping in St. Louis at the jeweler Phyllis's cousins Patti and John Strong had used. During our stay in Minneapolis, we had seen a ring with an emerald-cut diamond set at a 45° angle. That image stuck with us, and we asked the jeweler to do the same. He was skeptical, but when we picked it up five days later, he said with a smile, "You have a one-of-a-kind ring." We thought that was fitting for our one-of-a-kind marriage.

I left for Colorado the next day to staff the student leadership camp at Bear Trap. I managed to take off May 17 in the middle to attend the Colorado Springs wedding of Mike Clark, the friend who had driven me to Bear Trap two years before when I first met Phyllis.

On May 27 I began my work at IVP, reporting to Jim Sire. I rented a room in Glen Ellyn for the summer and eventually found an apartment on Fairview Avenue in Downers Grove, just south of the tracks, one mile from the IVP offices on Main Street. It would be our first home.

During late spring and summer we completed premarital counseling with Dave Winter, a friend of Phyllis's. He was a Plymouth Brethren elder who had worked with many other couples. We found him helpful as we discussed conflict, compatibility, and honesty with each other.

Throughout those months Phyllis and her mom worked on dresses, invitations, mailing lists, tuxes, a photographer, and the like. In the midst of it all, Phyllis made time to help Mary and Kirby get their new house ready to move into. Friends hosted a surprise shower, and the Sanders side of the family hosted one too. We also made a couple of trips from St. Louis to Chicago with furniture and household items for our new apartment in Downers

Grove. One of those trips involved John and Patti Strong driving a U-Haul up with Phyllis.

On one of my visits to St. Louis, when Phyllis and I went to see her parents, Gabe told me to come out back to help split some wood. Together we worked with wedges and sledgehammers. I didn't know if this was a test, a rite of initiation into the family, or if he just wanted some help. But I was no match.

As I labored to break off a piece or two, I kept hearing the steady pop, pop, pop of wood cracking. Though he was sixty-five, he could still leverage his 6'5" frame and his old-man strength to split off chunks in a single blow. After ten minutes I was spent. I kept going for over an hour, though, because he did too, without a hint of tiring.

Another time in St. Louis, we met with mutual friends, Rudy and Sara Mitchell. Sara said they didn't have money for a wedding gift, but she had something for us, nonetheless. She then pulled out her guitar and quietly began singing:

> There are places I'll remember
> All my life though some have changed. . . .
>
> Though I know I'll never lose affection
> For people and things that went before
> I know I'll often stop and think about them
> In my life I love you more.

Lennon and McCartney never sounded so good.

8

MARRYING

September 6, 1975, dawned clear and a mild 55°. I had spent the night with John and Patti Strong and hadn't slept at all. Phyllis stayed at her apartment and slept like a rock. I could hardly eat a bite for breakfast. Phyllis's appetite was unhindered. It wasn't that I had any doubts about Phyllis. Rather I was overcome by the magnitude of the step we were taking. Phyllis was simply being her lighthearted self.

A lot of activity had led up to that day. Keeping things economical was a theme. We priced traditionally printed wedding invitations which seemed high to us. But Phyllis had a friend who knew calligraphy and had made invitations for others. It was beautiful, but we printed it on regular paper stock and several barely survived through the mail. My mom was not happy with the condition they were in when her friends received them. Our instincts for frugality had, unfortunately, gotten the better of us.

The text of the invitation was warm and welcoming. Phyllis especially wanted it to come from both sets of parents, not just hers, as was traditional. After announcing the time and place that "Phyllis Jean Strong and Andrew Thomas Le Peau will vow their lives to one another forever," it read, "Mr. and Mrs. Gabriel B. Strong and Mr. and Mrs. Philip H. Le Peau invite you to witness their vows and worship with us. Our joy will be more complete if you can share in their celebration of their union in Christ."

Robert Fulghum said that since weddings "are high state occasions involving amateurs under pressure, everything *never* goes right."[1] Not surprisingly, even though we were both people who liked to plan carefully, we had our share of fits and missteps.

One point of tension came when discussing the rehearsal dinner. My parents picked a great spot, Musial and Biggies, a landmark restaurant in St. Louis co-owned by the legendary Stan Musial. Phyllis was concerned about serving alcohol, however. Memories of her Uncle Frank's alcoholism before his dramatic conversion were still strong in her mind. In addition, many on her side of the family were abstainers even though serving alcohol wasn't an issue for Phyllis's parents. When we brought this up, my dad was adamant. "It's my party. I'm serving alcohol. We'll also have water and juice if they want."

Phyllis realized he was right. It was his party, and the discussion was over. She let her family know the plans.

Since both of us had been attending various churches in St. Louis in the last couple of years, we didn't have an obvious home church in mind. After looking at our options, we settled on the stately Memorial Presbyterian Church on Skinker Boulevard, adjacent to Washington University and across the street from historic Forest Park, site of the 1904 St. Louis World's Fair. While it wasn't the home church for either of us, it was unofficially InterVarsity's home church since it hosted many student activities. The church was delighted and (yes) gave us a break in fees.

Phyllis suggested we ask George Stulac to officiate. We both knew him well since he was on our area InterVarsity staff team working at the University of Nebraska in Lincoln. He was also a Presbyterian minister and would soon become pastor of a church in Wichita. He was delighted to accept, especially because Memorial had been his home church when he was a student at Washington University. As Presbyterians would say, all this was providential because about six years later he became pastor at Memorial. His sermon at our wedding had stuck in the minds of those who ended up on the search committee.

Phyllis wrote in July asking George to wear his clerical robes and a cross to give the wedding a more liturgical feel. "And if you still have a beard—the marked effect would be great."[2]

By one o'clock the temperature had risen to a comfortable 74°, and the church was filling with a couple of hundred people. Phyllis and I had agreed, as tradition dictated, that we not see each other that day until she walked down the aisle. I was thus sequestered with my best man George Carthage and the other groomsmen.

As we neared one o'clock, Kirby came to relay a message to me. "People are having trouble finding parking spots on the street because of all those attending Rosh Hashanah at the synagogue next door." There were several houses of worship nearby and none had parking lots, including Memorial. "Phyllis," he went on, "wants to delay the start for fifteen minutes to give folks more time."

Only later did Phyllis tell me that someone relayed the exact same message to her, except she was told that I was the one who wanted the beginning delayed!

Also unknown to me was another drama that was unfolding. Keeping with our desire to be economical, we planned a simple reception with just a wedding cake, nuts, and punch in the church basement afterward. This was before the days when a catered reception was customary—at least in Phyllis's circles.

Phyllis, however, did want to supplement the fare with dozens and dozens of homemade chocolate chip cookies contributed by many, which had become something of her joyful trademark among friends, family, and colleagues. Again, my parents were a little skeptical of the low-key nature of the event. That was not what they were used to. But they said little since they considered this to be Gabe's and Louise's event.

Louise ordered a traditional triple-tiered cake from a local bakery. But as the hour of the wedding approached no cake was delivered. Louise made many phone calls to the bakery, but there was no answer. She was annoyed, angry, and embarrassed. As she walked down the aisle with my college friend Mike Clark holding her hand comfortingly, her face betrayed her feelings.

Eventually the groomsmen and I came out, and we aligned ourselves in front as the bridesmaids made their way down the aisle to Purcell's "Trumpet Tune." Someone gave me the wise advice to never take my eyes off the bride once she appeared. That was easy to do.

After we were all in our places, George Stulac's first words were, "We are here to worship God." Yes, it was a celebration, but Phyllis especially wanted it to be a celebration in God's presence and for his glory.

Gabe then gave me his daughter's hand. Though I'd been extremely wound up all day, once we were together, I completely calmed down.

After a few words from George, Phyllis and I then each briefly addressed the gathering, something I have rarely seen at other weddings. We alternated comments, first welcoming everyone. "We are glad that each one of you is here." I also said, "When you're going to get married, you get kidded a lot. One of the things people would say to me was, 'Andy, do you know what you're getting yourself into?' Each time I'd smile and answer, 'Nope!'" But we knew each other and affirmed that we knew the God who would watch over us.

Phyllis especially wanted to use this time to thank our parents. She took the lead in thanking her parents for their love and care for her. I echoed that for my parents and then said to both couples, "We thank you, too, for being wise enough and giving enough to not hold on to us but to give us to each other when we know you will never be able to forget that we were once babies in your arms. Now we look forward to a growing relationship with you as a new family, yet always, too, as your son and daughter."

We asked George to preach on Ephesians 5, which famously begins this section on husbands and wives by saying that one key way we are filled with the Spirit is when we submit to one another out of reverence for Christ. Marriage (which Paul says represents Christ and the Church) was a bond to be marked by mutuality, not by one lording it over or complaining about the other. As George said,

> A wife's submission is not intended to be a weak, unthinking passivity. Christ does not expect his church to become a vegetable before him. On the contrary, he expects us to become filled [with] more life than ever before, learning to love him with all our heart and soul and strength and mind. This is abundant life, and the wife should demonstrate her love for her husband with abundance of life. This will mean more vigorous thinking, not less. It will mean exercising all the energy, sensitivity, wisdom and ability of which she is capable.[3]

I expected and hoped for nothing less than that from Phyllis. And I was not disappointed. George's words about husbands, however, had the greater effect on me. They guided and shaped my entire life with Phyllis.

Paul wrote, "Husbands, love your wives, just as Christ loved the church and gave himself up for her to make her holy" (Ephesians 5:25-26). George said:

> This is self-sacrifice. The usual pattern of the world seems to be the opposite—the husband expecting the wife to sacrifice herself for the sake of the husband's job or schedule or goals or desires. The husband is called by God to sacrifice himself (his job, his schedule, his goals, his desires) for his wife. . . .

Instead a husband's main role is to see that his wife grows and flourishes in all the ways God desires and has gifted her. Husbands are to:

> Focus our lives on the goal of the wife's development into a full, mature, whole, sanctified woman of God. . . . This will mean

endeavoring to provide her with all the help she needs in every area of her personal development—spiritually, intellectually, physically, emotionally.[4]

As an example George said, "If my wife is not called to be a pastor's wife, then I am not called to be a pastor." To me, that was stunning, yet intuitively it seemed absolutely right. Even though Phyllis leaned toward traditional views about husbands heading the household, I wasn't so sure. I wanted her to give all the strength and help she could. I especially wanted to work and live with someone like Phyllis whose wisdom and character I respected so much. It made no sense to try to do this on my own.

Whatever Phyllis needed to grow and flourish—that was to be my focus. She would always be more important to me than any job or ambition. Though I wouldn't and didn't always succeed, I aimed for her to be first in all ways.

The congregation then sang "The Church's One Foundation," a hymn we picked because it was common to both Catholic and Protestant worship, and because it spoke of the unity of Christ's Church. We then exchanged vows and rings and lit a unity candle.

After George pronounced us husband and wife, we rapidly walked down the aisle to Widor's stirring Toccata from his Fifth Organ Symphony, still my favorite organ piece. When we made it back to the foyer, one of the ushers was waiting with a telegram for us from a friend wishing us the best in our new life together. I had never received a telegram and never have since, but it seemed entirely appropriate for such a momentous occasion.

As soon as Phyllis's parents were escorted out, Louise immediately found a phone and once again called the bakery. This time they answered. Cake? They delivered the cake at 10am. What did she mean it wasn't there?

Quickly what happened became clear. The bakery had two wedding cakes to deliver. One in the morning and one in the afternoon. The morning cake (ours) was delivered to the other venue. The bakers immediately rushed to retrieve the cake and set it up at our reception. But it didn't arrive till an hour later and was ever so slightly askew. Louise demanded a reduced fee and got it. But she never quite got over her dismay.

The outcome for us was different. A friend had wisely told us beforehand, "Don't worry if something goes wrong. Then you'll just have a fun story to tell for years afterward." And we did. Phyllis was also thoroughly pleased that the chocolate chip cookies that received so much skepticism beforehand had saved the day—as chocolate chip cookies can so easily do.

We invited our bridesmaids and groomsmen to be part of the reception line. Mike Aubart told us later that he got tired of saying over and over that he was Andy's friend from high school. "So," he said with a wink, "I told a couple of people I was Phyllis's first husband! But only a couple!"

Phyllis's young nieces and nephews couldn't wait for us to be done with the reception line. They were constantly bugging her, "Aunt Phyllis, have you seen the gifts? Have you been to the gift table?"

We finally made our way over and saw a beautiful bicycle built for two, a gift from our InterVarsity students and colleagues. To the shock of everyone, Phyllis immediately climbed onto the bike, wedding dress and all! She told me to get on too, and everyone laughed, especially Phyllis. People said then as they often did later, "Only Phyllis!"

After things settled down and people began drifting away, we changed clothes at the church and were driven to Paul and Kathy Woodard's house. We had hidden our car in their garage to keep mischievous hands from decorating it in unwanted ways. As we started up the steps to the house to get the keys, Phyllis said to me, "Let's just sit down at the kitchen table and act like we are going to stay there all day instead of rushing away. It'll be so much fun!"

And we did. We sat and chatted, but Kathy could hardly stand it. "Don't you guys want to go? Shouldn't you be leaving? Don't you have plans?"

Phyllis laughed and laughed, saying we had all the time in the world. But before too long we put Kathy out of her misery and took off.

After we got in the car it wasn't too long before something prompted Phyllis to say, "Oh, Andy, you're such a good husband."

I hooted in laughter. We'd only been married six hours! That seemed like a miniscule sampling from which to draw such a definitive conclusion. But Phyllis's default was to see the best. And for years after she'd be alert to opportunities to remind me of that moment and proudly say, "See! I was right!"

For our honeymoon we didn't go far. We reserved a few days at Tan-Tar-A, a resort in Lake of the Ozarks, about a three-hour drive southwest of St. Louis. That became the scene of two more iconic moments we often referenced throughout our marriage.

The weather was not great that week, with rain and cooler temperatures interrupting our outdoor plans. Once we were walking outside to a meal when I gestured and said, "Don't step into the puddle." Immediately Phyllis stepped right into the middle of it. We both laughed, and through the years the phrase "Don't step in the puddle" meant one of us could possibly do something obviously stupid.

Another time we were trying to find our way someplace in the resort, but it was a maze of passages and walkways and buildings that often left us bewildered. At one such moment, when we weren't sure which direction to go, I, with exaggerated stealth, looked one way and then the other to make sure no one was watching. I then pulled out a map of the resort to covertly sneak a look to find out where to go. I was intentionally mocking how men never like to ask directions, yet there was truth there too that we both laughed at. I just hated getting lost.

ᴼ ᴼ ᴼ

We had given the nurses from Kansas and Nebraska that Phyllis was discipling—Jane Bacon, Linda Gustafson, Cathy Marsh, and Joleen Brown—the job of transporting our wedding presents back to our apartment on Fairview Avenue in Downers Grove. They couldn't believe we had given them our keys. They took full advantage by removing all the labels from our canned goods, short sheeting the bed, and engaging in other mischief.

Within a few weeks of our wedding, Phyllis was inviting couples over for dinner. We were soon part of a small group mostly made up of people from IVP meeting weekly for prayer and Bible study—no doubt at her instigation.

Others joined us for meals most weeks. Family and friends made weekend visits, including John and Patti Strong. One wedding gift we unpacked was a guestbook that Phyllis was delighted to thrust in front of everyone who visited. She wanted all guests to write the date, their name, and a comment. Within our first four months of marriage, fifty different people signed it who had joined us for meals and often games—and some had come multiple times. I wasn't used to such an intense social life, but for Phyllis it was second nature. She couldn't get enough of people.

She also settled into her routine with the four nurses. They all worked at Hinsdale Hospital, and Phyllis met with them each week as a group and individually as part of the year-long discipleship program.

Unsurprisingly, Phyllis also made fast and deep friendships at the hospital. The administrators were impressed with those "Christian nurses" she led. Given that the hospital was deeply Seventh-Day Adventist, this was a bit of a surprising label for the group since so many employees were quite religious. Clearly the five of them stood out. They were hoping Phyllis would bring more people like them to work there.

The four nurses applied the content of the Love That Heals

seminar, learning how to connect with patients and nurses facing tough situations. Jane Bacon had her first opportunity to share about the peace of Christ with a patient who readily prayed to follow Jesus.

Hinsdale Hospital was about five miles east of us. I would usually walk the mile to IVP, and Phyllis often biked. I would get up about 7:00, but Phyllis was up by 5:00 or so to get ready for her early shift. The days were getting shorter, so she was starting off in the dark.

One morning she came into the bedroom to wake me up. "Andy, Andy, I've been in an accident." I had been sound asleep and was only semiconscious.

"Are you all right?" I mumbled.

"Yes, but you need to get up."

"Why? Aren't you ok?" I was groggy and hadn't quite caught on to what it took to be an attentive husband in that moment. I just wanted to go back to sleep.

"The man who hit me is here," she responded.

I struggled out of bed, and the three of us chatted. He was concerned that Phyllis was ok, which she was except for a bump or two. After that, Phyllis drove to work more often.

In that first year I was reading Richard Adams's *Watership Down*. Phyllis made great fun of me for reading a four-hundred-page novel about rabbits. For once I was smart enough to not argue or get defensive. I just started reading her a chapter a night before bed or out on the lawn on a lazy Saturday afternoon.

When we were about a quarter of the way through, we read that one of the main characters, Bigwig, got caught in a snare. As the other rabbits looked at the motionless body of their friend, I saw a tear coming down Phyllis's cheek. I knew she was hooked even before we celebrated Bigwig coughing his way back to life.

About that time Phyllis's old boyfriend, Walter, contacted her to say he would be in Chicago for a conference and asked to stop by. It had been ten years since he unexpectedly broke things off with

Phyllis, without even telling her, and became engaged to a different Phyllis. We both thought it was just a bit strange that he wanted to visit. But Phyllis was gracious and said, sure, he could come.

A few weeks later he stopped in for part of two days. One time I had to go to the office while the two of them had a bit of time together. Afterward Phyllis told me Walter had said, "Andy must be a bit concerned or nervous that an old boyfriend has stopped by."

Phyllis responded with a clear declaration: "Walter, there is no one in the world who is more secure in the love and loyalty of his wife than Andy Le Peau." That was the end of that conversation!

I still smile thinking of it. What a wife I had!

℘ ℘ ℘

Because of my work at IVP, we had the opportunity to meet well-known authors, including Walter and Ingrid Trobisch. They had been missionaries in Africa and had written best-selling books on relationships and marriage for Harper and Row as well as for IVP.

The two of us had lunch with Ingrid. As we chatted, she asked about our new life together, and Phyllis began to talk about some of her questions.

Eventually, Ingrid said to Phyllis, it seemed to me out nowhere, "You are afraid Andy will be a better husband than you will be a wife."

I was shocked, but Phyllis became teary. Apparently Ingrid had hit a nerve. I certainly didn't feel Phyllis lacked anything. She delighted me. I had no idea she felt any such insecurity. To me, Phyllis was simply the strong, settled, playful person I had always known. Maybe that's why I had missed this. Ingrid had not.

She reassured Phyllis that marriage was not a competition. It's an opportunity for each person to grow. Ingrid's words sunk in, and Phyllis never expressed such feelings again.

My problem was the opposite of Phyllis's. I was not at all insecure about how to be a good husband even though I should have been. I had my parents' good example, but otherwise, what did I really know? I was much too sure I was going to be great at this marriage thing. And I did enjoy Phyllis tremendously. But as with most things, I could have done with a tad more humility and a tad less arrogance. I had so much to learn.

WELCOMING

Phyllis wanted to have children right away, and, given her age, we knew we shouldn't wait long. I was hoping we could have at least two years to ourselves, however, before welcoming other members of the family. We didn't quite make that goal. Phyllis was thrilled when we found out she was due in November 1976. I was glad too, though as was typical, the two of us balanced each other—she was full of enthusiasm and confidence while I felt more the coming responsibility of parenthood.

When Phyllis was about two-thirds of the way through her pregnancy, the doctor began to ask whether there was a history of twins in her family because she looked rather large. He decided to do a sonogram (a rare procedure in those days). We were both pretty sure it was just one child, so Phyllis said it wasn't necessary for me to accompany her as I had other times.

On the appointed day I was at work and got a phone call from her. "Andy," she said, "I had the scan and everything's fine, but there aren't two babies in there."

"There's not," I said.

"No. There's three!!!"

I sat in stunned silence trying to absorb this staggering news. Then in the background I heard Phyllis's audience of several nurses stifling laughter, and I realized I had been had. We weren't having triplets. Just one!

"Don't you ever do that to me again," I demanded over the phone. But that never stopped Phyllis.

Knowing we were adding to the family, we began looking for a house. We knew Ham and Pat Borland from the Methodist church in town, and they were the obvious realtors to help us. "I know prices are high," she said, "but you've got to look around so you will recognize a deal when you see it." In May we looked at several in the area. They were small, unappealing, and, at $35,000, too expensive. We stopped looking, being a bit discouraged because prices were going up faster than we could save—and we were setting aside nearly all of Phyllis's salary for a downpayment.

Then in the middle of August Phyllis called me at the office. "Andy, Pat wants us to go see a house right now."

"Can it wait till tonight? I'm in the middle of work."

"No. She said it will be gone by then. We've got to see it now."

Half an hour later we met at 5340 Lane Place, just two blocks from the IVP office. The house was small and needed a lot of work, but it had a good floor plan. The man who lived in it had died, and his children were anxious to sell. They were asking $31,900. We offered $31,000, and by 8 p.m. we had an agreement. Our five-decade relationship with Lane Place had begun.

Our credit had to be reviewed by the bank for the loan. While only a dozen years before student nurses needed their fathers to cosign on financial arrangements, this time it was the reverse. I had been unable to qualify for a credit card, but after we were married Phyllis could add me to her account. Thus I got my first credit card, and Phyllis's longer work history and credit rating helped us get our loan approved.

The four nurses and friends from IVP helped us move at the end of August. Soon we were stripping wallpaper and painting. Because Phyllis loved natural wood, we set to work stripping and staining woodwork. I had never done that before, but she had plenty of experience and taught me how.

On October 23 we went to the wedding of my brother, John, and Nancy Sisty in Iowa City. Phyllis and I were both amused that Nancy was eight years older than John, the same gap we had. Yet John had gotten absolutely no questions from the family about the age difference that I had received. We happily teased the couple that we had paved the way for them.

At the wedding we could see that my dad was getting weaker, losing weight, and struggling to get around with a cane and leg braces. The doctors thought it might be Lou Gehrig's Disease (ALS), but they weren't sure. He endured all the events as best he could, but when John and Nancy asked him what he thought of the hour-and-a-half Nuptial Mass full of music and Scripture and prayer and the Eucharist, he said, "It was too damn long!" He laughed but he was so weak that the ceremony had worn on him.

Phyllis wanted to keep working until the last possible moment. She decided to make Friday, November 19, her last day. After we went to sleep the night of the 18th, her water broke at about 3 a.m. Though she was not having contractions, she knew she needed to get to the hospital right away. Off we went to Hinsdale Hospital, which she had left less than twelve hours before.

We had taken Lamaze classes because Phyllis wanted to have natural childbirth. After several hours with no contractions, the doctor decided to give her Pitocin to kick start her system. She was soon in hard labor. I had never seen anyone work so hard for so long. I knew Phyllis was strong, but childbirth required a whole new level. All our Lamaze techniques barely had any effect.

Finally, at 8 p.m., November 19, we welcomed Stephen Andrew into the world and into our family. I was so proud of Phyllis and so glad for Stephen. In fact, I was elated.

I was with them all the next day, but Phyllis was well enough that she said I should go to church like usual on Sunday. I was in choir practice before the service when the choir director came to me and said, "Phyllis is on the phone. She said everything is fine with her and the baby, but she wants to talk to you and said you need to go to the hospital." He may have seen a question on my face, so he added, "And you need to do what the new mother says. Go!"

When I got on the phone, she said, "Your sister, Mary, called and said your dad died this morning." I was in shock. The last time we ever saw him was when my mom and dad drove away with Mary and Kirby the day after John and Nancy's wedding. "Stephen and I can't go with you, but you need to go be with your mom."

I felt whiplashed between an exuberant high and deep devastation. But I went—without Phyllis, without Stephen.

While I was gone, friends brought the two of them home from the hospital. When I returned from the funeral I saw in action how quickly we had been welcomed into the lives of our neighbors, coworkers, and church friends. Phyllis had received round-the-clock help while I was gone, and we were flooded with meals and cards and flowers.

I had never experienced such care from so many. I had always been impressed with how Phyllis constantly extended hospitality. Now we were on the receiving end of the abundant generosity of others. I was beginning to learn how to extend welcome to all.

𝒫 𝒫 𝒫

Where had all those church friends come from? A year before we had just begun working out our church situation. We knew we would worship together, but where? We spent the fall visiting different churches. Several folks from InterVarsity Press, including Jim and Marj Sire, attended First Presbyterian just a few blocks down Fairview from our apartment. But Phyllis's mom said she remembered that their first pastor in East St. Louis, Farrell Jenkins, was now pastor at First United Methodist in Downers Grove, on Maple Avenue just a block from the IVP office. She thought we should at least look him up.

Three weeks after we were married, we went to the service there.

Phyllis hadn't seen Reverend Jenkins since she was a little girl twenty-five years before and didn't recognize anyone up front. But when she heard this robed, white-haired minister speak during the service with a distinctive rolling, resonant bass voice, she immediately knew it was him.

Downers Grove

Born in Vermont Territory in 1782, Pierce Downer settled down to farm and raise a family in New York. About 1830 his son, Stephen, left home to seek his fortune in northeastern Illinois, eventually arriving at Fort Dearborn along the Chicago River. Stephen encouraged his father to investigate the opportunities in the area. On his visit in 1832, Pierce traveled west on horseback through open prairie. After coming to the junction of two Indian trails, he laid a claim near a grove of Oaks.[1]

Other early settlers lent their names to streets near the center of what was called Downers Grove–Blodgett, Curtiss, Blanchard, Stanley, Lyman, and Carpenter. The Blodgett home also served as a stop on the Underground Railroad.[2]

In 1838 a log school was built near Maple and Carpenter that also housed Sunday services for a Methodist congregation. A new church was constructed in 1894, located at what is now 5321 Lane Place. Because of the lighted "Welcome" sign in front, it soon became known as The Welcome Church. In 1928 a new structure for First Methodist was built at its current location on Maple Avenue.[3]

The key event that transformed the town came when the Chicago, Burlington and Quincy Railroad was extended from Aurora to Chicago in 1864. With Downers Grove on the line, the stage was set for marked population growth.

The railroad line also allowed for delivery of Sears Catalog Homes built from "kits." Nearly 150 of these were erected in the village in the early twentieth century.[4]

The train line also allowed Chicagoans to travel to the first golf course in the U.S. west of the Allegheny mountains. Established in 1892, the course (now Belmont Golf Club) had nine holes. When nine more were added the next year, it became the first eighteen-hole course in the United States.[5]

The Tivoli Theater, built in 1928 in the classic French Renaissance-style with an initial capacity of 1,390, also became a landmark.[6] Downers Grove High School (now Downers North) was established the same year less than a mile north of the Tivoli on Main Street. Though Downers Grove was founded as a small, rural community about the same time Chicago was, over the decades the growth of the metropolitan area spread to and then went beyond the town, transforming it into a far western suburb.

After New Year's we decided on First Methodist. The next Sunday we went early enough to attend an adult Sunday-school class before the service. We were directed to a room with about twenty people in their twenties and thirties. Though we were nervous and didn't know anyone (okay, *I* was nervous) as Providence would have it, a get-acquainted game was scheduled that day. Within the hour we knew the names, origins, and Christmas activities of nearly everyone. It was our first introduction to Welcome Class, named for the former church building located half a block away on Lane Place.

True to the class's name, we were made to feel right at home. The people were friendly though the content of the class was traditional liberal, mainline fare and not exactly to our taste. We were a bit surprised at a Welcome Class party one Saturday evening when the president of the class came in drunk.

We enjoyed the people, nonetheless, including Ham and Pat who invited us over for dinner in April 1976. Of course our conversation turned to the class and what we thought of it. We tried to be diplomatic. We enjoyed some material and some not as much.

"Well, what would you like?" they asked.

"We'd like to see more Bible study."

"Do you two know anything about leading Bible studies?" Ham asked.

"Well, yes. We've led a few Bible studies," we said, underselling our experience by a fair amount.

"Great. Why don't we sign you up? I think that's just what we need."

We were stunned. That was not like anything the class had done before. Though, yes, leading Bible studies was in our wheelhouse.

In his enthusiasm Ham got up and continued, "I'm going to call the president of the class right now and tell him you guys will do that." It happened so fast, I'm not sure he took time to get our consent. But away we went.

Phyllis had been somewhat disappointed when I took the job at IVP because she had dreamed of us doing ministry on campus together. But here we were, thrown into an exciting ministry opportunity. Most of the class were nominal or cultural Christians. If they had made a childhood commitment to faith, they had not grown much beyond that. Yet they were open, discovered that they liked Bible study and wanted more.

Previously the class had had a variety of teachers and different series throughout the year. But we were suddenly installed as the permanent, year-round leaders. And it was always a Bible study. We simply did what we had been trained to do in InterVarsity—we led inductive discussions on a passage, emphasizing observation, interpretation, and application.

We started with topics like success, failure, doubt, faith, marriage, and prayer. But in each session we covered a chapter of the Bible or several paragraphs of a chapter rather than cherry-picking prooftexts. Then we did whole books like James or Amos, or a section of a book like the upper room discourse in John 13–17.

The people loved it and the class grew. Because they came from only lightly churched backgrounds, they came to the Bible with a wonderful freshness, without preconceived notions of what the passage should mean.

When we discussed Jesus raising Lazarus from the dead in John 11, Sandy said, "I don't like this at all. I am just mad at Jesus about this whole business."

"Why?" we asked, a bit bewildered.

"Because when Jesus' friends die, he gets to raise them from the dead. When my friends die, they just stay dead. And that makes me mad."

We loved Sandy's honesty. She was tapping into something real. Death is an enemy, and though we see in the Lazarus story the beginnings of the defeat of Death, Sandy was right. It is still something we grieve and can even be mad about.

We heard other stories too. Sandy's husband told us he was on a business trip, out with his colleagues at a bar after a day's work. And what did they discuss? Paul's letter to the Romans. Over beers they were having their own spontaneous inductive Bible study.

In a typically liberal, mainline church, Phyllis and I stood out. The staff knew we were far more conservative than they were, but they loved us—not least because we were attracting people to the church.

Once I told a couple of staff that I had just read a review of an IVP book in the Iliff School of Theology journal, which came from the staunchly liberal Methodist seminary in Denver. I said the first line read, "Despite the fact that this book comes from InterVarsity Press, you can't immediately dismiss it." I told them I thought that was the highest praise possible, and they howled.

Farrell Jenkins left for a church in South Carolina shortly after we started attending. Bill White, the new pastor, discovered that we didn't exactly line up with his theology, but we were all on friendly terms.

After a while, we decided we should invite him to lunch. On our way to the restaurant Phyllis said, "You know, Bill, I've been enjoying your sermons much more lately." I was a bit surprised. I had not heard her mention that before.

"Why, thank you, Phyllis," Bill responded, "I appreciate you saying that."

"I just have one question," Phyllis continued.

"Oh," he said, quite open to hear. "What's that?"

"Are you getting better, or am I losing my faith?"

Bill roared with laughter.

Soon Ham and Pat approached us again. "We need to have a class retreat. Would you guys be willing to put a program together if we handle all the logistics?" That seemed like a dream to us, but they thought we had the harder job. Again, InterVarsity was our model as we patterned the weekend after the many student retreats we'd been to and led: quiet times, small group Bible study, a speaker, and recreation. Those with kids brought them along, and it became a whole family event. The spring retreat became an annual feature of our life together.

We also led mid-year, one-day marriage seminars. I still am amazed they thought we had something to offer, having only been married a couple years ourselves. But Phyllis, as always, was full of confidence, and off we went.

During those years, some in the class made fresh commitments to faith. Some renewed the ones they made as children. We also offered training in how to lead small group Bible studies. But try as we might, no one wanted to pitch in and lead an occasional class. Probably they felt intimidated by us being there. However, later, when couples moved out of town, we heard reports that they had started leading Bible discussions in their new churches that had nothing like that to offer.

ⅈ ⅈ ⅈ

With the new baby, Phyllis took the year off work, but she was not one to stay idle long. Soon she was making plans for another discipleship program during 1977-78, something she could do at home. Linda Stirk, Nancy Hanselman, Anne Grossman, and Chieko Fukushima moved to the area to work at Hinsdale Hospital and meet regularly with Phyllis for study and prayer.

Phyllis was thrilled to find out she was pregnant again in early 1978. After we told our next-door neighbors the news, they started making a pitch for us to buy their house. They were moving and had more space to offer us. While it only had two bedrooms, it also had a back porch and a partially finished basement. We had been working hard on fixing up 5340, but we still had a long way to go.

Moving right next door into a place that was mostly redone held a lot of appeal. So did the fact that the wood trim was already stripped, stained, and varnished—appealing to Phyllis because of her love for natural wood; appealing to me because it was already done!

As was always the case, everyone knew what Phyllis thought about everything. So when Ham and Pat visited the new house, they wrote in our guest book, "Love your new home but think you should paint the wood trim!"

Our neighbors were glad we were staying on the block. We had already become good friends with several of them, enjoying block parties and more. When they saw the "Sold" sign in front of our first house, a group gathered to hear about who the new neighbors would be.

"Who did you sell to?" Russ asked.

"Oh, the Blacks," I said.

He looked utterly shocked. It took me a moment to figure out why. Then I laughed and said, "It's Jim and Sandy Black. That's their name."

"Well, I wouldn't be surprised," he said, "that you would be the first ones on the block to do something like that!"

Redlining was just beginning to fade at that time, but I was still surprised (probably because I was a bit naïve) that he'd be upset about us selling to a family of color. Yet we were gratified that somehow he knew we were the kind of people who would do just that.

The move next door to 5344 Lane Place had happened in August, once again with the help of an army of friends. Phyllis was delighted that we saved money by not needing a moving truck. We could carry everything out one door and into the other.

We were thrilled that Susan joined us on the morning of December 18, 1978. When the nurses announced our healthy baby girl weighed 8 lbs., 10 oz., Phyllis said, "Oh, a small one!" She got just the surprised reaction she was aiming for. Quickly she explained to them that our first child was over 10 lbs.

A parade of visitors came to the house to admire Susan's beautiful red hair and Stephen's energy. My mom arrived a few days before the baby was born and stayed till after Christmas. She was just in awe when we brought Susan home at less than a day old. "I have never held such a new baby."

Before she left, Mom wrote in the guestbook, "You have made me so welcome and comfortable. Hope someday Steven and Susan will do the same for you." It was another prayer-prophecy said over us that decades later would come to pass.

♯ ♯ ♯

We made return visits to be with my mom, including one to help her recover from cataract surgery (which was much more of an ordeal than it is today) and for Easter week. Though I'd grown up Catholic, that visit, going through the services for Palm Sunday, Holy Thursday, Good Friday, and Easter made a marked impression on me. I suddenly saw the liturgy as a weeklong immersive drama, like going to a play in which the audience takes part, a play extending over several days.

We were especially struck by Good Friday. The unaccompanied music was haunting as the choir sang through the chapters in John's

Gospel from Jesus' betrayal to his burial. At the end all candles and other objects used in the liturgy were removed or covered. The church was bare. We left in silence. That stark emptiness, which reminded us of what the disciples felt, hung with us all that day and the next.

At the Easter Vigil, however, all became light, with trumpets sounding and golden banners now dramatically announcing the resurrection. The contrast from Friday was visceral. Jesus was risen indeed.

I still felt a bit awkward with my mom about having left the Catholic church. Though disappointed, my mom courageously accommodated herself to that reality. She also grew to love and appreciate Phyllis more and more. My mom once told me that Phyllis was never the problem. It was me!

Mom had grown to appreciate Phyllis so much that my very Catholic mother didn't mind at all when, shortly after we were married, her very evangelistic daughter-in-law sent a letter to Mom's non-religious husband. Phyllis wrote about how much she loved Phil and wanted him to know about Christ's love for him as well. After reading it he turned to my mom and said, "Tell her to stop trying to convert me."

Always hoping her husband might show more interest in God, my mom responded, "Tell her yourself."

But, a couple of years later, as we stood in my mom's kitchen, the three of us began to review those early tensions, various Protestant and Catholic similarities and differences, what we appreciated about each, and how we all saw things now.

As the discussion wound to a close, Phyllis, never one to let five hundred years of church history get in her way, blurted out, "Oh, Mom, you know you wouldn't trade me in for seven Catholic daughters-in-law!"

My mom shook her head, in bemusement, and with a wry smile said, "You're right, Phyllis, I wouldn't. I wouldn't."

PARENTING

Sometimes it is said there are two kinds of people—those who are people-oriented and those who are task-oriented. Though many took Phyllis to be decidedly the first, she was in fact both. She loved being with people, laughing with people, crying with people, and talking with people as much as she loved getting things done. Phyllis was an industrial-strength planner.

She was a skilled juggler who somehow could keep both knives and colorful water balloons moving continuously before her in amazing patterns and without mishap—nonstop! Though Phyllis often liked the lift that a cup of coffee would give her, she didn't need it. She was naturally caffeinated and had enough self-generated energy to power a medium-sized city.

She took such satisfaction in completing tasks that she'd become even more animated with every item she finished. Back in her nursing days she would start every Saturday by writing "Make a list" at the top of a sheet of paper. Then she would itemize everything she wanted to do that day. When she finished writing the list, she'd go back to the top and cross out "Make a list."

I was goal-oriented too, but I was a rank amateur compared to the elite, Olympic-level organizer I had married. Each year Phyllis made sure we scheduled a weekend or at least a day to make goals for the year. We had goals regarding our spiritual lives (daily, weekly, monthly, yearly), our physical well-being (exercise, diet, rest), our finances, major and minor house projects, and of course people. We listed all those we wanted to connect with—family, neighbors, church people, and many others. Though all this simplified as the years went on, in 1978 our annual plan ran to eight pages!

That prompted me to institute a new category: Things we would *not* do. I wanted to make sure we didn't completely overextend ourselves by adding too many activities in the course of the year. I had more limited energy. As a matter of self-preservation, then, I tried a bit to reign in Phyllis's wide-ranging passions—a near hopeless task. We also needed to leave space in our lives for the unexpected crises or opportunities that always arise.

When it came to parenting, Phyllis was no less deliberate. One goal was to try to make Sunday special by not letting it become just another day to get things done. (Yes, the irony was not lost on us that we were making rest something *to accomplish*.) Nonetheless, as tired parents of young children, a Sunday afternoon nap was a glorious pattern for both of us.

A few months after Susan was born, we had a quick lunch one Sunday after church before putting her and two-year-old Stephen down as usual. We had just begun to drift off when we heard *bang!* A pause was immediately followed by a loud wail. I jumped out of bed and went into the hallway to find Stephen, looking like he was in a horror movie, coming toward me, arms outstretched, with his face half covered in blood.

I scooped him up and called, "Phyllis!"

Stephen had decided to be Superman. As soon as we put him down for his nap, he had climbed up on the chest in his room and leaped to his bed. Unfortunately, he miscalculated the distance and hit the side of his head on the top corner of the footboard resulting in a deep, one-inch gash.

I was not at all sure what to do, but Phyllis's ER training took over. Calmly she put pressure on the wound and said, "We need to get him to the hospital for stiches." We called a neighbor who took Susan and off we went.

Stephen was hurt and crying, but Phyllis held him and talked to him quietly, telling him everything that was going to happen at the hospital. She wanted him to know what to expect so he wouldn't be scared. We'd go into a room with the doctor and a nurse. His wound needed to be closed so the bleeding would stop. They would give him something for the pain before using a needle and thread to stitch it. That would sting a bit though not much, and it wouldn't last long. But he would need to be still, to not move, so they could get it done quickly.

I thought this was way too much detail and might only make Stephen panic more. But nurse Phyllis was exactly right. She topped it off with another brilliant move that was perfect for our dessert-loving boy.

"And when we are done, we will take you to get an ice cream cone!"

Stephen did great. He was calm and cooperated fully with his mom who was right there with him the whole time.

✎ ✎ ✎

We were so glad when Philip joined us about two years after Susan on October 30, 1980. Phyllis was in awe of the miracle of each child. She wrote:

> The moment our first child was born had a great impact on me. . . .
> To hear that cry, to know that at one time Stephen did not exist but
> that now he does, to ponder that he was made in the image of the
> Almighty God, to receive Stephen as a gift from God to be nurtured
> and cared for—all of this made us grateful and humble. That awe
> continued as we watched two more children come into the world.
> God is indeed a great Creator!
>
> Seeing the world through the eyes of small children also
> increases my appreciation for creation. The wonder of a lightning

bug, the beauty of a butterfly, the taste of an ice-cream cone, the uniqueness of a leaf or a snowflake—all take on new meaning as I see them through the delighted eyes of a child. Susan never takes a walk without bringing home a very special rock. Stephen readily exclaims, "Isn't that a beautiful flower!" Even on his fussiest days, Philip is content when we go outside.[1]

Yet neither of us lived in such reverie all the time. Phyllis often said, "It wasn't marriage that made me realize what a sinner I am. It was being a parent!" Having two-year-old Susan look her straight in the eye and say, "I don't *want* to brush my teeth," or telling Stephen for the third time not to play with the hose, would sometimes send her over the edge. Phyllis wrote:

What have I learned? That I am inwardly an angry person. My kids can make me angrier than anyone else in the world. It's hard to admit that about a two-year-old and a four-year-old. . . . I don't like my anger. God doesn't like it either. He says in James 1:20, "For the anger of man does not work the righteousness of God." But he forgives. And my children are quick to forgive.[2]

And they were. When we realized we had overreacted, we tried to acknowledge that to the kids. Phyllis wanted to model apologizing and not get caught in a dysfunctional cycle of pretending unacceptable behavior was normal or okay.

We loved our children deeply, and so we were a bit surprised when Walter and Ingrid Trobisch said that children are guests in the family. They aren't there when the family is formed, and they aren't there at the end. They aren't the center of the family. Husband and wife, with Christ, are. I suppose this is like the adage that parents are to give their children roots and wings, to help them be grounded and secure enough to meet the challenges and opportunities of life they will inevitably face without us.

Still, Phyllis loved having babies and I was a proud dad. We so enjoyed these little people and building a family that losing one in miscarriage was a massive blow.

Phyllis was halfway through her fourth pregnancy when she realized the baby was not kicking. The doctor confirmed there was no heartbeat, and they would need to induce labor. No one knew why this happened, he said. Sometimes it just does. They took Phyllis away, and I waited.

When Phyllis came back, she said, "He was a perfect boy."

Did I want to see my son? the nurses asked.

I was devastated. I just couldn't. I felt I should and wanted to, but I couldn't. It was all too painful. Phyllis, of course, told me that was okay. Even in the midst of her own profound loss, she was able to offer me understanding and comfort. We all needed to deal with our grief in our own way, she said. Yet, because our boy was so young, there would be no funeral, no burial. Three times we had gone home from the hospital with joy and a wonderful baby in the back seat. This time it was empty.

Fifteen years later someone suggested we have a service for our baby. Even after such a long time, they said, it could be good to have some kind of closure. We decided to ask our pastor and his wife, Bob and JoAnn Harvey, if they would help us.

The four of us met. Bob modified a liturgy for us, and JoAnn read Scripture. For the first time, we named him—Michael. Phyllis and I wrote letters to our son. Though I had never seen him, I wrote that I could see him now, in my mind and in my heart with his brothers and sister, tall and at ease and laughing. The picture brought me a measure of comfort and peace, remembering we would see him again in heaven.

When Phyllis became pregnant with Michael, I wondered if I was at the limit of my capacity as a parent. But after he died I passionately wanted another child. Phyllis was always ready. We were both excited, then, when David arrived in June 1983.

Not long before, we got ready for his arrival by moving a few hundred feet down the street to 5313 Lane Place, "the third and final house" on the block, as Phyllis called it, which gave us additional room. We loved the Lane Place location with easy walking distance to my office, downtown stores, and the Baptist school the children attended. In addition, we loved our neighbors.

Even so, one time Phyllis got herself on the wrong side of someone. After having such a positive relationship with the family for years, the neighbor suddenly turned against her.

Neither of us could quite figure out what might have happened to generate this reaction. Phyllis tried to find out, but her queries were rebuffed. The neighbor wouldn't talk. After months of silence, shortly before the family moved, the husband indirectly and diplomatically affirmed that the breach had little if anything to do with us. Nonetheless, because reconciliation was so important to Phyllis, it was a hard reality for her that sometimes rifts are not healed.

℘ ℘ ℘

The frugality Phyllis grew up with carried into her adult life. During her nursing days she would tell her mom, "Don't buy me anything for Christmas. Let's just do the big January sales." Her tendencies were reinforced in our early years of marriage by the emphasis some Christian leaders put on living simply. Doing so was a way to stand with the poor, to lay aside distractions from ministry, to practice a spiritual discipline that focused our dependence on God, to enable being more generous, and to be good stewards of the earth by consciously resisting overconsumption.[3]

We usually bought used cars and ran those vehicles till they had no more useful life. We got a good roof antenna for our TV instead of paying hefty cable fees each month. Phyllis went to a lot of garage sales both out of an ethical commitment and because she just loved getting a deal.

When Stephen was not quite three, she came home with a used Big Wheel which he was delighted to ride down the slight incline of the sidewalk on our street time and time again. Garage sales also supplied much of our Christmas needs. Phyllis would bring home toys and games throughout the year, store them secretly in the attic, and then wrap them up for Christmas morning.

Halloween costumes were always bare bones. We didn't like spending money for a costume kids would wear once. The problem was, neither of us were particularly creative or crafty. (How many times can a kid go trick-or-treating dressed as a soccer player? Apparently quite a few.) The one or two ragged costumes we had were used year after year, passed down from one child to the next as they grew. Why was Philip dressed as Little Bo Peep for Halloween one year? Obviously because his sister had the same costume the year before.

We did most of our grocery shopping at ALDI because they had the best prices. Our family frugality was also reinforced because neither of us liked grocery shopping, although I tolerated it a bit better than Phyllis. Since she loved planning, she mapped out ten meals to cover two weeks (with leftovers or with me cooking to cover weekends). She then made a shopping list for me, doubling everything. That way the meals for the first two weeks of a month were repeated the last two weeks of a month.

Powdered milk was a staple that saved us hundreds of dollars with four growing kids who didn't know any better. Steve and Susan, however, noticed that the Special K they had when visiting Phyllis's mom was the best cereal ever. They didn't realize until years later that it wasn't the cereal that was so good. It was the real whole milk Granny had that made the difference. As the kids hit their teens, they started protesting. We relented and began buying regular milk. As Steve remembered later, "We had powdered milk all the time. I just thought we were poor."

Passing on the value of a simple lifestyle had other hits and misses. Once when Steve was about ten, he told his mom, "I wish I was an only child."

"How come?" she asked. "Don't you like your brothers and sister?"

"Oh, they're fine. It's just that if I was an only child, then I could have all the stuff."

"But Stephen, even if you were an only child, we still wouldn't give you all the stuff. It wouldn't be good for you to be spoiled like that. It wouldn't be good for your character."

"Yeah, I guess you're right," he said reluctantly. "It's not the kids that are the problem. It's the parents."

We also gave each child a "bank book"—a small notebook for tracking their money. Instead of giving them cash each month that might encourage spending, we had them note down their allowance with ten percent going to savings and ten percent to give to the church or other causes. They could use the rest as they wished. Money management became a monthly habit.

Another less-than-appreciated pattern was weekly house cleaning. Protests and grumbles accompanied every Saturday morning when Phyllis made assignments for picking up the house, cleaning the kitchen, dusting, and vacuuming. When we decided to get a dog, Phyllis emphasized the fun but also the responsibility. She made it part of the routine that each of the four would take Tumpkin, our black Cocker Spaniel, out for a walk once a day.

Phyllis not only loved people but loved gathering groups of people. She couldn't help but bring young moms together to study God's Word and to encourage each other in practical ways with the stresses babies can bring.

She also gladly teamed up with neighbors like the Blacks and Remperts who also had kids the same ages as ours. Each year the mothers would gather to decide on similar rules and guidelines for all their children regarding playing in the street, riding bikes, or whatever seemed prudent to codify. The kids were dismayed because this common front meant they didn't have two parents. They had eight. All the adults knew the rules and were ready to enforce them when they saw a child transgressing. The kids on the block also had a joke about the hierarchy. They called one mom the pope and other moms the priests.

Phyllis also coordinated play groups that rotated among several homes. Once a week all the kids would show up at a particular house for the morning, giving all the other mothers time on their own for chores, errands, or just some R & R.

Though she didn't want to go back to work when the kids were young, Phyllis was happy to do childcare at home for a few years. Once Phyllis got a call from the county Department of Youth and Family Services, however, that someone had reported her for potential violations. They scheduled a visit. We didn't know for sure who had called but we had a good idea. Our neighbor next door, Merv, was a bit crotchety in his old age and was known to do this sort of thing.

A case worker showed up and found that since Phyllis only had a few children, she was under the limit requiring a license to do childcare. A few days later I saw Merv across the fence, went up to him and said, "I thought you would like to know that the county family services department cleared Phyllis of any potential childcare violations."

His eyes got big and he said nervously, "Oh, I didn't call them."

"I didn't say you called them," I responded with a smile, knowing he had just given himself away. "I just said that I thought you'd like to know she was cleared."

We sent the kids to the First Baptist Christian School which was just two blocks away. I would walk them to school each morning and then walk another two blocks to the InterVarsity Press office. Phyllis would then walk them home each afternoon, sometimes with a friend or another mother from the block.

Once when Philip was in first grade, he saw his mom was engrossed in conversation with her friend as the three of them walked back home from school. He knew how absorbed his mom could be when she was talking to someone, so he decided to hide behind a tree to see if she'd notice he was not there. On the pair walked, and on they talked. After half a block Philip was afraid she'd totally forgotten him, so he ran to catch up. When he reached her, he realized she had not even noticed that he was ever gone.

Phyllis was very conscious of the faith that had been passed down to her from her parents and grandparents. She deeply desired to do the same. As a result, we were quite intentional about making faith part of the family.

We went to church regularly, and First Baptist Christian School offered a solid education in the Bible as well as the other standard subjects. We often played tapes of Christian children's songs in the car as we traveled. Agapeland's *Bullfrogs and Butterflies, Psalty's Praise Songs* and *Music Machine* stuck with us all as we sang together, "Have patience, have patience, don't be in such a hurry. When you are impatient, you only start to worry."

We prayed and often read from a children's Bible at meals. We also offered the kids the opportunity to pray before meals. Once when Stephen was about five and Susan about three, Susan volunteered. But Stephen interjected, "Oh, Susan. Your prayers are so boring. You always say the same thing."

We thought for sure World War III would break out, but Susan simply bowed her head and began praying the sweetest, most sincere, and most theologically astute prayer you have ever heard come from the mouth of a curly-haired, redheaded three-year-old. When she said, "Amen," Phyllis and I looked at each other in wonder, as if to say, "Are we not the most amazing parents ever?"

At which point Susan turned to her brother and with fire in her eyes said, *"See, Stephen!"*

That wasn't the only time the amazing results of our Christian parenting became evident. Some years later when Philip was about eleven and David was nine, Phyllis, Stephen, and Susan had gone to church early. That left just me and the two boys silently munching our cereal on Sunday morning. Finally, apparently bored, Philip looked at me and said, "Dad, don't you think we should tell Dave?"

I was still in a morning stupor and looked at him a bit bewildered.

"Dad," he said more insistently, "I think we need to tell Dave."

I looked at Dave to see if he had any clue as to what his brother was talking about. Dave shrugged his shoulders, so I turned back to Philip, still clueless.

Finally, in exasperation, Philip looked at his brother and said, "David, this morning in church, you are going to be *sacrificed!*"

We kept TV to a minimum but usually had a couple of shows we would watch as a family. Phyllis especially loved the wholesome goodness and gentle humor of *Little House on the Prairie* with Michael Landon that ran from 1974 to 1983. That was followed by another Phyllis favorite, *The Cosby Show,* which chronicled the humorous escapades of the Huxtable family over the next eight years.

We did learn, however, to never say *never*. When VCRs were introduced, we said we'd never get one. Of course, it wasn't long before we were recording shows on tape. We also said we'd never get video game players such as those from Atari and Nintendo. Life (the culture and persistent children) can humble even the most determined parents, however. Our compromise was to buy used units and limit their time.

Another family tradition was the "100 monthiversary." A friend told us that at eight years and four months, a child is 100 months old. That provides the opportunity for a surprise party. Since Stephen was just a year away, Phyllis began planning.

On March 19, 1985, we strung a big sign across the kitchen reading, "Happy 100 Monthiversary." As Stephen walked into the kitchen that morning, Phyllis led us all in cheering. He wasn't quite sure what was going on, but he soon caught on. After school we celebrated with cake and presents in "the hundreds"—such as a hundred mints, a hundred cards (two full decks), a hundred Legos, a hundred each of pennies, nickels, dimes, quarters, and dollars. We capped it off with a list we compiled from family and friends— "One Hundred Things We Like about Stephen."

Phyllis especially liked the list of affirming things we had to say about our oldest. Stephen especially liked the cash.

The beauty of the celebration is that while all children know when their birthday is coming, they don't keep track of a hundred months. Because of that each one of them was surprised.

By these and other common experiences, repeated over the years, we sought to build a solid family culture.

℘ ℘ ℘

Phyllis began to get the writing bug in this era. It started when a coworker of mine in the editorial department suggested the three of us write a discussion guide to Habakkuk. Jack Stewart was attracted to this Old Testament minor prophet because of the emphasis on justice, injustice, and the ways nations tend to run over their own people and those of other countries. In 1979 *Just Living by Faith* was released by IVP.

Then in 1981 Linda Doll, the editor for InterVarsity's HIS magazine, asked Phyllis to write an article on the value and worth of raising children. Though the magazine was aimed at college students, Linda sensed that this generation felt a reluctance to bring children into a world with so many problems. She thought Phyllis was just the person to offer a counterbalancing perspective. "Life's Little Blessings" came out in the December issue.

That same year IVP released two Bible study guides based on studies we had done in Welcome Class. One was on the letter of James, released as *Faith That Works* and later revised for the LifeGuide series and retitled *James*. The other was a series of discussions on aspects of marriage, entitled *One Plus One Equals One.*

That opened the floodgates for Phyllis. She published eight guides in the Caring People series in 1991 (based on NCF materials) and in the same year three guides in Zondervan's series on the fruit of the Spirit. Among her other projects were guides based on books by John Stott and N. T. Wright.

Many considered the most ironic guide she ever wrote to be *A Woman of Rest.* Yet because she knew of her tendency to be constantly on the go, she aspired (not always successfully) to balance her activity not just with relaxation but with quiet trusting in God's grace.

Perhaps her favorite was the last guide we authored together—*Grandparenting.* Family was always a deep passion, and if she could help others love their grandchildren as she loved hers, well, it couldn't get much better than that.

Her guides were also translated and published around the world in Arabic, Indonesian, Italian, Korean, and Portuguese. Over the decades, all of them cumulatively sold over a million copies.

Bible Study Guides by Phyllis J. Le Peau

Just Living by Faith and A. T. Le Peau, J. D. Stewart (IVP, 1979)

James and A. T. Le Peau (IVP LifeGuide, 1981, 1987, 1999)

One Plus One Equals One and A. T. Le Peau (IVP, 1981)

Ephesians and A. T. Le Peau (IVP LifeGuide, 1985, 2000)

Joy (Zondervan, 1991, 2001)

Kindness (Zondervan, 1991, 2001)

Gentleness (Zondervan, 1991, 2001)

Caring for People in Conflict and NCF (IVP, 1991)

Handbook for Caring People and Bonnie J. Miller, NCF (IVP, 1991)

Caring for People in Grief and NCF (IVP, 1991)

Resources for Caring People and NCF (IVP, 1991)

Caring for Emotional Needs and NCF (IVP, 1991)

The Character of Caring People and NCF (IVP, 1991)

Caring for Spiritual Needs and NCF (IVP, 1991)

Caring for Physical Needs and NCF (IVP, 1991)

Acts (IVP LifeGuide, 1992, 2002)

Women of the New Testament (IVP LifeGuide, 1996, 2003)

Love (IVP LifeGuide, 1997, 2003)

A Woman of Rest (IVP, 1997)

Ephesians based on John Stott (IVP, 1998)

Acts based on John Stott (IVP, 1998)

1 & 2 Timothy and Titus based on N. T. Wright (IVP, 2009)

James based on N. T. Wright (IVP, 2012)

A Deeper Look at James and A. T. Le Peau (IVP LifeGuide, 2013)

Grandparenting and A. T. Le Peau (IVP LifeGuide, 2017)

℘ ℘ ℘

One priority Phyllis made sure we included in our annual plan during those early years of marriage was trips to see our families. We would usually alternate between St. Louis and Minneapolis for Christmas and Thanksgiving. We also often found ourselves in Kalamazoo with Phyllis's sister and her husband, Diane and Dick O'Day, along with their four kids.

At Thanksgiving in 1979 my side of the family gathered in Minnesota. John and Nancy Le Peau brought little Lucy while Mary and Kirby Heyns came with their three young girls (Kim, Rachel, and Becca). Phyllis instigated the first all-cousins birthday party (a tradition these same cousins have continued with the next generation) complete with cake and hats for everyone.

Phyllis also thought it would be perfect to buy toy musical instruments for the kids. Proudly, from room to room, she led a boisterous parade of beating drums, banging cymbals, and tooting horns. Though the other adults tolerated the noise, Phyllis was only aware of the joy and fun.

Phyllis's instinct that we visit my mom as much as possible turned out to be more than just the appropriate thing to do. We had no idea how brief our time with her would be. We went to Minneapolis in August 1983 for what was to be a routine procedure to clear her renal artery. Due to complications from surgery, however, she never came home.

I was crushed. I felt like a homeless orphan. In the months that followed I was mad at God and sometimes couldn't bring myself to go to church. Phyllis allowed me to grieve as I needed and loved me steadily, never reproving me for falling into acute depression. Her patient, nonjudgmental care was key over the next year as I began to heal from this deep loss.

Another trip just a few months later also had a profound effect. One winter day we traveled down Interstate 55 in sub-zero temperatures to St. Louis to be with Phyllis's parents. All too soon we experienced white-out conditions and ended up in the middle of a fifty-car pileup.

With the blizzard still raging, our car was eventually able to limp to a nearby exit and a small town. Phyllis and I sheltered in a restaurant with our four young children, all of us dazed and uncertain. As we stood among dozens of other stranded motorists, we heard rumors that the town was going to open the local high school gym so people would have a place to stay that cold winter night.

Soon a local woman eyed us and our four small children and said, "You're not staying in the high school gym."

"We're not?" we responded, confused.

"No," she replied, "you're staying in our house tonight."

That night, instead of hosting others as we usually did, we were the strangers being cared for. That night we were in need of a warm place, warm food, and friendly faces. This family welcomed us into their home, fed us all we wanted, had us join in their activities, and as we left the next morning, I was astonished to hear them say, "It has been wonderful to have you here. You blessed us. You've reminded us of what's important in life, of how good God is."

I could hardly believe it. We were the ones in need. We were the ones who had been helped, but somehow they were the ones who were blessed.

That night in their home we were all reminded vividly how God welcomes us into the hospitality of his love through the gift of his Son sent to all of us. We were reminded that God calls us to find ways to follow his example by also reaching out to those in need, those who are weak or oppressed—just has he had done for us, entering this world as a baby who would give us the greatest welcome of all.

This was especially vivid because that winter night in which the six of us were stranded and helpless, that night in which we needed rescue—that night was Christmas Eve.

11

SUMMERING

"Why don't you come with us on vacation for a week in Michigan?" We didn't know it at the time, but this question, posed to us in the Spring of 1979, would have a profound, multigenerational impact on our family.

We met Tom and Cindy Walthour in Welcome Class at First Methodist in Downers Grove. We had had them over for dinner a couple of times, and enjoyed their children, John and Diana.

The previous two summers, the Walthours had spent a week at two small cottages on Fremont Lake in western Michigan, just four hours away. They took one cottage and a brother's family took the other. Each family had their own space, they told us, but they usually had dinner together on picnic tables under a huge willow. The rest of the day was free for water fun, fishing, reading, or playing games.

But their relatives had other plans for the upcoming summer. Since Tom and Cindy wanted to go back to Fremont, they wondered if we'd like to join them.

So it was, then, that on Saturday morning, July 21, 1979, we packed up the car with two-year-old Stephen and six-month-old Susan and followed the Walthours to Fremont. That afternoon we moved into two fishing cottages that had been built in the 1920s. Originally there were seven cabins but two had burned down some years before. Though owned by different families, the five shared a common well. The two we rented were owned by Rich and Marlene Hiemstra who lived just up the hill. Rich was the credit manager for Gerber Baby Food which had its headquarters in Fremont. Tom, who was credit manager for Dean Foods, knew Rich through industry connections.

When we arrived, we saw a beautiful, roughly oval, eight-hundred-acre lake in front of us. The cottages had been built on cinderblocks set right on the ground. They each had two bedrooms, a kitchen, and a living room, with a toilet and shower stall squeezed between one bedroom and the living room. The only sink was in the kitchen where we brushed our teeth and bathed the baby. The walls were just an inch thick.

The most beloved feature was a screened-in front porch that spanned the entire side of each cottage facing the lake. We spent hours there playing games on the table and gliding back and forth on the porch swing.

We also had use of a rowboat secured to a wooden dock that stretched seventy feet into the lake. Almost miraculously, the sandy-bottomed lake was shallow, only a couple of feet deep at the end of the dock. With a hundred and twenty feet of lakefront, this provided a huge surface area where kids could play safely while parents joined them or watched nearby. A few inner tubes got plenty of use each day.

The huge willow tree, which we estimated to be more than two hundred years old, was a landmark feature of the property. Old Man Willow provided wonderful shade from the summer sun and a place for the children to spend hours climbing. (In 2025, at 22 ft., 1 inch in circumference, it was listed as the girthiest tree in Newaygo County, and thirty-third in the state.[1])

Fremont

At the end of the last ice age, about 12,000 years ago, the glaciers receded. Within about a thousand years people began occupying western Michigan. (In October 2010, when digging a hole to plant an autumn blaze maple sapling on the west side of the property, I found a full grooved stone axe head. Such tools can date from 3,000 to 9,000 years ago.[2])

The Hopewell Indians were mound builders who lived in the area from about 400 BC to AD 400.[3] The Ottawa (Odawa), Chippewa (Ojibwa), and Potawatomi (Bodéwadmi) people were likely descendants of the Hopewells who established villages in the region around 1700.

European traders began arriving about 1620, soon followed by an increasing number of settlers. The area was considered part of French Canada from 1668 to 1763 when it was turned over to Britain after the French and Indian War. The pressures on the native population by settlers and the government were exacerbated when a devastating smallpox epidemic swept through the Grand River Valley in western Michigan from 1835-37.[4] On January 26, 1837, Michigan became the U.S.A.'s twenty-sixth state.

Weaverville, named for the area's first postmaster, was founded in 1854. When Weaver moved to Hesperia in 1862, the name was changed to Fremont Centre because it was in the middle of what was then Fremont Township and to honor Union army officer, explorer, and politician John C. Frémont.[5]

The expanding and then contracting glaciers of the last ice age had created sandy soil, deposited sediments, and scraped the landscape flat, making western Michigan ideal for agriculture. It was a natural place for the Fremont Canning Company to begin business in 1927, which soon became famous for its baby food, changing its name in 1941 to Gerber Products Company.

The receding glaciers also left behind the five Great Lakes and eleven thousand inland lakes in Michigan, one of which was the spring-fed Fremont Lake.

We had two fun summers with the Walthours, but in 1981 they made other vacation plans. We deeply missed being at Fremont that year, so we decided to invite Paul and Kathy Woodard and their three children to be with us for a week in July 1982, and they joined us most summers after that.

We barbequed many nights and enjoyed the fresh produce of the summer months—sweet corn and peaches. We often picked our own blueberries and raspberries. S'mores were always a favorite treat. The kids were constantly in the water, and Phyllis's competitive spirit and fondness for trash-talking were given space when the adults played Five Hundred (a variation of Four-handed Euchre) late into the nights.

We delighted so much in Fremont that Phyllis suggested we book the cottages for two weeks in 1985 and invite another family to join us the second week. The summer after that we invited the John Le Peaus and Heynses to join us one of the two weeks for a first-ever family reunion.

In the middle of that week, on July 29, Phyllis received the hard news that her dad died. Years earlier he had developed adult-onset diabetes (now called type 2 diabetes), no doubt because he was such a sugar lover. After we were married this tall, lumbering, gruff, good-natured man had to have one leg amputated and a year or so later the other leg was also removed.

The man who turned out so well, despite being ill-treated as a young boy by his aunt, kept up his spirits by reminding everyone that for decades, when he was surprised at something, he would always say, "Well cut off my legs and call me shorty!"

He had been hospitalized for a couple weeks, so the news though difficult was not unexpected. Phyllis and I reluctantly decided she should leave me and the kids at the lake while she went to southern Illinois with her mother and sisters to bury her father near Shawneetown. She had sent me off alone to my father's funeral ten years before. Now, with very mixed feelings, I did the same.

She reported back that she took great comfort at the graveside service when the minister looked at Phyllis and her two sisters, and said, "Girls, your dad is home."

After a couple years of enjoying two weeks in Fremont during the summer, Phyllis thought three weeks would be even better. This gave her even more opportunity to be the party host and queen of fun. She was so delighted to invite different families to join us each week. The Woodards typically had a week. Lane Place neighbors also came with their kids including Jim and Sandy Black as well as Mary and Terry Rempert on occasion. Others who enjoyed a week were Steve and Jackie Eyre with their boys, and Judy and Wayne Paney with their children.

Traveling and sightseeing were fine with Phyllis, but those activities didn't satisfy her cravings for deep, focused interaction with people, for the adrenalin rush that games gave her, and for initiating all the merriment. Since she still couldn't get enough of lake fun, we rented the two cabins for four weeks in the summer of 1989. Because I had limited vacation time, I went back to work in Downers Grove for the fourth week, leaving Phyllis and the kids in Fremont with our last group of friends for the summer.

Right before I left we noticed the Hiemstras were measuring the rooms in the other cabin. When we asked about it, they said they were planning on selling. The cabins had always been an investment intended to help with college tuition for their three kids.

"Will we still be able to rent from the new owners?" we asked.

"That's hard to say. It depends on the new owners," they replied, reasonably enough.

Later Phyllis said to me, "We should think about buying them."

"I can hardly stand the thought of not being able to come here in the summer," I replied. "But I'm not sure how that would work. We'd need to rent, and having rental property four hours away seems crazy."

But all that week, I kept thinking about it. Could we buy it with friends or neighbors? Could we do it on our own? The more I thought, the more I wanted to do it. I just wasn't sure how.

I drove back to Fremont Friday afternoon and started to help pack up since we needed to be out by early Saturday morning. Phyllis stood on the porch steps silently watching me as I sat between the two cottages getting the air out of the big inner tubes. Then, without any preamble, she said, "Andy, let's do it."

Not just because we'd been married for fourteen years, but because Phyllis was always an open book, it was not hard for me to know what she thought about anything and everything. At that moment I knew exactly what she was talking about. She had been more interested in and more certain about taking this step than I had been.

I simply replied, "Okay."

She was shocked. "You mean it? Are we talking about the same thing? You mean we should buy the cottages?"

"Yes, I do."

"Then we need to talk to the Hiemstras right now, before we leave, before they sell them to someone else."

Rich and Marlene were happy with our interest. Having neighbors next door they already knew and trusted would be an advantage from their perspective. Over the next few months we negotiated terms, and in January 1990 we drove up to Fremont to close the deal. Phyllis's energy and willingness to take risks once again propelled us into a new phase of life.

The Hiemstras passed on to us the contact information of previous renters, and we began scheduling them for the next summer. We also invited new families such as the Fines. Phyllis knew Gary and Cheri Fine from Wellness, Inc., their new business, which had first hired Mary Rempert and then Phyllis.

Our relationship with the family up the hill from the cottages, Dar and Darrell Crawford, immediately changed when we bought the cottages. We were no longer renters they would occasionally interact with; we were now neighbors. Within a few months they asked if we'd like to buy a boat together. Dar's boss was selling an old ski boat for $1,000, and she and Darrell thought it would be great for their kids and ours who were near in age.

Their three boys and our four children all learned to ski behind the old yellow boat the kids christened The Eggbeater. While they all popped up after two or three tries, it was a different story for Phyllis. Every day we were at the lake over the next three or four summers, Phyllis tried to get up and fell, tried to get up and fell, tried to get up and fell.

We'd tell her: Don't stand up too fast. Sit back. Keep your skis straight. Tighten your ski boots. You fell forward that time. You fell backward. You fell left. You fell right.

Our tips never did any good. Phyllis was still determined, however, trying to get up five or six times or more before she tired out. But she never made it.

Years before I had read a humor piece in the *Chicago Tribune Magazine* about names and their supposed significance—Mabel was a waitress, Hazel was a maid, etc. With uncanny accuracy, the comment for "Phyllis" was "happy but uncoordinated."

I wondered if Phyllis would ever get up. But because I knew how desperately she wanted to, I kept that to myself and kept taking her out on the water, week after week, year after year. Then late one afternoon, when the water was calm, Phyllis wanted to try again. Gary Fine drove the boat, and I was the spotter. Astonishingly she got up and stayed up. Gary drove steadily and took as wide and gentle a turn as he could when we got to the cove, a quarter mile down the shore.

I thought Phyllis would be ecstatic, but she had a pronounced scowl on her face. I yelled for her to smile, but she couldn't hear. Gary drove the boat back past the cottage and a celebration erupted. Everyone on shore waved, cheered, and yelled as loud as they could. A minute later, after a highly successful first ride, she finally fell.

"Why didn't you smile?" I asked when we picked her up.

"I thought it was a dirty trick and I was just going to fall again."

She hadn't quite realized she was up and skiing since she had never experienced it before. At age fifty, she skied for the first time and kept skiing for the next twenty-five years. Later she often used a pair of ski gloves to help her keep her grip when getting up. But Susan would call out to her, "Mom, the magic is not in the gloves! It's *in you!*"

A summer or two after she first skied successfully, I was once again pulling Phyllis. Suddenly, she fell awkwardly. I was surprised because by that time she'd become very consistent. Skiing was routine for her.

When I guided the boat back to her as she floated in the water, I asked, "Are you all right? What happened?"

"Oh," she laughed, "I thought I'd drop a ski and try to slalom."

"That's okay," I said, thinking she would never succeed in this new endeavor, "but if you are going to try just one ski, let me give you a couple of tips."

On the next try she got up on two as usual, and following my instructions, dropped a ski, slipped her foot into the back foothold on the remaining ski, and continued down the lake on one ski. We were all shocked and amazed that after failing to get up on two skis for four years Phyllis was able to slalom on her second try.

"It was the greatest lesson I ever had on fear of failure," she told us. "I wanted to ski so badly and feared never being able to, that I was always tight and nervous. I was my own worst enemy. But having finally learned to ski, I didn't care at all if I ever learned to ski on one. After you gave me those instructions, I wasn't tense one bit. I just did it."

The joy and stimulation of skiing made it a lifelong passion. Fifteen years after first learning Phyllis wrote in her journal, "Skiing is still emotionally refreshing as it is physically. I am so grateful the Lord allowed/helped me to learn."[6] She had found another way to kick her adrenaline into high gear.

One major addition to cottage fun came from the hands of Phyllis's brother-in-law, Dick O'Day, Diane's husband. Dick was a bricklayer by trade and, because of his hyperactive nature, was constantly building and rebuilding things for his kids in the backyard of their house in Kalamazoo—swing sets, forts, a basketball court. As soon as we bought the cottages, he built us an 8' x 8' floating dock.

The sturdy frame was made of thick treated wood, floated on four empty, fifty-gallon yeast barrels he had obtained from a local brewery, and was covered with decking and indoor-outdoor carpeting. He brought it up in his pickup truck one weekend and supervised as his teenagers attempted to anchor it one windy, wavy day. They eventually managed to get it out a hundred feet from shore, securing it just beyond the drop off.

The floating dock provided hours of fun for diving practice, playing King of the Dock, and generally pushing, shoving, and throwing each other off. Phyllis loved seeing a dozen or more kids squeezing on it at once.

The dock did, however, have a tendency to float away in the middle of the night since it only had a cinder block or two tied at each corner keeping it in place. That was not nearly enough weight to do the job. Eventually, I laid down a permanent anchor of more than a dozen cinderblocks on a heavy chain, which was cabled to the shore when we brought the dock in each winter.

Dick's original dock lasted almost three decades. Though we replaced the carpet every few years and the decking twice, the basic frame stayed within one inch of square through storms and hard use all those summers.

℘ ℘ ℘

Paul and Kathy Woodard and George and Barbara Stulac not only joined us at Fremont, but they also regularly led family camps together at Bear Trap each summer in Colorado during the early 1980s. One year they asked us to join them there. The idea of bringing our kids to the place where Phyllis and I met that had been so formative for me as a college student was very appealing. In addition, Phyllis loved working as a ministry team with both couples. As a result, we drove a couple of days west, and on June 14, 1986, we rolled into that narrow, sequestered mountain valley for the first time with our four children.

George often directed the work crew of college students and gave Scripture expositions to the families. Speaking and codirecting duties were usually split between us and the Woodards. Phyllis especially loved leading the group in singing hymns with Barbara Stulac at the piano. We went every summer for the next ten years.

Even with the range of ages of our kids, they all had something to enjoy at Bear Trap's family camp—trail riding, hiking, rappelling, bonfires, overnight camping, horseshoes, archery, hikes to see the lights of Colorado Springs at night from the Duffield Overlook, getting wet in Little Fountain Creek that ran through camp, and more. They also loved the time they had in the Bible in small groups led by InterVarsity college students on summer work crew.

One highlight was the Wrangler's Breakfast. Every morning a different group of about two dozen adults and children walked or rode horses up the hill to a cookout site. There the "wrangler" (or just someone from work crew) served up bacon, eggs, and pancakes on an open fire. The specialty was a bullseye—a pancake with an egg in the middle.

Somehow the early morning mountain air made everything taste extra good. (Later we realized that much of the amazing flavor came from the pancakes being cooked in bacon grease, giving the pancakes slightly crispy edges!) It wasn't long before this Bear Trap tradition became a Fremont tradition where we started enjoying

Wrangler's Breakfast at the lake, which was cooked in cast iron skillets over the grill.

Phyllis loved the people at Bear Trap and loved the opportunity to speak about marriage and family life. Once when our kids were reaching their teens, we took a chance and let Susan and Philip say a few words to the parents about what life was like for them in the family and in school, and about their desires for independence. They did a great job. Then we took an even bigger chance and let the parents ask the two of them questions.

"Don't you think," asked one parent, "your parents have the best in mind for you, and that when they put limits on you it is for your own well-being?"

"Oh, of course, I do," answered Susan. "And when I have kids," she went on with prophetic humor, "I will probably put limits on them too. But for now, I want my independence!"

🐚 🐚 🐚

In the 1990s all of Chicago, all of the U.S., all of the world was about the Bulls. Michael Jordan was the most recognizable athlete, if not person, on the planet. With Scottie Pippen, B. J. Armstrong, John Paxson, Steve Kerr, and others, Jordan won six championships for the Chicago Bulls—repeating the threepeat.

Phyllis was a rabid fan who was sucked into the glory and excitement of each playoff run. As the family gathered around the TV to watch each game she'd cheer and scream and yell.

In a bit of role reversal, our kids even tried to get her to quiet down during games. "Mom, not so loud!"

But I tried to offer some perspective, saying, "Kids, let your mom have some fun!" They got it and they did.

One of the challenges, however, was that sometimes our trips to family camp in June overlapped with the NBA championship series. We planned stops on the road to allow us to watch games. But in 1993 a major conflict was unavoidable. The first night of family camp overlapped with what could be the deciding game six of the final series. The Bulls were up three games to two, playing Charles Barkley's Suns in Phoenix.

Stephen and the other kids were desperate to watch the game. But TV reception in the 1990s at 9000 feet, tucked between mountain peaks, was a dicey affair at Bear Trap. Only one TV, in the residence of a permanent staffer, got reception. The kids promptly talked their way into the house to watch the first half. The Bulls were up 56-41.

The second half would happen just as the first all-camp meeting was taking place. Phyllis and I were in a quandary. We didn't think it was appropriate for us as leaders to excuse our kids when everyone else was expected to be there. Reluctantly, we told them they could catch the very end of the game as soon as the meeting was over.

With much grumbling, they went up to the balcony for the meeting. What we didn't know was that as soon as the meeting started, they snuck out to watch the conclusion of the game. As it turned out, Phoenix came back, and the Bulls were down 98-96 with four seconds left. Horace Grant, who was under the basket, received a pass but saw John Paxson open beyond the three-point line. Grant fired the ball to Paxson who sank the shot for the 99-98 win, securing the Bulls' first threepeat.

Our four bounced into the meeting just as it was concluding with the announcement. We were excited, but some of the other campers were annoyed with our Bulls' mania. When Phyllis and I found out the kids had skipped out early, she had a mixed response. She wished they had obeyed, but she also decided we were just being too strict to not let them go watch. We had leaned toward law, but that time our parenting should have leaned toward grace.

At the end of our decade of family camps, Susan and Steve were in college and had their summers tied up. Since the summer was full and Phyllis had a job assignment with InterVarsity the same week as family camp, we decided to skip it that year.

When we sat Phil and Dave down at the kitchen table to tell

them the news, their shoulders slumped, and they both hung their heads in silence. Phyllis and I looked at each other, not knowing what to make of their reaction. None of our kids were ever reluctant to speak their minds. We often joked to each other that we wished we had at least one sweet little spineless thing. But this time the two boys said nothing.

"What?" we asked. "What's going on? What are you thinking?"

"Don't you guys know that a week at Bear Trap is worth a year of Sunday school? It's the most significant week each year for our spiritual growth and development."

We were stunned. Indeed, how could we not have known that! I suppose these two astute teens might have figured out exactly what they needed to say to manipulate their parents, giving us the precise reason that would get us to change our minds by playing the "spiritual growth" card. Regardless, it worked!

On the spot we decided I could take the two of them on my own. Bear Trap meant that much to all of us.

ॐ ॐ ॐ

We made one major exception to our normal routine of family trips to Fremont and Bear Trap. And it didn't even happen in the summer. Phyllis realized that Christmas vacation, 1997, would be the last time we would be able to have a large say in the schedule for all four kids. Stephen would be graduating from the University of Colorado the following May, and after that his work schedule would mean we couldn't assume he'd be with us on holidays.

We had been to Hawaii two years before with John and Patti Strong. At each point we kept saying to ourselves, "The kids would love this." So we planned our one big family vacation to Hawaii between Christmas and New Year's.

Everyone was excited. When Dave and Phil started telling friends at church about it, Brandon, Jenny, and Lindsay Jones said they were going too! At the exact same time! To the exact same place! We took advantage of this serendipity to make arrangements with their parents, Stan and Brenna, to join them for a day hiking Diamond Head and another on Waikiki Beach.

That was the scene of a legendary debacle. Phyllis loved playing in the waves but was having trouble keeping her balance—especially, let it be said, with Dave pushing her underwater. Finally, as she tried to make her way back to the beach, a six-inch wave rolled in—and knocked her down! Happy but uncoordinated, indeed!

While on Oahu, Phyllis made sure we visited the moving USS Arizona Memorial at Pearl Harbor. Highlights on Maui included whale watching, having a few hours with Cousin Becca Heyns who was in Maui for a swim meet with Pitt, biking down the ten-thousand-foot dormant volcano Haleakalā, and driving the scenic Road to Hana on Christmas Eve.

Each was a moment that lived in our collective memory, perhaps reaching a climax with Steve being thoroughly exasperated that he was trapped in a too-small rental car on our way back from Hana as his siblings joyfully sang Christmas carols in their annoying private language.

℘ ℘ ℘

Each fall we winterized and closed the cabins in Fremont, usually in late October or the beginning of November. Often Dave would drive up with me to help, and we'd stop at Sherman's Ice Cream on the way back to reward ourselves.

In the fall of 2001, as Phyllis and I were busy with such jobs as draining the waterline and putting things away in the bedrooms, the leg of a bed went through a rotten place in the floor. We couldn't do much about it then. We just put a piece of plywood down as a temporary fix.

In the spring of 2002 we had a handyman come to check things out. He pulled up the slats of the wooden floor in the bedroom and found nothing but sand underneath. The joists for the floor had completely rotted away. Since the cabins had been built seventy-five years before without a foundation, it was surprising they had lasted that long.

The handyman also pointed out that the roofline looked like a swayback horse. Below that the gutters followed a similar curve. And that was because the floor joists supporting the walls were rotting or gone. The whole thing would need to be torn down. While the other cabin didn't show the same problems, it would soon. The township authorities wouldn't allow us to rebuild both cabins because we would violate code by having two structures on a single plot. (The original cabins had been grandfathered in when the current code was adopted.)

Should we take this as the moment to sadly say goodbye to our beloved Fremont? "No," came the resounding answer from our four twenty-something children.

"But you guys don't like the cottages that much."

"Yes, but don't sell the land! Build something nice," they said, always happy to spend our money for us.

Should we build a duplex so we could continue to give two families their own space? That would be more expensive and wouldn't have the best resale value. We decided then to go with a single-family structure.

If I were designing a lake house, along with the usual kitchen, dining room, living room, and screened in porch, it would have one bedroom, one bath, and a study. That would suit my personality just fine.

Phyllis had other ideas. "Andy, we've should make this into the ideal place for family reunions and retreats." Each fall I had jammed my editorial team into the cottages for a few days of planning and Phyllis had done the same with her InterVarsity area team. Now she had even more in mind.

She wanted room—lots of room for lots of people. As a result, her design squeezed in as many bedrooms as possible. Never mind that they were small. That didn't matter since people wouldn't be spending time there anyway. They'd all be outside or together in one place, just the way she wanted. Thus she planned out a great room spanning the whole side of the house facing the lake, consisting of an open-plan kitchen-dining room-living room combination.

To top it off, remembering how much we all enjoyed the screened-in porches, she definitely wanted two porches to hold the porch swings from the original cottages. The new lake house fully reflected Phyllis's love for being with and hosting as many people as she could.

We hired a contractor who got us a good price by having a factory-built modular home constructed for us. At a factory in Flint, Michigan, the main floor of the house was built in two long, rectangular sections. The wiring, the plumbing, the cabinetry, and the wallboard were all finished there before being trucked to Fremont on two semis.

In January 2003, the two rectangular sections were set on the foundation that had been laid the month before. The next day the roof (which had been shipped flat on top of the two sections) was raised to a peak and secured. The dormers and porches were then added on site.

During the winter Phyllis was in her glory collecting beds, mattresses, and other furniture that filled our house and garage in Downers Grove. In late May we rented a truck and moved it all to Fremont, ready for our summer renters and family fun.

Phyllis had designed a house that was the architectural reflection of her personality.

Months before, as we were planning all this, however, Phyllis said, "Let's not tell the extended family and let them be surprised when they show up for the family reunion this summer! That'll be so much fun!" With nieces beginning to get married and have kids, we did get a few questions about where we were going to put everyone. But Phyllis happily gave them a reassuring non-answer:

"Oh, it will be fine. We've got it all figured out."

Sure enough, the family was delighted with the surprising spectacle. Lucy Le Peau said, "When we drove down the hill and saw that house, I thought, *How rude of someone to build that big house in front of the cottages!*"

℘ ℘ ℘

Over the years Fremont was the site of innumerable stories and episodes that became part of family lore. Once, before Steve and Kristen married, Steve had a girlfriend visit for a few days. After she left the lake, we were all talking outside along the shore.

Phyllis wanted to know what he thought of her. "Steve," she said, "how would you rate her on a scale of one to ten?"

The rest of the family hooted and howled. We couldn't believe she was asking a question like that which seemingly reduced a person to a number, especially one associated with diminishing women to a purely physical evaluation. In vain we tried to get her to withdraw the question. "No," she said, not quite understanding our objection, "I just want to know what he thinks."

I tried once more, "Phyllis, you just can't ask that kind of question. Try another way." But I got nowhere.

At that point Phil gently put his arm around me and with a smile, gestured out to the water, and said, "Dad, sometimes you've just got to let Mom sail out into the stormy waters and be glad you're standing on solid ground!"

Phil was right, of course. Often when I felt Phyllis's questions were too intrusive, I would try to get her to back off. It took me a long time to realize that Phyllis and the kids could handle their relationships with each other just fine. I didn't need to jump in and referee because I was uncomfortable with someone else's conflict. In any case, when Phyllis had her teeth clamped on a question, she was not about to let it go.

Phyllis also loved a story about Phil at age sixteen. She got special pleasure telling it five years afterward to the InterVarsity chapter Phil and Dave were a part of at the University of Arizona. She was speaking that night at their weekly meeting and thought a story about her boys would be the perfect way to start things off.

"We were with our neighbors at the lake," she told the sixty or so students, "when we were shocked one summer afternoon to see an apparently very territorial duck systematically breaking the necks, one by one, of a brood of ducklings. Eventually a neighbor threw rocks at the perpetrator to try to stop the carnage, which distracted the attacker long enough for the mother duck to break its neck. But it was too late. That afternoon and into night the mother duck forlornly and ceaselessly quacked up and down the shore, calling for her ducklings who were no more."

As the girls in the group began to respond sorrowfully by saying, "Oh, no," Phil slunk further and further down in his chair, trying vainly to get out of sight since he knew what was coming.

Phyllis cheerfully went on, "Eventually, Philip, tired of the incessant racket, mustered all the compassion he could and yelled out to the mother duck, 'Get over it. Your babies are dead!'"

The boys howled. The girls cried out in distress, "Phil, how could you?"

Phyllis couldn't have been more pleased with the reactions.

℘ ℘ ℘

When it came to vacations, Phyllis did not gravitate toward amusement parks or cruise ships with individuals going off to their own excitement. She was willing to travel a bit and do some sightseeing. What she valued most, though, was vacations that emphasized time together and common activities like playing games, having water fun as a group, or hiking up a mountain together. Bear Trap and Fremont were perfect for a routine of knitting us together in just those ways. Hawaii fit in as a grand exception.

Phyllis instinctively built traditions and a thick family culture that bound our lives together. Fremont and Bear Trap were two major components of that. Activities repeated on a daily, weekly, and yearly cycle created a sense of stability and belonging. Celebrating milestones like birthdays, the 100 monthiversary, and graduations for each member gave a sense of value and worth. Half-birthday breakfasts with one or both parents also became institutions.

Eating the evening meal together as much as possible signaled how we valued each other. Going to church weekly impressed the importance of our church community and of our faith. Time-honored menus and treats on holidays—heath bars, chocolate cherry cookies, gooey butter cake—built bonds of delicious memories together.

Tradition creates a dense web that securely holds a sense of identity and of belonging as a result of common experiences, a common history, and common memories. At one point, the family even developed this list:

You Might Be a Le Peau If . . .

- you get louder when someone doesn't agree with you because obviously they aren't hearing you

- you grew up on powdered milk but still ended up six feet tall

- after your dad told all the kids around the dinner table, "Put your bottom on the chair and your feet on the floor," you all said (and acted out) in unison, "Feet on the chair, and butt in the air!"

- at some point you thought swimming across the lake was a good idea

- your idea of camping involves speed boats and jet skis

- someone calls you Pepe and laughs real hard 'cuz, "Yeah, buddy, I'm thirty years old and that's the first time I *ever* heard that!"

- you compare all extroverts to your mother (or mother-in-love) and find that they all just don't measure up

For Phyllis, family was a place to know and be known, to love and be loved, to serve and be served, to celebrate and be celebrated.[7]

12

HOME OPENING

In 1978 we wrote in our annual plan, "We would seek to build a family and home that is wide open to friends, neighbors, coworkers, and strangers, one that is consistent in discipline, one that is just plain fun, and one that is centered on Christ." That sounds like something Phyllis contributed. I agreed, however, and my introverted self went along for the ride.

She loved having people over for a meal—neighbors, coworkers, family, friends from church. Though we didn't continue at the frenetic pace of fifty different people during our first four months of marriage, hospitality was a cornerstone of our family culture. As the four children got older, they usually joined us for the meals and sometimes helped with preparations. But they definitely became accustomed to a parade of people making their way through our lives.

Phyllis especially loved setting a beautiful table. Candles, flowers, tablecloths, attractive place settings all said, "You are important, and because of that we have taken a lot of time and care to get ready for you. We want you not just to enjoy the meal and the conversation but to delight in the visual experience as well." Phyllis didn't have much artistic sense in painting, photography, or crafts, but having a beautiful, welcoming environment was a way to say, "We are glad you are here. We want you to feel welcome and comfortable."

She also loved loading up family and friends with her kitchen specialties. A recipe for Refrigerator Rolls came from a friend's mom everyone called Mimi. They would rise up big and hot and yeasty. She also adopted my mom's recipe for Chocolate Cherry Cookies. She was an expert at making homemade Heath Bars. St. Louis's signature dessert, however, may have been her own as well—Gooey Butter Cake.

Often family who were visiting from out of town would stay with us several days or a week. Then, when our four young kids were in middle school, a local family friend was in a crisis. Issues from the past with her family of origin were coming to a head. Because Phyllis saw that it wasn't good for her to be living by herself, we invited her to come stay with us long term, to offer a secure environment for her while she worked through these difficulties. After several months, she transitioned back to her own apartment.

That began a pattern of people living in our household for months at a time for various reasons. Diane's daughter Kim O'Day lived with us for a year before she was married while working in the Chicago area. She thought ten-year-old Philip was hilarious, which didn't make it any easier for us to keep his behavior in check.

Next came a college student, Scott, who just needed inexpensive housing, which Phyllis insisted on providing at no cost. He earned his keep by putting up with four, sometimes annoying, youngsters and even teaching us all a game with five dice he called Farkle. Many other guests followed.

In the summer of 1992, Steve and Jackie Eyre came for the summer with their three boys. We had known them from our InterVarsity connections in St. Louis. Now they came for a bit of a sabbatical. One hot summer day several of the seven children joined forces to set up a lemonade stand at a busy intersection nearby. They did a booming business. But Jeremy Eyre, their oldest, never got over the fact that when their picture came out in the local newspaper, Jeremy was identified as Susan's assistant—even though the whole thing was his idea!

We enjoyed lots of stimulating conversation and small group Bible study. Steve and Jackie also served us as well. When Phyllis and I were working through some ongoing tensions, they were able to provide calm, wise, supportive counsel that was instrumental in getting us over the hump.

As our four began entering high school, we learned of two high school girls who for different reasons needed housing. We knew of Jen through church and Alicia from other local friends. When Phyllis heard of the need, her immediate reaction was, "Andy, let's have them stay with us." That was not my first thought. Yet they stayed with us two years until they both graduated.

Even these two caught the rhythms and personality of the family. Once at a meal with the eight of us, Alicia asked Phyllis to pass the potatoes. Phyllis picked up the dish but held it as she got distracted telling in some detail a story from the day that suddenly came to mind. When Phyllis took a breath, Alicia dryly interrupted and said, "Phyllis, I don't want your life story. I just want the potatoes!"

When people from out of town were hired by InterVarsity Press, Phyllis took it upon herself to act as IVP's unofficial human resources assistant. For example, she found Jim Hoover's first place to rent at Kenilworth Apartments across from the library and two blocks from the office on Main Street. So many folks from IVP rented there it became known as InterVarsity Arms. For those wanting to buy, Phyllis put them in touch with our realtors, Ham and Pat Bourland from Welcome Class.

In addition, she told many, "Come stay with us while you look for housing." And that did not just mean a weekend house-hunting trip. It meant, "You and your spouse and your kids can all stay with us for weeks or months till you get settled into your new place." And many did—including Joel Scandrett, Jeff Crosby, Cindy Bunch, and Brannon Ellis, to name a few.

So many different people lived in our home that those on the block had a running joke. Thieves could pull a moving truck into the driveway in broad daylight, remove all the valuables from the house, and the neighbors would just smile and wave thinking it was just another person moving in or out of the Le Peau household.

Phyllis's hospitality extended beyond merely finding or providing accommodations. Jim and Paulette Hagen and their kids moved to Downers Grove in the mid-1980s when Jim took a job with IVP. Paulette wrote Phyllis years later:

> I was such an emotional wreck when I arrived. Your friendship, care and inclusion into your life was an indication of God's love for me and the "rightness" of His moving me into a new locale, against my wishes. God, true to His word, turned all that into good for me and our family. . . .
>
> I think of our many Omega [restaurant] breakfasts. Talking about where we were spiritually and praying for each other. Years of sharing ministry together. All our shared experiences make my heart fill with joy for God's gift to me of you as a friend.[1]

Phyllis was also alert to those who found themselves between housing. Paul and Priscilla Heidebrecht from our church, Immanuel Presbyterian in Warrenville, had a gap between vacating the house they sold and moving into their new house that was still under construction. Tom and Cindy Walthour were doing major remodeling work and had to be out of their house for several months. Two missionary families who transitioned back to the U.S. needed a few months to figure out their next steps. They did it at our house (fortunately, not all at the same time).

Phyllis's radar was finely tuned to pick up on all these situations. She was always ready to jump in and offer what we had.

When she enjoyed her second stint with InterVarsity as the kids went off to college, she found other excuses to have people stay with us. She found housing for groups of staff coming in for weeklong team meetings and training events. Not only did she fill up the bedrooms vacated by our kids, but she recruited neighbors to host staff as well.

After full days of work, all those from out of town found their way to our kitchen and dining room for wine, cheese, and Six-handed Euchre. One of the greatest gifts the Midwest InterVarsity team gave Phyllis was teaching her how to play what became her favorite card game.

Two features of Six-handed Euchre made it addictive for her. First, it was a team game and Phyllis loved working and playing in teams. The six players were divided into two groups of three who had to work together (without saying what was in their hands) to take tricks. Second, the game allowed for high-risk opportunities. The adrenaline rush of betting nearly everything when "Shooting the Moon" was more than Phyllis could resist. Though some thought she was too risky at times, she proudly pointed out her high success rate.

ℕ ℕ ℕ

We had the opportunity to welcome even more into the family when our four children got married within three years of each other. In their teens we predicted Dave would be the first to marry since in fourth grade he had the first "date" of the four, and we good-humoredly decided that the firstborn would be last. We were half right.

In March 2005 Phil married Tyler Wager, a Tucson hometown gal he met at the University of Arizona. Susan and John DeCostanza, who got to know each other during a year of missionary service in Peru, followed shortly in July of that same year. On John's and Susan's first anniversary, July 15, 2006, Dave married Christe Brickey. Those two also met at the University of Arizona where they both were part of the InterVarsity chapter. Steve and Kristen Scaglia followed two years later, also in July, having met online though discovering later they had a Denver friend in common.

Each wedding had something special about it that Phyllis loved. Phil and Tyler were married in the enchanting and intimate

Mission in the Sun, a "chapel" built by Arizona artist Ettore "Ted" DeGrazia, especially known for its open-air roof. Susan's and John's Chicago wedding was officiated by the two priests they worked with in Peru, Fathers Ned and Al, who Phyllis so enjoyed. She thought the big, white lighted tent in our backyard for Dave's and Christe's rehearsal dinner was magical. Steve and Kristen had a beautiful outdoor wedding in Estes Park, Colorado.

Of all the families who lived with us in Downers Grove over the years, probably the one Phyllis was happiest to host long term was the DeCostanzas. In the fall of 2009 John and Susan told us that they wanted to live in community with their friends Heath and Thais Carter. The two couples were trying to find housing that could accommodate all of them, but in the meantime they could use a place to stay. How would we feel about them all moving in with us while they were looking?

Phyllis had no hesitation. Just three months earlier, in June, Susan and John were delighted to become adoptive parents when they welcomed three-day-old Lina into the family. What could be better for Phyllis than to be with her new granddaughter every day (oh, and of course, Lina's parents too)! That fall the two families squeezed in with all kinds of baby furniture and paraphernalia. I joked with Heath, "You get half a bed, I get half a bed, and Lina gets three rooms."

Besides Lina, one of the best features of the arrangement was sharing cooking duties. John and Heath were excellent chefs who helped me elevate my game. Susan and Thais were no slouches in the kitchen either. It was hard to see them all go just half a year later, but they found a duplex in the Brighton Park neighborhood of Chicago that worked well as both families started adding children.

After a few years of community living, the Carters moved to Indiana where Heath had taken a job at Valparaiso University. The DeCostanzas asked to move back with us for a year while they figured out next steps. By then Luke (age 4) and Gabe (age 2) were added to the mix. And again Phyllis and I had no hesitations. *What a treat!* we thought.

After a year, John and Susan asked about staying one more year. Again—not a problem! Lina and Luke were going to Hillcrest, the neighborhood school their uncles had attended, while Gabe took a five-minute walk with his mom to preschool at the Congregational Church. After Susan dropped him off, she walked five more minutes to the train station and caught the express to the Loop for her job. John drove to Dominican University where he worked in the ministry department.

Two delightful years blossomed into a third. But finally (and understandably) the hour-long commute (one way) was wearing on John. They bought a place a little over a mile from Dominican. When they showed the kids the new house for the first time, pointing out who would sleep in which rooms, Gabe asked, "Where are Mimi and Poppo going to sleep?" An understandable question. All he had known was our wonderful multi-generational living experience.

What effect did Phyllis's superabundant hospitality have on people? Jaime Wong offers just one example. Jaime was friends with our sons Phil and Dave and Christe Brickey (later Le Peau) during their years as undergraduates at the University of Arizona. They became great friends through the InterVarsity chapter on campus. Phyllis and I then got to know Jaime when we visited Dave and his brother Phil on campus, and when many from their chapter stayed at our house in Downers Grove after an Urbana Missions Convention.

Jaime wrote:

When I was growing up, I had to share my parents with many other people—often kids and young adults who came to church through our various different ministries to the San Francisco Chinatown community. My siblings and I were constantly told we were so, *so, <u>so</u>* lucky to have such amazing parents and that they would do anything to have grown up with my parents. *Hey*, I thought, getting my snark on, *they are mine, please get your own!* Ha!

At school, my mom and dad were always at our after-school activities—most memorably when my brother and I were on the track team and for our track meets, my parents would *always* bring a giant container of Red Vines and the largest carton of Goldfish (Costco size) for the team to share. Throughout the track meet, we'd pass those two containers around the field and both containers would be polished off by the last race.

When I first met Phyllis, I wanted to be a Le Peau. *Ha!* I *finally* had the other perspective of wanting to "have a parent like yours!" and it made me really understand all those kids/young adults in my past who wished they had parents like mine. She made me feel like I was home.

When I decided to go to U of A, little did I know that I would be so homesick—but also, little did I know that I made the best decision of my life going to the desert for four years because I got to meet friends that I would have the pleasure of calling family. Spiritual family. But we really do have the best parents, and everyone else should be jealous.[2]

Many experienced what Jaime did. For them, Phyllis felt like home.

Above: Gabe Strong's parents, John and Dorothy Strong, with their first four children: Nancy, Pauline, Judith, and Charles (c. 1902). Gabe was the ninth of their eleven children.

Left: Solon and Sara "Sadie" Sanders (c. 1905), the parents of Louise Strong who was the fifth of their seven children.

Louise and Gabe Strong, Phyllis's parents, not long after they were married in 1938.

Gabe and Louise, about 1955.

Phyllis (center) with her sisters Judy (left) and Diane (right) about 1952.

Above: Aunt Nova and Uncle Frank Sanders, Louise's older brother, were instrumental in helping Gabe and Louise when their marriage hit a crisis.

Right: Gene (Louise Strong's brother) and Dorothy Sanders, with son Dale and baby daughter Daryl (c. 1953). Uncle Gene was a Baptist pastor and Aunt Dorothy was a nurse who influenced Phyllis's career choice.

Phyllis through the decades: (left to right) her St. Luke's Nursing School yearbook picture (1963); her employee photo when she began working with Nurses Christian Fellowship (1973); while living in Downers Grove, Illinois (1982).

Below: The most unique gift at the wedding was a bicycle built for two. "Only Phyllis" would jump on, wedding dress and all.

Above: Phyllis with Andy, Susan, Philip, and Stephen, in a photo taken for her article "Life's Little Blessings" (1981).

Andy and Phyllis at the bell at Bear Trap Ranch in Colorado in 1985, a dozen years and four kids after they first met there in 1973.

Stephen and Kristen were married in Estes Park, Colorado, in 2008. Left to right: John and Susan DeCostanza, Andy Le Peau, Kristen and Steve Le Peau, Phyllis Le Peau, Christe and Dave Le Peau, Philip and Tyler Le Peau holding sons Corbin and Eric.

The third and final house on the block, 5313 Lane Place in Downers Grove, Illinois, purchased by the Le Peaus in 1982, was the family home for over forty years.

After renting two small cottages in Fremont, Michigan, for ten summers beginning in 1979, the Le Peaus bought the property in 1990. When the cottages (originally built in the 1920s) began to collapse, Phyllis created a plan for a house to replace them, ensuring its continued role as a gathering spot for the family. (Artwork: Adrian Morozan. Used by permission.)

Even after failing to get up on skis for years at Fremont Lake, Phyllis's persistence finally paid off and she found skiing exhilarating every summer for twenty-five years.

Phyllis loved talking to people about Jesus regardless of age, ethnicity, or background. At InterVarsity's spring-break outreach at Panama City, Florida (2012-15), students loved talking to Phyllis too.

The Family Tree: At the 2017 reunion, the grandchildren joined Phyllis and Andy (aka Mimi and Poppo) at the willow tree on Fremont Lake.

Pictured: 1) Eric Le Peau. 2) Beniah Le Peau.
3) Dhrasti Le Peau. 4) Sonal Le Peau.
5) Corbin Le Peau. 6) Eli Le Peau.
7) Lina DeCostanza. 8) Adelaide Le Peau.
9) Mitiksha Le Peau. 10) Phyllis Le Peau.
11) Gabriel DeCostanza. 12) Andy Le Peau.
13) Luke DeCostanza. 14) Haneul Le Peau.
15) Ana Le Peau.

Zeno and Dimas Le Peau were Phyllis's last grandchildren to join the family. Here they visit Phyllis with their brother and sister in 2021 (top to bottom: Beniah, Zeno, Haneul, Dimas).

13

OPPOSITES
ATTRACTING

In 2008 I spoke to the InterVarsity college students attending chapter camp training at Cedar Campus in Michigan's Upper Peninsula. Since I was talking about marriage, I had their complete attention. I told them that having different personalities was not necessarily a barrier to a good marriage.

"For example," I said, "Phyllis and I have long been the poster children for opposites attract." I explained:

Phyllis is an extrovert. I am an introvert. *[silence]*

Phyllis cares passionately about the world. I love *to think* about the world. *[a few chuckles]*

Phyllis is full of life and energy. My mom said I was born tired. *[some laughs]*

When we were first married, Phyllis was a morning person and I was a night person. Now Phyllis is a morning *and* a night person, and I am neither. *[louder laughter]*

Phyllis thinks everyone she meets is fascinating. I think the dictionary is fascinating. *[lots of laughter]*

Phyllis has a heart as wide as the horizon. I have the emotional range of a turnip. *[uproarious laughter]*

> Phyllis is a wonderful conversationalist who can make a fence post talk. *[pause]* I *am* the fence post. *[the room exploded]* [1]

While personalities can be quite different, I said that it was critical for couples to have similar values. Our common commitments to God were foundational. We also had similar attitudes toward the frugal use of money and the importance of family. Those commonalities helped bind us together.

And the differences? Mostly they were a great source of fun.

Phyllis was so upbeat that December 21, the darkest day of the year, was her favorite day on the calendar because (living in Chicago) for the next six months, each day would bring more daylight.

Me? Some people seem to think I am a pessimist. No, no, no, I tell them. I am just being a realist.

Our differences in perspective were revealed in deep contrast when a phone call woke us up one morning at 6:30. Phyllis answered. A neighbor said their basement had flooded because of the overnight storm. Could either of us come over to help? I told Phyllis I would go and started to get dressed.

Then she said, "Shouldn't we take a look at our basement?" We both went down.

With Phyllis right behind me, I opened the basement door and flipped on the light. I looked down the stairs and then sat on the steps in disbelief. A dozen items floated in eighteen inches of water. All were bobbing at odd angles like derelict ships in a harbor after a hurricane.

I uttered several phrases that were less than entirely sanctified, but Phyllis instantly said, "Isn't this great! I've been meaning to clean out the basement for years. And now we don't have to sort stuff or decide anything. We can just throw it all away! That is so super!"

While that didn't immediately cheer me up, she was right. Her upbeat outlook was always good for someone our kids nicknamed Eeyore.

◌ ◌ ◌

Then there's the matter of me being fairly quiet and Phyllis not being so at all. Nonetheless she didn't like chit chat or talking about recipes. She wanted to talk about substantive issues. It was appropriate, then, that she was terrible at *Trivial Pursuit*, claiming that her brain was too full of important thoughts to leave any room for insignificant facts. She said that instead she was going to create a game called *Profound Truths. The Ungame*, a box game popular in the 1980s, was her favorite for years. It had cards with dozens of questions that people could discuss to get to know each other.

For Phyllis, talking was not for its own sake. It was a pathway to show love, to go deeper into someone's life, or to have fun and laughter. That carried into our life together.

In the early years of our marriage, Phyllis and I struggled with our different ways of resolving conflict. Unsurprisingly, she wanted to talk things out, right there on the spot. I wanted time alone to calm down. That way I could be more objective (and more gracious) without being afraid I'd be overwhelmed by my feelings and say something I'd regret.

Phyllis was insistent, though. She wanted to reconcile— immediately . . . during the argument! Perhaps part of her urgency came from the history her parents had of a near divorce and from the wrangling they often continued to engage in.

Over those first years I learned to shorten the time between argument and resolution, and she learned to trust that I would always come back to ask and grant forgiveness. But those early quarrels were challenging.

Once we were in the middle of one such heated disagreement. To break the tension a bit and to make a gentle plea for more time to get my emotions under control, I asked, "Phyllis, don't you think that every husband deserves the silent treatment . . . at least once?"

"Listen, Buster," she responded with cheery firmness, "the only time you're getting the silent treatment is when I get laryngitis."

℘ ℘ ℘

Like many married couples, Phyllis and I had our catchphrases and inside jokes.

After hunting together for a lost item like keys or glasses, whoever found it would hold it up and sunnily ask the other, "Does it look like this?"

Another phrase we stole from a Mark Lowry comedy routine. If I was helping set the table and Phyllis told me I wasn't doing it quite right, I'd say, "I'm just trying to be a blessing," and she'd respond with mock sternness, "Try harder."

Likewise she'd use the opening line if I was getting on her case about something. I'd respond with the required reply, and we would smile, laugh, and hug.

In the midst of a quibble, the "blessing" exchange reminded us of the laughter we shared when we first heard the joke, and in microcosm it recalled all the experiences that bound us together in countless small ways.

The exchange would also help diffuse tensions small or large by reminding us that we should assume the best intentions of the other, not the worst.

With Phyllis, that was always easy to do.

℘ ℘ ℘

Because Phyllis was so outgoing some people suspected she ruled the household. She didn't like that image at all. She didn't want people to think she was domineering. And she wasn't. We were both strong personalities. Nonetheless, I wasn't above teasing her when the opportunity arose.

When I was writing *Paths of Leadership*, I began thinking about the dedication for the book. Many authors rightfully acknowledge the support, help, and input they receive from their spouses to make a project like that possible. And that was true for me too. But I told her (and many others, with good effect) that the dedication was going to read:

To Phyllis
who helped me write
this dedication

She knew it was funny, but she was nervous, not knowing if I was serious about doing it or not. When I handed her a copy of the printed volume, she was relieved to read instead:

To Phyllis, my love

Phyllis's talkativeness could continue through most of her waking hours, even into the late evening. Although she was a high-energy person, she fell asleep almost instantly. I, on the other hand, needed at least fifteen or twenty minutes to wind down before slipping into dreamland.

One night we were lying in bed with the lights out. For about ten minutes Phyllis talked about some event of the day or some topic that was on her mind.

Suddenly, she paused for a breath and said, "Andy, I can't sleep."

"Phyllis," I responded flatly, "try not talking."

"Oh!" she said, as if the thought had never occurred to her.

She became silent, and in ninety seconds her breathing had become heavy and regular. She was out. Phyllis had two speeds: Stop and Go.

℘ ℘ ℘

The last chapter of the book of Proverbs closes with an amazing portrait of a strong, omni-competent wife who takes initiative in the family and community for the sake of others. While this portrait of the Proverbs 31 woman is sometimes revered among evangelicals, ironically it is far from a picture of a narrowly focused, stay-at-home mother who is often idealized in some groups.

In reality, it sounds more like Phyllis.

A wife of noble character who can find?
She is worth far more than rubies.

Her husband has full confidence in her
    and lacks nothing of value.
She brings him good, not harm,
    all the days of her life.
She selects wool and flax
    and works with eager hands.
She is like the merchant ships,
    bringing her food from afar.
She gets up while it is still night;
    she provides food for her family
    and portions for her female servants.
She considers a field and buys it;
    out of her earnings she plants a vineyard.
She sets about her work vigorously;
    her arms are strong for her tasks.
She sees that her trading is profitable,
    and her lamp does not go out at night.
In her hand she holds the distaff
    and grasps the spindle with her fingers.
She opens her arms to the poor
    and extends her hands to the needy.
When it snows, she has no fear for her household;
    for all of them are clothed in scarlet.
She makes coverings for her bed;
    she is clothed in fine linen and purple.
Her husband is respected at the city gate,
    where he takes his seat among the elders of the land.
She makes linen garments and sells them,
    and supplies the merchants with sashes.
She is clothed with strength and dignity;
    she can laugh at the days to come.
She speaks with wisdom,
    and faithful instruction is on her tongue.

She watches over the affairs of her household
   and does not eat the bread of idleness.
Her children arise and call her blessed;
   her husband also, and he praises her:
"Many women do noble things,
   but you surpass them all."
Charm is deceptive, and beauty is fleeting;
   but a woman who fears the Lord is to be praised.
Honor her for all that her hands have done,
   and let her works bring her praise at the city gate.

Proverbs does not hold up the model of having a spotless home or makeup applied to perfection or matching children neatly lined up in a row. (Aware of this, Phyllis joked with a friend that they should coauthor a book titled *Dirty House for the Kingdom.* "I'll do the chapter 'Dirty Oven for the Kingdom,'" she volunteered). Instead Proverbs talks about someone making real estate deals, running a business, proactively meeting the needs of the poor, and handing out sought-after counsel to the people lined up outside her door. If a Proverbs 31 woman like that ever showed up in some churches that say they follow the Bible, surely she would scandalize the congregation.

Like the Proverbs 31 woman, Phyllis was constantly on the go. She transacted business on behalf of the family, including once putting a bid on a house for sale when I was out of the country. She was, in addition, usually the point person when it came to buying and selling cars for the family. She (and we) believed in buying used cars and running them into the ground, believing this was the most economical strategy. She also got an adrenaline rush from the process of negotiating and getting a great deal. And since I didn't, I was happy for her to take the lead, to let her use her gifts for the good of us all.

Phyllis also acted compassionately on behalf of the disadvantaged.

While she wasn't pushy, she was not afraid to offer her wisdom to others about life, whether about new jobs, church, marriage, or relationships.

As in all things she didn't take herself too seriously. Phyllis was well aware that she often came off to others as a force of nature. Rather than deny or minimize this, she happily exaggerated the image. "I'm not a Proverbs 31woman," she would say with gusto. "I'm a Proverbs 32 woman!"

Throughout the years we both paid attention to our anniversary, trying to mark it in some way, though usually neither of us made it a big production. My dad's practice was to give my mom a long-stemmed rose for each year of marriage. I followed that pattern and added a bottle of champagne to the tradition. Never one to drink much, on one of those first anniversaries, Phyllis confessed, "Andy, I feel so champagne-y!"

If schedules were tight, we didn't feel obligated to celebrate on *the* day and picked another. I thought, however, that I needed to do something special for our twenty-fifth.

Blue star sapphires had become something of a tradition on my side of the family. My mom didn't want a diamond when she got married and loved the star sapphire she got instead. My sister, Mary, did the same for her engagement ring. Later she gave one to Kirby. My brother, John, and Nancy each got one after they were married.

I conspired then with John and Nancy to get a ring from their jeweler. When the six of us were together at a posh restaurant a couple of weeks before our anniversary, I stunned Phyllis with the surprise gift. For one of the few times in her life, she was speechless. She loved it.

Afterward she realized, to her dismay, that she had nothing planned for me. Then one morning after I had left for work a week later, our oldest, Steve, called from Colorado and unexpectedly said,

"Mom, you've got to buy dad a PT Cruiser." Chrysler had just come out with the compact that stylishly evoked vehicles of the 1930s.

"What? Why?"

"It's the only car Dad has ever shown interest in."

"But we don't buy new cars. You know we are frugal. We buy used cars."

He was unfazed. "Mom, you need to get Dad the car."

After the call, Phyllis sat in shock. *A new car? Really?*

She decided to ask the other three. She couldn't get hold of Phil at the University of Arizona, but she thought he'd just have the same opinion as Steve. She was sure that Susan at Boston College, with her deep concerns for the world, would have a sensible perspective.

"I think you should do it," Susan said, surprising her mom. "You and Dad have been very generous to many, many people over the years. It's fine to be generous to each other for a change."

For the second time Phyllis sat staring, not quite sure what to think. Just then, Dave came home from an early morning cross country practice and flopped down on the couch.

"Dave, you've got to get showered and dressed. We're going to buy Dad a PT Cruiser for our anniversary."

"What!" he said, jumping up in excitement. Then he sat down again, deflated, and said, "Don't kid with me, Mom. That's not cool."

"No, really. Steve called and Susan agreed. We've got to go now." Steve had told her they were popular, selling fast and hard to get.

Within a few minutes they were at the local Chrysler dealership. "Yes," the sales rep said, "they are in short supply, but I happen to have two on the lot. Would you like to look?"

They picked the silver one and were soon handed the paperwork. Phyllis was about to sign when Dave, thinking he needed to sound at least a little responsible during this uncharacteristically lavish and spontaneous act by his mother, said, "Mom, are you sure about this?"

"Yes," she said, "I'm sure."

Well, great! Dave thought, relaxing. *This is gonna be super.* He was already planning his wheels for Homecoming.

Phyllis told Dave to take the car immediately to get an upgraded stereo and CD player. He drove the car home, and they hid it in the garage, just before I got back from work.

When I walked in, the two of them had huge smiles on their faces like the proverbial cats who had swallowed canaries.

"What?" I said, quite suspicious. "What's up?"

They handed me a small box in wrapping paper that could have held a watch. Slowly I opened it and saw a car key. *That looks like the key to a new car,* I thought. *But it can't be. Phyllis would never do that. And it says "Chrysler" on it so it must be for a PT Cruiser. But it can't be. They are all sold out.*

I didn't move or say anything, my thoughts running rapidly in circles.

"Dad," said Dave with some exasperation. "Don't you want to look in the garage?"

We walked out and opened the garage door. Because the day was bright and sunny, the inside of the garage was dark. All I could see was the back of the silver car, and I stood there motionless and silent, thinking, *That's beautiful!*

"Dad," Dave said, once again interrupting my thoughts, "don't you want to go for a ride?"

I remained motionless. He then grabbed the keys from me, backed out the car, opened the driver's door, handed the keys back to me, and firmly said, "Go for a ride!"

Phyllis got in the passenger seat, and I got in too. It was the surprise of my life. She loved successfully pulling this off with the advice and help of her kids. But she woke up in the middle of the night worried about spending all that money in a way so contrary to our normal patterns. Her mind was set at ease when she realized the money that made it possible had come from my folks, and it was really a gift from them to me.

I had the car for eighteen years, the favorite car I ever owned. My wife and my children made our twenty-fifth anniversary one we never forgot.

Forgetting played a different sort of role with another anniversary. One early fall day, Phyllis and I were peacefully sitting on our porch swing in Fremont. It was a perfect, beautiful, warm, sunny afternoon with puffy clouds dotting the sky and water gently lapping on the shore of the lake.

"Andy," Phyllis said as we swayed back and forth quietly, "we ought to come here sometime on our anniversary."

"Phyllis," I said with a half-smile, "we *are*." She was so caught up in the moment that she didn't realize that day *was* our anniversary.

At that point I left the swing briefly. I came back with one rose for each year we'd been married and then prepared the special meal I had planned. Phyllis was highly organized, yet, ironically, she was so often focused on what needed to be done that special days could slip from her mind.

ꟼ ꟼ ꟼ

Phyllis loved the Bible. Phyllis read the Bible. Phyllis memorized the Bible. Phyllis believed the Bible.

But there was one verse in the Bible she was sure was wrong— Mark 12:25: "When the dead rise, they will neither marry nor be given in marriage; they will be like the angels in heaven."

No marriage in heaven? Preposterous! As she would tell me when this verse came up, "You're not getting off the hook that easily, Le Peau!"

What was the best thing about marriage for me? Phyllis, of course. Because she was fun, our marriage was fun. Since she was full of activity and care for others, our marriage was too. Here was a person full of energy, full of good ideas, full of love. The words George Stulac spoke about Ephesians 5 at our wedding were so on-target for me. The best thing I could do for those around us and the kingdom of God was to set Phyllis free to flourish.

When my sons and son-in-law got engaged, I wanted them to know what I had learned. I remembered what George Stulac said at our wedding about Christ showing his love for the Church by giving himself up for her, and that's how husbands were to act. I told them, "Wives may be called to submit, but husbands, like Christ, are called to die. So maybe we have the harder job. Our job is to make whatever sacrifices are needed for our wives' well-being."

We don't throw our weight around. We don't demand that wives submit. After all, Ephesians 5 does not say, "Husbands, make sure your wives submit." The instruction is addressed to wives, not husbands. The issue of submission is between a wife and her Lord. It's not the husband's responsibility.

What might it look like for a husband to sacrifice so his wife could flourish? One moment gave me a clear picture. For several years Phyllis had told me of her dissatisfaction with our church. Immanuel Presbyterian had lots to offer, but she sometimes felt out of place. Yes, she certainly had fun joking about being one of Immanuel's token extroverts. But sometimes she wondered if she was so much of an outlier that she might bother people.

More importantly, she yearned for the church to move forward in the areas of her passions, particularly corporate prayer, diversity, and evangelism. She was delighted when the church adopted the Alpha Course which aimed to introduce people to Christ who had little church background. But she felt such efforts at the church were rare. Certainly she had all the outlets she could want in these different areas within her work with InterVarsity and elsewhere. But for Phyllis that was not enough. She wanted it all.

It's a truism that no church is perfect, and everyone has some complaints. As a result I probably didn't take her issues seriously enough. In addition, I was happy at Immanuel. I liked the choir, the worship, the people, the emphasis on education for children and adults. I didn't want to move. While she saw Immanuel's strengths, she also knew its weaknesses and had another church in mind for us to go to instead, a church that wasn't as appealing to me.

I gladly supported her as she took on various leadership roles and sought to grow in different areas of life. But it took years of discussion for me to finally remember that I am supposed to sacrifice so my wife can flourish spiritually. Being the spiritual leader didn't mean finding the church I thought was right. It meant finding a church together that was right for my wife. And if she was feeling her gifts and passions were being thwarted, I needed to act.

I finally told her that if she wanted us to change churches, we would. It was up to her.

"You're saying it's my decision?" she asked.

"Yes. It's your decision."

"Then I'm going to have to think about this."

She did just that for the next several months. Shortly after Easter, at a morning prayer meeting at Immanuel, Phyllis sensed the Lord asking, "Are you willing to be blessed here at Immanuel?"

She was surprised. Later when she told me about her experience, she said, "I think we should stay."

I did not know that was how it would turn out. If she had decided to go elsewhere, we would have. In one sense I would have been disappointed, but in another I would have taken satisfaction in doing what I could so she could grow in all the ways she should.

We stayed. Some of the frustrations remained. But she also found new opportunities for service that fit her passions and her many abilities.

Yes, our contrasting personalities caused some frictions. But Phyllis's life, love, and laughter made all the difference for this fence post.

14

JOY BRINGING

Not long after we were married, a friend asked me, "What first attracted you to Phyllis?"

Without hesitation I said, "Oh, she is a zoo!" She was crazy and fun and crazy fun, and I loved it. She took such pleasure in the big things and small things of life. Her energy and joy were infectious.

I was (and still am) a pretty heady guy. Ideas and books get my blood pumping the way many people get excited about their team vying for a championship. You see, I grew up in Minnesota. Even though I am not ethnically Scandinavian, I seemed to have absorbed some of that Nordic reserve and coolness.

I became fluent in speaking Minnesotan. If I am euphoric about something, I'll say, "Not too bad." And if I hate something with a pure hatred, I'll say, "Not so good." No wonder I found Phyllis's freedom of spirit and unfettered sense of humor so refreshing and appealing.

Before we married, Phyllis gave a book to her parents by one of her favorite authors, Joseph Bayly. The title, *Out of My Mind*, was also the name of his regular magazine column. In the book were brief, random, humorous, and sometimes profound musings, on whatever occurred to him.

Once when we visited her mom and dad, she pulled the book off their shelf that she had given them as a gift and proudly showed me the inscription she had written to them on the short title page.

To Mom & Dad,

To remind you of me [with an arrow pointing to the title *Out of My Mind*]

Love,
Phyl

Phyllis delighted in making others laugh, in being known for her zany persona, and in cultivating that image.

I am reluctant to stand out too much. I am in the habit of carefully thinking through what I want to say before I say it. My filter is always working overtime to make sure I don't say anything that could be stupid or embarrassing or hurtful. Despite my best efforts, occasionally something unfortunate would pop out of my mouth, and I would feel so bad that I would double my resolve to not let that happen again.

Not Phyllis. If it came to mind, it came out of her mouth. And if it came out of her mouth before it came to her mind, also not a problem. If she said something awkward or confusing, she'd laugh all the more at her own craziness. She was a free spirit.

𝒫 𝒫 𝒫

One time Phyllis, our granddaughter Dhrasti, and I were driving through western Michigan on our way to Fremont when we stopped for lunch at an Arby's. Soon a group of thirty motorcyclists rolled into the parking lot next to our car in which we were eating. They were mostly men, mostly Black, and mostly leather clad. Some were large human beings.

Almost immediately Phyllis said, "I'm going to go talk to those people," and she popped out of the car before we had a chance to say a word. She plunged into the group and, to our amazement, had them laughing within exactly fifteen seconds. Together they talked animatedly for ten minutes while Dhrasti and I did the only reasonable thing. We finished our meal in the car.

After forty-five years of marriage to Phyllis, I suppose I should have been used to such doings. Still, when she got back in the car, in wonder I asked, "What did you say to get them laughing?"

"Oh, I reminded them that their mothers said they should always wear their motorcycle helmets. And, yes, they agreed and promised they would."

Everyone just felt better about life and themselves after being with Phyllis. One of the staff she supervised with InterVarsity Christian Fellowship said, "There is no one I would rather be fired by than Phyllis." And he meant it. He knew he'd be encouraged by her, loved by her, and more prepared to meet his future.

No moment was too large or small for Phyllis that she couldn't include some fun and laughter. Sometimes she would take a deep dive into a person's life in a way that expressed love and care. But she was also happy to touch others briefly and lightly, making their day just a little bit better.

Once Phyllis was called for federal jury duty. For two weeks she took the train to downtown Chicago to the Dirksen Federal Building for the trial. She couldn't talk to me about the trial, but she did tell me about the commute.

She was amazed that the thousands of other commuters were often grim-faced as they went to work. She told me she was setting herself the challenge of making people smile. But she came home frustrated because no matter how much she smiled at people, they didn't smile back or even look at her at all.

A couple of days later Phyllis came home triumphant. "I got people to smile back at me!"

"What did you do?"

"As people walked into the building, I held the door for them. That made them look at me, and I gave them a big smile. And they smiled back." She took immense joy in bringing even just a bit of happiness to others.

ℙ ℙ ℙ

Phyllis also loved bringing out joy in group games like *Codenames*. The more people the better. The more trash talking the better. *Qwirkle* was another favorite. She probably gave away two dozen of these games for birthdays, anniversaries, or just because. She also took great pride in trouncing her adult children and the rest of the extended family at the biennial Le Peau Ladder Golf Tournament at Fremont.

She'd often play Hand and Foot with her side of the family, a card game that could easily expand to eight or ten people. She took special delight in cheating by covertly dropping bad cards under her chair. She even looked forward to the moment she'd get caught—another opportunity for laughter.

Cheating often gave her such a thrill, she'd even do it while playing solitaire. "Phyllis," I'd ask, fully engaging my inner cranky old man, "why don't you just start by arranging all the cards in order by suit?"

"Oh, Andy. You're no fun!"

If there was any fun to be had, Phyllis did not want to miss a minute. As Susan and Stephen told it:

> If we were staying up late and having fun with friends, and mom started to feel tired but she didn't want to miss anything, she would stand up, pat her thighs and say, "Okay, let's all go to bed." And when no one moved she'd sit back down and try to stay awake and stay in it.
>
> Once I remember being at Aunt Diane's house. It got very late and when no one would go to bed at her prompting, she finally left the room seemingly to go to bed on her own. But she walked back in a moment later with floss. My cousins and aunts and uncles and I were laughing and talking, and there was Phyllis right in the middle of the mix, flossing away.[1]

What does it take to have that kind freedom to experience life without inhibition? I think part of it is knowing we are loved. For

Phyllis, a lot of that came from her parents. Gabe and Louise weren't perfect. They were both plain-spoken people from rural southern Illinois whose rough edges and rough attitudes were often not well hidden.

These two strong-willed people could regularly be in conflict about things small and large. Yet they found a way to love each other, and they never wavered in their love for their three daughters. While Phyllis knew early on that she never wanted a marriage like that of her parents, she was secure in her relationship with them. That gave her the confidence to be herself in school, in the neighborhood, and in church.

Because she was secure and because she loved making people laugh, Phyllis was happy to make herself the butt of her own jokes. Everyone knew she loved to talk, loved to laugh, and loved to laugh at how much she loved to talk. While Immanuel Presbyterian is warm and caring, all of us knew that we were a largely introverted group. Not surprisingly, in this environment Phyllis stood out in vivid contrast.

Once when she gave a report to the church on Sunday morning about her ministry with InterVarsity Christian Fellowship, she introduced herself by saying:

"I am Phyllis Le Peau and I am Immanuel's token extrovert. [chuckles]. . . I am trying to be a quiet intellectual. [laughter] . . . It's not working. [roars]"

On another occasion she showed a picture on the church's big screen of the beach evangelism she and other InterVarsity staff and students had done that spring in Florida. She paused for a moment, looking at the picture behind her, and then turned toward the congregation and said, "They say a picture is worth a thousand words. . . . I'd rather have the thousand words!" The place erupted.

She often compared herself to the boisterous, blundering apostle Peter who always said what was on his mind even if he didn't know what was on his mind. After all, speaking first and thinking later was her joyful modus operandi. "Peter and I are soul friends," she would say. "Remember when he goes up the Mount of the Transfiguration with Jesus, James, and John? When Peter is so shocked at seeing Jesus with Moses and Elijah, it says, 'And Peter, not knowing what to say, said. . . .'" Proudly she'd conclude, "That's me!"[2]

Phyllis loved talking and connecting with people so much that more than once while she was in the bathroom off the kitchen, she would yell out her contribution to the conversation that was going on around the table. With little effect I asked her to wait till she was done in the bathroom and had rejoined us.

She also had a habit of walking into a room talking. Once or twice I suggested that she walk into a room and first take five seconds to assess whether there was another conversation going on that she might be interrupting. This likewise had little impact. She just loved to talk.

When most people had already left church each Sunday morning, Phyllis would still be deep in animated conversation. In such situations, two of her teenage children would often get on either side of her, link an arm with her, and escort their mother out the church, holding up free hands on either side of her head to act as blinders so she wouldn't see someone she just had to have a word with.

As she wrote in one of her InterVarsity prayer letters, "I guess it is rather superfluous to say that Andy and I enjoy our grandchildren beyond words . . . and that is saying a lot for me. I have words for everything."[3]

As much as she loved talking, Phyllis had a complicated relationship with the English language. She would often utter phrases her mother tongue never imagined. We called these inventions Phyllis-isms. Some favorites?

Like any sensitive husband, sometimes I would get a bit nervous about how she would react to something I said or did. Once when she noticed this, she said, "You don't have to act like you're walking through the tulips." Fortunately, that wouldn't be as tricky as walking on eggshells.

On another occasion, however, I wasn't cautious enough, so she warned me, "Andy, you're treading on thin ground." At least in such a case I wasn't in danger of breaking through the surface and drowning!

Phyllis, being a very intuitive person who apparently also had X-ray vision, once said, "I see it in my bones."

Another time her intuition got so intense it engaged her entire circulatory system. She said, "I know it's true. I feel it in my blood." The English language was never safe when Phyllis Le Peau was around.

Being a person of absolutes, she told me, not entirely unexpectedly, "It either rains or it doesn't do anything." There was no drizzle in Phyllis's forecasts.

She also worked to teach her grandchildren how to be polite. She was known to tell them, "Do not eat with food in your mouth." Miss Manners, watch out! A new standard was in the making.

Sometimes, however, she'd twist lines on purpose. One of her favorite movies was *The Hunt for Red October* with Sean Connery and Alec Baldwin. But once she accidentally referred to it as *The Hunt for Red Lobster*. After that, although she knew the right title, she always had great fun calling it by her unique variation.

That also happened with one of the phrases she always relished telling me, "I love you more than yesterday, less than tomorrow."

In addition to that, however, Phyllis loved saying it wrong on purpose: "I love you less than yesterday, more than tomorrow." I think she said it to me more often the wrong way than the right way. And each time she'd laugh and laugh because it was so much the opposite of what she felt.

Phyllis had a wonderfully active mind, but she primarily saw and understood the world through the lens of her emotions. Once we were watching for the third or fourth time Ron Howard's *Apollo 13*

about the astronauts whose spacecraft going to the moon became disabled enroute. As the movie progressed her grip on my arm got tighter and tighter.

"Why are you squeezing me?" I asked. "You've seen this movie before. You know how it ends."

"Yes," she said with a half grin, "but what if they don't make it this time?"

AREA DIRECTING

When the children all started going to school full days, Phyllis joined her neighbor Mary Rempert at Wellness, Inc. They would get up at 4 a.m. to get set up at various locations all over the city for early morning health screenings at businesses and organizations, which involved drawing blood from fasting participants. I'd get the kids off to school, and she'd be back in time to welcome them home.

Gary Fine owned and ran Wellness (later Empower Health Services) which provided medical testing on site, benefiting employers and workers because they didn't have to take time away to go to a doctor's office for lab work. That was on top of the main advantage of greater health awareness.

Phyllis had been trained as a phlebotomist in nursing school, but nurses knew that taking blood samples from someone's arm was a specialized skill that took extra training and practice. Because Phyllis was determined to excel, she began practicing at home—on the kids and me! Soon she took pride in drawing blood on the first attempt to find a vein and without it hurting.

Wellness even showed up annually at the IVP office. When Jim Hoover first came, he told Phyllis, "You need to know that I faint every time I get blood drawn."

"Well," Phyllis said with a big, confident smile, "this will be the first time you don't." She began by taking his blood pressure which showed a rather alarming spike. She suggested trying again later.

After a few minutes Jim came back. Phyllis started asking some basic questions: How are you? What are you doing this week? Though Jim had trouble focusing enough to answer them, the distraction worked. He didn't faint, and he hasn't done so since that time Phyllis drew his blood.

She not only did blood draws with Wellness, she also started doing sales. Her upbeat, outgoing nature made her a natural for signing up new businesses to the program.

After she had been working at Wellness for several years, people from InterVarsity began talking to Phyllis about coming back to work for Nurses Christian Fellowship (NCF) as the national head of NCF's college ministry division. Over the year that these discussions took place, three different people offered her the same job. The apparent string of leadership changes and accompanying reorganizations made Phyllis cautious. In addition, she had doubts about NCF's strategies for ministry with student nurses. Though she loved NCF, it didn't seem wise to wade into those uncertain waters.

Soon, however, Jeannette Yep began recruiting Phyllis to be area director for InterVarsity's campus ministry in Northern Illinois. This immediately caught her interest. She already knew Jeannette well since she was Linda Doll's roommate and had an office at the IVP building. Since the territory included all the colleges west of Chicago to Rockford, she'd have much less travel than she would with NCF.

As a result, in the late 1990s she threw herself into the work with students and her team. Byron and Michelle Graham were staff at Northern Illinois University in DeKalb, one of the few residential schools in the area. Most of the other InterVarsity chapters in her area were at commuter schools, which were more challenging because students weren't on campus as much, and had jobs and family responsibilities as well. But when college faculty or administrators sponsored InterVarsity at the College of DuPage, Harper Community College, and Joliet Junior College, the IV staff and students had a center around which to build a chapter.

InterVarsity Christian Fellowship (IVCF)

The roots of IVCF go back to evangelical students at the University of Cambridge, England, in 1877. Feeling that their spiritual concerns and convictions were sidelined by existing churches and associations, they "began to meet together, in spite of the disapproval of some university officials, to pray, study the Bible, and share their faith with fellow students."[1] Over the next fifty years, similar student-run organizations sprang up at other universities in Britain.

Only in 1928 did this loose association of student-run groups officially become Inter-Varsity Fellowship, hiring its first employee. In the 1930s the movement sent staff to Australia and Canada where students had asked for help in starting similar campus groups. As World War II was beginning, students at the Universities of Michigan and Washington asked Canadians to do the same for them. In 1941, InterVarsity Christian Fellowship was incorporated in the United States.

InterVarsity Press (IVP) was established as the publishing division of IVCF in 1947.[2] Nurses Christian Fellowship began in the 1930s as an independent organization, joining InterVarsity in 1948.

Originally focused in its first decades on helping students grow in evangelism, discipleship, and mission, IVCF later formulated its purpose as: "to establish and advance at colleges and universities witnessing communities of students and faculty who follow Jesus as Savior and Lord: growing in love for God, God's Word,

God's people of every ethnicity and culture, and God's purposes in the world."[3]

By 2020 IVCF had approximately fifteen hundred employees serving more than forty thousand students and faculty in chapters on more than seven hundred campuses nationwide. Specialized ministries focus on the arts, athletes, graduate students, sororities and fraternities, international students, law students, and students from a variety of ethnicities.

Phyllis's work was helped by being part of the strongest region in the country. Wisconsin-Illinois-Indiana under Jim Lundgren had competent, qualified staff and well-established programs Phyllis and her team could plug into. Fall and winter conferences were attended by hundreds of students in each state, offering excellent training and encouragement. Thousands of students went through week-long training events (called Chapter Focus Week) in May and June each year. Working and playing with all those staff and students so intensely for days or a week made her extroverted self happier than usual.

She also loved the opportunity in the summers of 2000 and 2001 to help train new staff at IV's national office in Madison, Wisconsin. During those ten-day events she had great fun encouraging them and welcoming them to their new role.

The free time with other staff was a highlight. She loved trash talking during card games as much as the game itself. Six-handed Euchre often occupied her into the wee hours. Phyllis realized, however, that her appetite for card playing could make some people feel left out. She then worked hard at conferences to include other staff in games during evenings and other free time.

Two of her many passions were Bible study and evangelism. A two-day consultation in July 2000 combined both. Phyllis enjoyed working with Rick Richardson to strategize on how Investigative Bible

Discussions could become more central to IVCF's evangelism strategy in the region. She wanted this to be key in the Chicago West area as well. In her student days and at Welcome Class at the Methodist Church, she had seen the impact of small groups of Christians and seekers discussing together the source documents of the Christian faith.

She also knew that her passions were decidedly not "administrivia" with all its forms for budgeting and hiring, especially if it involved learning new computer software. Phyllis had a hate-hate relationship with technology. On the one hand she felt technology was a wonderful servant and a terrible master. On the other hand, she thought technology was from the devil.

For months (years?) I had tried to explain to Phyllis how to search for something using Google. But it never clicked with her. I tried to make it as simple as possible. "You type into the search box what you are interested in and hit enter. That's all there is to it." But nothing helped. Because it was technology, she had a massive mental block. I eventually gave up.

But later when I was away on a trip, she called me with the exciting news. "Andy, I Googled!"

I gave a big laugh and startled my colleague Dan Reid enough that he asked what happened.

I told him, "Phyllis Googled for the first time!"

With mock shock, he asked loud enough so Phyllis could hear, "By herself!!??"

She loved the story, but she still hated technology. She didn't mind being busy, but she did mind the busy work that often went along with her role.

Having a job that was never done could also be stressful. In her journal she wrote, "I am very irritable. As I woke up this morning, I realized I am carrying the weight of the fall on my shoulders. And the irritability is in spite of taking a reading day yesterday which was great. I need to do that more often—still haven't read the Staff Director's Handbook."[4]

Even for an activist like Phyllis, she looked forward to reading days. She drank in *Traveling Light* by Eugene Peterson and *Rees Howells: Intercessor* by Norman Grubb. The latter made a lasting impact. As she wrote in her journal, "I want our team to be a team of prayer as much as of training and strategy."[5]

She reread *The Pursuit of God*, a classic by A. W. Tozer. She had even met one of Tozer's grandchildren while doing a Wellness blood draw in downtown Chicago. Noticing the client's last name she asked, "Are you related to the author A. W. Tozer?"

"Yes, I am," she confirmed.

"Are family members still Christians?" Phyllis wondered.

When the reply came, "Not like him," Phyllis chuckled inside.

Receiving the Day by Dorothy Bass also impressed her with its call to resist busyness and welcome openly what God has for us each day. But the calendar was getting to her. Dave graduated from Downers Grove North High School and Susan from Boston College in 2001. That summer we drove him to the University of Arizona and sent her off to Peru. And the pressures of the upcoming fall as area director were weighing on her, often waking her in the middle of the night. She wrote emphatically in her journal with more than a hint of frustration at herself, "I am *not* Receiving the Day!"

Being too busy was a lifelong struggle for Phyllis. She did better than most in taking time for quiet or prayer. But to succeed in doing less? That was largely aspirational. You might as well tell the stars not to shine, the wind not to blow, the river not to run to the sea, or the bee not to gather nectar. And Lord knows I talked to the bee many times, with little effect.

Back in December 1991 when Phyllis worked for Wellness, Inc., the family went to see the movie *Hook*. Robin Williams played the role of a grown-up Peter Pan, a lawyer who was always on the phone and unable to pay attention to his kids. At one point his daughter grabs Peter's phone and in frustration throws it out the window into the snow.

While the audience gasped, our four kids immediately agreed, "Always being on the phone—that is so much like *Mom!*" We laughed because we both expected them to say, "like *Dad.*"

Another more sober wake-up call came years later when, as she wrote, Philip said to her:

"The only time you have time for me is when you have something for me to do!"

Philip wasn't angry. He was hurt. I could barely breathe because I knew he was right. Too often I had allowed myself to become so busy with what seemed like important things that my son was now deeply wounded.

We were running late. We were scheduled to leave for Philip's freshman orientation to the University of Arizona that morning in the northern burbs of Chicago, about forty-five minutes away. We had two dogs that needed to be walked before we left. Did I mention that we were running late? Phil had ignored my request to take out the dogs. My anger got the better of me, and Philip responded with his piercing shard of truth. . . .

After I recovered from the shock of Philip's statement, I told him I was wrong and asked him to forgive me. And he did. That gave me the freedom to change, to take some things off my calendar, and to better see the people right in front of me.[6]

Phyllis knew in her head that fasting from activity was a way of expressing trust in God to take care of us. She readily took retreats of silence, had quiet times for reflection and Bible reading many mornings, and in May 2001 wrote in her journal, "I am so glad Andy puts his foot down about being busy on Sunday. The quiet Sundays without a list have been wonderful."[7]

She enjoyed having her college-age, young adult children around much of the summer of 2001. But she also regretted getting angry while at the lake when she didn't feel like they were helping her enough. They were ready to forgive, knowing it was an aberration and that probably, yes, they could have been more helpful.

They knew and loved their mother for the person she was, taking her outbursts in stride. Once, after Phyllis was grumpy with Susan, she apologized saying, "I'm sorry, but menopause has just got the better of me."

"Well," Susan responded flatly, "that explains yesterday. What explains the last forty years?"

Seven years later her journal sang the same refrain as her bête noire of busyness kept appearing: "I'm trying once again to slow down and spend meaningful time with God in quiet times and retreats of silence, to listen, reflect, read scripture, journal and pray."[8] And a year after that: "I am coming to the close of a very full semester. . . . I have not slowed down."[9]

I was proud of her abilities, the leadership she provided, the impact she made, the lives she touched, and all she accomplished. But this meant she often felt stretched thin, was tired, and had no margins. Though this ironically had the effect of distracting her from people, perhaps only those closest to her noticed. That was because she had so much energy that she could still give twice as much care and attention to people as us ordinary mortals.

Her motherly instincts went on high alert on the morning of September 11, 2001. She was shocked when two commercial airliners, piloted by hijackers, slammed into and brought down the Twin Towers of the World Trade Center in Lower Manhattan. The national and international implications of this surprise attack, killing more than at Pearl Harbor in 1941, sent her and the country reeling. But she immediately thought of Steve. He had been working at CBS in Midtown Manhattan for the previous year. We had visited him there not long before. But where was he now? Was he okay?

With communications disrupted by the attack and millions of people trying to make phone calls to loved ones, it was almost impossible to get through. Finally, two hours later, Steve called her. He was fine. CBS was five miles from the attack and was not directly affected; nonetheless, most everyone was being sent home. Since the subway system for a city of eight million people was shut down, it would take him hours to walk to his apartment in the Bronx.

Phyllis was immeasurably relieved. Though it was unlikely Steve would have been a casualty, he could have been anywhere in New York for a variety of reasons. She immediately called his brothers and me.

Susan, however, was in Bolivia for language school leading up to her two years of mission work with the Christian Brothers in Peru. She had to go to an internet café with her friends to find out what was happening. When she logged on, an email from Steve waited for her. Not only was he okay, but he thoughtfully included news that Susan's good friend from Boston College, Maire, who was also working in New York, was fine as well.

The intense gratefulness we all felt was muted by the cloud of questions and uncertainty that enveloped the country. Schools in Chicago were immediately closed, and all downtown workers were sent home that day as a precaution against other potential attacks. All commercial flights in the U.S. were grounded immediately and for most of the next week. But the legacy of that moment has lasted for decades.

When Phyllis began as area director, she had her office in our house. That meant she had no separation between home and work. She was constantly drawn back to and distracted by her desk. I suggested for her sake and the sake of the family that she find office space elsewhere to gain some separation.

For several years First Presbyterian Church, just a mile away, donated space to her. When that wasn't available anymore, she found space at Parkwood Church (later Christ Community

Church) which had several InterVarsity staff and students, mostly Asian American, as founding members.

Phyllis asked the pastor what the fee would be. He responded, "We're not going to float the church budget on your rent. What we could use is someone to mentor the women in our church. Would you be open to that?" That was like asking a lion if it wanted prime rib.

For more than twenty years, long after she stopped using the office at the church, she met every month or two with eight or ten professional women from the church for Bible study and prayer about what was going on in their lives at work and with their families. Often they traveled to Fremont for weekend retreats. Though the makeup of the group changed as some people moved away and new ones joined, everyone involved found it a delight, especially with Phyllis at the center. As one of them said, "Slowly over time she completely reshaped the way I understood Jesus."

Phyllis was always quick to listen, creating a safe space for them to spill what was on their hearts. She heard so many stories about complicated relationships with their mothers that she once said, "I need to meet all your mothers to talk with them." Even as she wanted to challenge those mothers to show love to their daughters in better ways, she also helped these daughters to see their mothers as God sees them.

Phyllis's month-in-month-out work as area director consisted of meeting individually with the eight or ten staff she supervised from Chicago West. The Northwest Indiana Area team was added later. She had the ability to deal straightforwardly with performance issues in an upbeat way. As one of her team members, Phil Nordquist, later wrote, "She is one who wants to see the best come out of people and does it in a caring and purposeful way. When I think of Phyllis, I know that I am loved."[10]

During his early years on staff, Phil was not much of a reader. But Phyllis knew that reading was vital for personal and professional growth. "Fifteen minutes a day equals fifteen books a year," she told him, repeating an old IVP slogan. Even reading at a modest pace, people can make their way through fifteen two-hundred-page books in twelve months.

Despite his reluctance, Phil agreed to start. A few months later, when Phyllis asked him how the plan was going, she remembered him saying, "It's great. Now I have something to talk about to students besides girlfriend and boyfriend problems!"

All the staff loved working with students, but many had difficulty with personal fundraising, which was the financial model InterVarsity used to make student ministry possible. She helped them overcome their fears and reluctance with patience, practical guidance, an upbeat spirit, and by example. Often the team gathered for an evening at the IVP offices where they had multiple phone lines available to call prospective donors. In between calls they encouraged each other and celebrated successes.

Phyllis enjoyed bringing her team annually to Fremont, first to the two cabins and then to the lake house, for week-long training or a retreat. Since the two original cabins were small with only inch-thick walls, going to the bathroom was not a completely isolated affair. Once when she was playing Six-handed Euchre, Phyllis, never one to enter or exit a room quietly or unobserved, announced, "I have to use the bathroom, but you can't listen!" Then, once inside, she belted out at full volume, "I'm singing in the rain, I'm singing in the rain, what a glorious feeling, I'm happy again!" The group completely lost it in laughter.

Under Robert Burdett's leadership, Phyllis regularly staffed Formation, the regional training program for those in their first two years as InterVarsity campus staff. WinterFest, a weekend conference for hundreds of Illinois and Indiana students, was always a highlight with its energy, vibrant worship, excellent teaching, and practical training.

At spring Chapter Focus Weeks, she was always ready to volunteer my help as well to co-lead tracks on apologetics, Bible overview, or the gospel of Mark. In 2005 she was anxious about doing the plenary exposition on John 13–17 during one week at Cedar Campus in Michigan. But her thorough preparation paid off, and her concerns fell away once she was in front of the crowd.

After four years of Jesuit education at Boston College (BC), Susan had signed up for a year of serving the poor with the Christian Brothers in Peru. She learned Spanish and stayed an extra year with Fr. Ned and Fr. Al to live and work in the *Pueblo Joven* ("young town" or *favela*) in Chimbote, north of Lima. Phyllis and I along with each of her brothers enjoyed, at different times, visiting her, her fellow volunteers, and the two priests she worked with.

While Susan was in Peru growing more serious about becoming a Catholic, Phyllis was growing more excited about what was happening at Lewis University in Romeoville, Illinois. At Lewis, a LaSallian Brothers institution, a mix of Catholic and Protestant students had formed a vital campus group and wanted to affiliate with InterVarsity.

Phyllis was thrilled with the cooperative ministry that developed. She found the Brothers and the students delightful and thoughtful. Steve Zlatic from the Lewis ministry department was supportive and saw to it that an IV campus staff was put on part-time salary to work especially with the chapter. Skillfully she also helped several of her team overcome their questions and concerns, if not skepticism, about such a cooperative ministry.

Soon Phyllis connected to other IV staff working on Catholic campuses, such as Chris Nichols at the University of San Diego. A chapter of Catholics and Protestants was flourishing there too.

Together Chris and Phyllis developed the Exploring Common Ground conference on Catholic-InterVarsity relations held in January 2002 on the University of San Diego campus. Peter

Kreeft and Fr. Ron Tacelli from Boston College and several others addressed the forty students and staff who attended, several from Lewis. A Catholic friend of Susan's from BC, Maire, spoke on "How InterVarsity Made Me a Better Catholic."

Two years later another Exploring Common Ground conference was held at Lewis. Because of my Catholic background, Phyllis made sure I spoke at both conferences and participated with her in InterVarsity's Catholic Ministry Task Force.

When Susan came back from Peru, she joined the Catholic Church and married John DeCostanza, another volunteer she had gotten to know in Peru. As mentioned earlier, the two of them called on Fr. Ned and Fr. Al from the program in Peru to concelebrate the Nuptial Mass at St. Procopius in Chicago's Pilsen neighborhood.

Some asked me what I thought about this, especially people who knew my background. Those who still had issues with Catholicism and those who were themselves Catholic were curious. I told them all, "I trust the work of the Holy Spirit in my daughter."

Concerning Susan and how her InterVarsity work connected with Catholics, Phyllis often thought back to the months before we were married when Fr. Pendergast said to us: "I see the two of you being bridge people throughout your lives between Catholics and Protestants, between these two branches of the Christian family. That could be a wonderful calling on your spiritual journey." Now Phyllis beamed as she saw that same calling alive in John and Susan.

16

PEOPLE LOVING (1)

Phyllis lit up every room she walked into. Suddenly the space was brighter from her warmth, her laugh, her presence.

Though she spread her joy widely, one of Phyllis's superpowers was the ability to give people her complete, focused attention. She made each person feel loved, seen, and heard, as though each was the only one in the room.

Whether friends or family or neighbors or coworkers or college students, each knew her good-heartedness and genuine care. One reason was that she took such simple joy in the people around her. Life and love and relationships made up the air she breathed.

She was able to be present with others because she lived in the present. She rarely regretted the past and seldom worried about the future. Of course her prayer journal revealed her distress about times she had created a rupture in a relationship and had to look for ways to reconcile. But those episodes didn't distract her when she was with others.

I and the four children were the privileged, daily recipients of this undivided love which made us feel like we were just the greatest. We all knew we weren't as amazing as Phyllis thought, but what a magnificent gift for anyone to receive each day! And there was more.

She was a wonderful model to me of how to engage with and build up others. Too often worries and distractions got in my way. I have to work hard to achieve even a fraction of what she offered others.

℘ ℘ ℘

Though everyone was in Phyllis's line of sight, due to her growing up in East St. Louis and her summers at Cedine Ministries youth camp in Tennessee, people of color were especially important for her.

Movies and books about slavery and the holocaust always drew her in because of the intense feelings they elicited in her and her sense of compassion. In 1994 we had a Valentine's Day planned without the kids and had a choice of movies. Her friends urged her to see the comedy *Grumpy Old Men*. But she was afraid *Schindler's List*, a movie about one man's efforts to rescue Jews from the Nazis, would be gone from the theaters soon. So that's what we saw.

We went to dinner afterward, but the movie had put us in such a depressed mood that we were the grumpy ones. We bickered and could hardly eat. When she told her friends afterward what happened, they all said, "We told you that you should have seen *Grumpy Old Men!*"

Nonetheless, she still made sure we saw movies like *Twelve Years a Slave*, Spielberg's *Amistad*, and *Amazing Grace*, the story of Wilberforce's efforts to outlaw the slave trade and slavery in the British Empire. She also read books like Dee Brown's *Bury My Heart at Wounded Knee*, Frederick Douglas's autobiography, and *Uncle Tom's Cabin*. We were both struck that Tom is portrayed as a man of strength, virtue, and courage, not as the stereotype of the weak-willed bootlicker we often associate with the name Uncle Tom. She also read and was moved by more recent books like Bryan Stevenson's *Just Mercy* which tells how this Harvard-trained lawyer worked to help unjustly condemned prisoners on death row in Alabama.

Once while we were stuck at an airport due to weather delays, I naturally settled down to read a fat book I had brought along. Phyllis naturally walked around talking to people so she could make some new best friends.

After a while she came back to sit with me, but she was nearly in tears. "What happened?" I asked.

"I talked to a man from Springfield, Missouri. He was so proud of his town and started listing all the great things he loved about it—the parks, the schools, the culture, the climate, the landscape. Then he told me, 'And the best thing is that the population is only ten percent minority.'"

Phyllis had been stunned by the comment, but she managed to ask him evenly, "Oh, and why is that an advantage?"

She had never seen anyone backtrack so fast in her life. "Oh, I didn't mean to offend," the man said. "Sorry, I meant nothing by it." And on he went. They exchanged a few more pleasantries after that, but the conversation soon ended.

From her lifelong experiences, Phyllis knew that those from other cultures and ethnicities rather than detracting from had enriched her life, enriched her walk with God, and enriched the community. She also knew that too often we in the majority culture often do not call each other on our attitudes and assumptions. I know I've been one of those.

But Phyllis had the courage to make the issue explicit, as well as the grace to ask a genuine question rather than to merely accuse or lecture. Courage, grace, and compassion. That was Phyllis Le Peau.

When the Bush-Gore election was up for grabs in December 2000, and everyone was consumed with the hanging chads on voting punch cards, Phyllis was watching a lot of news. During that time she saw a spot on a local news program called "Wednesday's Child." That day they featured three siblings from Chicago in need of "a forever home." Even though all our kids were grown, Phyllis's big heart opened wide. "Let's do it, Andy," she said when I got home from work.

Well, I knew immediately I had to bring out the big guns. "Let's go talk to Jim and Ruth," I said. The Nyquists had continued to be dear, older friends, full of love and good judgment. We still considered them our mentors and still went to them for counsel when major (and sometimes minor) issues arose.

We set a date, and Phyllis poured out her desires. After hearing Phyllis in full, Ruth (who had worked as a counselor) straightened up in her chair, taking on a professional posture I hadn't quite seen in her before, and said, "Now Phyllis, [pause] how old are you?"

Phyllis was momentarily silent and then erupted in laughter. "Fifty-six!" she blurted out, and all four of us howled. Without having to say more, Ruth had brought reality to bear on the situation. "Maybe these next years," Ruth said, "will be ones where you will be able to pour all that love into grandchildren." Her near clairvoyance was uncanny as Phyllis was delighted, before many years passed, that seven of fifteen grandchildren came from other ethnic groups and cultures.

At that moment, though, Jim concurred and was also the epitome of kindness and optimism.

"Oh," Phyllis said with mock indignation, "how come all three of you are always against me?"

"Because," said Jim, "it takes all three of us to handle you!" And we all howled again. Even "sweet Jim Nyquist," as she called him, had her number.

☙ ☙ ☙

Phyllis would sometimes say to me, "No one is immune." When talking about famous singers or world-class athletes or amazing Christian leaders, anyone who seemed to have it all, anyone whom the stars had shone down on with success or talent or wealth, she would say, "No one is immune."

She meant that no one was immune to the effects of living in an imperfect world, to the permeating influence of sin either as victim or perpetrator or both. She meant we are all subject to the finite limits of being human—to sadness, to grief, to trial. She also meant, don't be jealous of others.

Phyllis did not say "no one is immune" because she wished evil for others but to reorder our attitudes (hers and mine) toward other people. We should have compassion for others even when they had wronged us.

Everyone has a backstory. If someone snaps at you for lightly touching their car in a parking lot, if a clerk treats you rudely and won't offer any extra bit of help at a store, if a neighbor calls the authorities because they think you may have violated an ordinance— they all have backstories, and we should respond with kindness.

Who knows what grief they have experienced, perhaps with a parent, a child, or a spouse? Who knows how they might have been mistreated as child? Who knows if they are grieving a miscarriage? Who knows if they are estranged from their family? Who knows how unappreciated they may be on the job or with friends? Who knows how rudely customers have treated them? Who knows what illnesses they are fighting? Who knows if they are unemployed, are locked in a dead marriage, or have a child living on the streets?

Who knows what they have lived through that has festered only to erupt from them unbidden in hurtful or angry ways?

Everyone has a backstory. Everyone carries great burdens. Everyone deserves our compassion. Everyone.

℘ ℘ ℘

Christine Wagoner's experience as a new InterVarsity staff member was typical of the way Phyllis approached people. "Phyllis not only laughed a great deal with me, she also wanted to know more about me. I remember feeling so connected to this woman who I hardly knew, but she had such warmth and love that overflowed from her, I couldn't help but want to spend all my time with her. She created space in her schedule to walk the camp road with me, ask me thoughtful questions about my life and listened to my stories. I felt so special."[1]

What Phyllis sensed intuitively—that people want to be known, to feel connected—intersects with a larger issue in society. In recent years I've read three books—by a conservative, a liberal, and an independent author—all of which give the same surprising reason for the increased rancor and divisions we see in our culture: Loneliness.

Jared Diamond in *Upheaval* says that when he entered academic life in the 1950s, he was friends with those with whom he had scientific disagreements. Now, he says, "my lecture hosts have been forced to hire bodyguards from angry critics."[2] What shifted?

A hundred years ago, he says, Americans participated in book clubs, bridge clubs, church groups, community organizations, town meetings, unions, veteran's associations, and more. This fostered trust and reliance on each other. In his book *Them*, former Republican Senator Ben Sasse also notes that "between 1975 and 1995, membership in social clubs and community organizations such as the PTA, Kiwanis, and Rotary plummeted. Same with labor union membership and regular church attendance."[3]

In addition, since World War II single-person households have tripled to twenty-six percent while rates of depression and addiction have increased.[4] Jeff Bilbro writes, "Loneliness has become an epidemic in Western liberal democracies. And, apparently, being lonely is worse for someone's health than being a smoker."[5]

Radio, then TV, then video games, then the internet, and then smart phones have increasingly kept us in our homes for entertainment. As a result, "heavy TV viewers trust other people less, and join fewer voluntary organizations than do people who are not heavy TV viewers."[6]

Our divisions are not due to Russian bots, cable news, or social media, though these have taken advantage of our situation by fueling outrage. "In other words," says Bilbro, "perhaps it is *because* we are lonely and detached from our places that we put such outsized importance on the news of the day."[7]

What can we do? No one silver bullet will solve this. Sasse offers more than a hundred pages of options on becoming Americans again, on setting tech limits, and on finding ways to be rooted even in our nomadic culture.[8] An obvious option is to push against the trend of disengagement and instead join a voluntary association—a community theater group, a golf league, or a tutoring program.

Bilbro says that one of the simplest ways to combat our isolation is to go for a walk.[9] When we walk out our front door, rather than drive, we have the opportunity to chat with a neighbor walking her dog or weeding his garden, or with kids playing basketball. We find out they aren't political units. We get to know flesh-and-blood people who have problems with aphids or are celebrating a birthday or have an elderly parent living with them.

Phyllis's version of this was to take a plate of cookies to people who moved into the neighborhood. When our children were young, other families with young children became a point of natural connection. After our kids were grown, she took walks for exercise with a neighbor and her dog. As any dog owner knows, that's how in no time you get to know the other dogs . . . *and* their owners. Whether those she met were liberal or conservative, young or old, Phyllis fought against the loneliness that she instinctively knew affected so many, and she enjoyed them all.

𝒫 𝒫 𝒫

Phyllis's legendary ability to focus on others did fail her occasionally. Once while I was driving, neither of us had been talking for a while as Phyllis scrolled through her smart phone. I decided to initiate some light conversation.

"I've accumulated over a hundred emails recently that I need to look at."

I got absolutely no response. On Phyllis scrolled.

After a few minutes I thought I'd try again. "It's been so hot recently, I haven't been able to get out for a bike ride."

Scroll. Scroll. Scroll.

Now I began to think of this as a challenge. What could I say that would get her attention away from her phone? Then I had it—something so out of character for me that she'd *have* to respond.

"I think I'll start using marijuana."

And yet, nothing. She just kept scrolling. I gave up, thinking there was no way to dislodge her focus from her phone.

Then a couple of minutes later she looked up and casually said, "Oh, is it legal now in Illinois?"

ℝ ℝ ℝ

This may make you wonder: with Phyllis giving so much of her love and care to others, did I ever get jealous? Because she filled me with so much of her focused affection, I never did.

Except once.

At a large get-together, as a friend and I chatted, he asked me what surprised me about being an empty nester. Our youngest of four had gone off to college just few months earlier. Since I am a world-class internal processor, I always know what I'm going to say before I say it. But this time I surprised myself by saying something I hadn't realized before.

"Well, I knew my son would be gone. What I didn't realize was that Phyllis would be gone too."

For several years Phyllis's job often took her on the road, for days or a week at a time. But it never bothered me since we still had kids living with us, and I never came home to an empty house—until they were all gone, and Phyllis's absence became strikingly apparent. As I talked with my friend at dinner, I realized that the cumulative effect of the empty house had begun to wear on me. I was lonely.

That night I told Phyllis about the conversation. Even though we had an extremely open relationship, I have always had a hard time admitting weakness. While it took a lot out of me, she listened well, compassionately, and without judgment.

As it turned out, the next day she left for a previously scheduled weeklong trip, but I wasn't concerned. We'd talked it through. That night I waited for her call.

And I waited.

And I waited.

I knew she could have meetings scheduled into the evening. Being in a remote area, her phone might also have trouble and finding another phone that worked could be difficult. Yet given our emotional conversation of the night before, I thought for sure she'd call.

But she didn't.

As the evening wore on, I suspected I knew why. It had nothing to do with schedule or phones. I guessed she had gotten caught up in a late-night card game of Six-handed Euchre with coworkers, something she loved. She was having a blast. I was alone. She was totally present with the people she was with. And I was not one of them. Yes, I felt sorry for myself and was jealous.

Sometime late the next day she called. Immediately she could tell I was a bit distant. "What's wrong?" she asked.

"Do you remember what we talked about the other night, right before you left?"

"Yes."

"And you didn't call last night?"

A moment's silence and the pieces came together for her. Then came deep and heartfelt apologies. I told her I thought a card game might have been involved, and she ruefully confirmed it was so.

I knew I had no reason to be upset since I was completely confident in her loyal love. But I was human, with feelings. She said she was glad I told her.

We reconciled. She apologized; I forgave. I apologized; she forgave.

The next day, she called me three times. And the day after that three more times.

"Enough," I said. "You don't have to call so much. I appreciate it, but I'm fine. It's over. We're good. Once a day is enough. I love you."

But she kept calling anyway. That was Phyllis. There was no middle ground. She was always all in. Totally focused.

PEOPLE LOVING (2)

How did Phyllis work her magic? By what alchemy were people so happily drawn to her? Over the years our guest book was filled with testimonies of many who came under her spell.

"Happiness is visiting you!"

"Such joy you give to all who know you."

"I love to visit you."

"The world needs more people like you."

"Thanks for the love you give."

Though the "you" could theoretically have referred to both of us, it was Phyllis who filled their hearts. How did she do it?

I found one apt description in Heather Holleman's *The Six Conversations*. In a day when so many people feel isolated and long for deep ties with others, Phyllis embodied what Holleman calls the four mindsets that are needed to connect with people.[1]

First, *Phyllis was curious.* She knew everyone had a backstory. Everyone had childhood memories. Everyone had learned hard or happy life lessons. Discovering these things about someone could be as easy as saying, "I'm so curious. Tell me about ___________."

Phyllis didn't show her concern only when people were overtly hurting. She took delight in getting to know everyone she encountered—on a bus, standing in line, sitting in a park. Because of her genuine interest and ready laugh, they were quite willing to engage her in conversation.

When our children went away to college and into the world of work, they knew the question their mother would always ask during a visit or a phone call: "How is your heart?"

With loving mockery they would reply, "Tender. Tender." Though her question may have been overly saccharine, they also knew their mom deeply cared. She wanted to know not just about their activities and classes. She genuinely wanted to know what was going on emotionally and spiritually with them. Talking about the weather was not going to satisfy.

Once several of us stopped in a crowded picnic area. While everyone else got the food and drinks together, we sent Phyllis to claim a spot. The only space available was a big table, which already was occupied by an older African American couple. Phyllis asked if we could join them, and they readily said yes.

Before the rest of us arrived a few minutes later, Phyllis already had them in deep conversation. We were shocked when we found out later that she had asked them what it was like to grow up as African Americans in the U.S. This was probably an example of "Professional Driver on Closed Course. Do Not Attempt at Home." Perhaps the couple was not about to genuinely open up to a stranger on such a personal topic and just humored this well-intentioned but naïve White woman. Nonetheless, they seemed at ease talking to Phyllis. She could often get away with such gambles because of her cheerful, accepting demeanor.

For many years we invited several neighbors to join us for a fall weekend at Fremont Lake. Once Phyllis told everyone beforehand that we were going to take time for each person to share his or her story—our growing up years, significant events that influenced our lives, and so forth. When I later told Fr. Ned (who had been with Susan and John in Peru), what she planned, he said with wistful humor, "I want Phyllis to ask me to tell my story."

Dan McAdams, a Northwestern psychology professor, in one research project, paid participants to tell their life stories over a four-hour session because he wanted to study how people constructed personal narratives. Though many cried at some point in the retelling, most were elated at the end. "I don't want to take money for this," they said. "This has been the best afternoon I've had in a long time."[2] Like our friend Ned, many people have a deep desire to be truly known.

Phyllis genuinely wanted to understand people and valued them. She assumed that others wanted to talk about themselves, and so she showed them love by giving them the opportunity to do just that. While we can certainly listen to the ins and outs of someone's day—errands, doctor visits, chores, work, and so forth—Phyllis thought most people would welcome deeper conversations about their hopes, disappointments, successes, and sorrows. Therefore, she asked questions like, "How did you two meet?" or "Tell me about your spiritual journey?" or "What do you like about that line of work?"

Once a question like that was asked, it can get turned back to the asker. "Okay, I told you how I like to relax. What about you?" Phyllis was not afraid for openness to be mutual.

Second, *Phyllis believed the best in others*. Social media and news media have trained us to start with a mindset of judging, shaming, and correcting others. Phyllis, on the other hand, began with acceptance, sympathy, and respect. Her face lit up when she saw you.

We all know that at work or in friendship, marriage or parenting, relationships just go better if we don't jump to conclusions about motives or intentions. You may have heard the saying, "Be kind. Everyone you meet is fighting a hard battle." That's the assumption Phyllis started with.

Third, *Phyllis expressed genuine concern*. Holleman says this means we are invested in another person. So yes, we start with sympathy or empathy, but we try to find appropriate ways to act too. "Investment doesn't mean to take on everyone's problems as your own, but it does mean you position yourself to support others as you can."[3]

Phyllis was not only ready to celebrate with those who celebrate but also to mourn with those who mourn. And if she wasn't sure what the best way would be to do either of those, she would ask by suggesting specific options. "I want to hear more. What would be best—a walk, a call, going for coffee?" Or "How can I help—taking the car in for repair, watching the kids, bringing a meal?"

Fourth, *Phyllis shared herself.* As Holleman points out, the first three mindsets can have an amazing effect. But if we never talk about our own victories or defeats, the other person can feel like they are our project.

Phyllis would share similar or related experiences, including what she had learned from them. But she knew enough not to say she knew exactly how someone felt about trouble at work, a parent being sick, or conflict with a neighbor. She would, however, let people know her own story and how she felt: "I am so sorry you are in such a hard situation."

In these ways Phyllis gave people what Carl Rogers famously termed unconditional positive regard. She let people know she loved them and cared about them just the way they were, even while she would challenge them to be better.

Phyllis was human and didn't get along with everyone. Sometimes her feelings got hurt which made it hard for her to reach out as she normally did. Occasionally people felt her questions were intrusive rather than friendly. She also had a hard time if she sensed being taken for granted. Like most of us, she sometimes wanted recognition.

She could become a mother figure for many because of her large, welcoming personality. Those with dysfunctional parents were drawn to her as the caring, nurturing mother they never had. But this could backfire. Occasionally she "got other people's mail" when they imposed on her their negative images or history with their own mothers.

Nonetheless, she had a marvelous effect on almost all she met. Strangers would open up, and these four mindsets explain much about why that happened. She was a natural at loving people in these concrete ways.

℘ ℘ ℘

David Brooks's volume, *How to Know a Person*, also made me think of Phyllis. She didn't need a book, even one as good as Brooks's, to understand how to do this. She did it instinctively and intensively. Yet Brooks put into words much of who she was and what she did automatically just because she loved people.

His chapter on empathy especially impressed me because of how closely he captured the way Phyllis perpetually went about life. He writes: "Empathy is involved in every stage of the process of getting to know a person. But it is especially necessary when we are accompanying someone who is wrestling with their wounds."[4] If you were hurting, Phyllis was the person you wanted beside you. Brooks goes on:

> The problem is that a lot of people don't know what empathy really is. They think it's an easy emotion: You open up your heart and you experience this gush of fellow feeling with another person. By this definition, empathy feels simple, natural, and automatic: I feel for you.
>
> But that's not quite right. Empathy is a set of social and emotional skills. These skills are a bit like athletic skills: Some people are more naturally talented at empathy than others; everybody improves with training.
>
> Empathy consists of at least three related skills. First, there is the skill of mirroring. This is the act of accurately catching the emotion of the person in front of you.[5]

Phyllis couldn't tell you afterward that she saw muscles tensing, an eyebrow twitching, or the rate of breathing increasing. But she knew something was happening with the person she was with because she was feeling it too.

> A person who is good at mirroring is quick to experience the emotions of the person in front of them, is quick to reenact in his own body the emotions the other person is holding in hers. . . . People who are good at mirroring also have what the Northeastern University neuroscientist Lisa Feldman Barrett calls high "emotional granularity," the ability to finely distinguish between different emotional states.[6]

Phyllis paid attention to the sometimes-subtle clues that you were sad or mad, depressed or stressed. She knew herself well and knew her own emotions—but not in a way that made her self-absorbed. Rather it was in a way that meant she could be attuned to the nuances of your emotions as well.

One example came in the early days of our marriage. "I was doing dishes with my mother-in-law one evening," she wrote. "I began asking her questions about Lucy Rae, her daughter who had died at age seven some thirty years before." Lucy Rae had died of polio within twenty-four hours of contracting the dreaded disease.[7] She was healthy one day and gone the next. "Mom's blue eyes filled with tears as she spoke. Though it did not surface often, the pain was still deep within her being."[8]

As my mom talked, Phyllis was likewise filled with a sense of grief and loss. She didn't give a hint of a suggestion that after thirty years, my mom should somehow be over it. Rather she validated my mom's sorrow by feeling it herself.

The second empathy skill Brooks mentions is mentalizing.

> We do this by relying on our own experience and memory. As with all modes of perception, we ask, "What is this similar to?" When

I see what a friend is experiencing, I go back to a time in my life when I experienced something like that. I make predictions about what my friend is going through based on what I had to go through. . . . We don't see "woman crying." We see "woman who has suffered a professional setback and a public humiliation." I've been through a version of that, and I can project some of what I felt onto her.

When practiced well, this mentalizing skill helps us see emotional states in all their complexity. People generally have multiple emotions at once. . . .

Mentalizing also helps us simultaneously sympathize with a person while also detaching to make judgments about them. I may feel genuinely bad that you are miserable because somebody scratched your Mercedes. I may also think you are reacting childishly because too much of your identity is wrapped up in your car.[9]

Phyllis had penetrating insight into people. She made accurate judgments without being judgmental. "You are great, and you can be better," was the message she communicated to person after person.

Because Phyllis was a natural leader with a strong personality, many younger women were drawn to her as a role model. They would often confide to her how they had been hurt by people who didn't think women could or should lead. They felt frustrated, wounded, and often beaten down by some in their family, in the church, or at work. Though Phyllis grew up in conservative Christian circles, she never had those negative experiences. She never felt put down or restricted in any kind of ministry she wanted to do. InterVarsity offered a similar environment. She led many small groups, published a dozen Bible study guides, often spoke to groups, was a supervisor of men and women, and directed a task force.

Nonetheless, Phyllis could give all these women her full empathy. She had known disappointment in other ways. She had been wounded in other settings. As a result, those she spoke with felt heard and understood.

The third empathy skill, says Brooks, is caring.

If mentalizing is me projecting my experiences onto you, caring involves getting out of my experiences and understanding that what you need may be very different from what I would need in that situation. This is hard. The world is full of people who are nice; there are many fewer who are effectively kind.

Let's say I'm with somebody who is having an anxiety attack. Caring is not necessarily offering what I would want in that situation: a glass of wine. Caring begins with the awareness that the other person has a consciousness that is different from my own. They might want me to hold their hand while they do some breathing exercises. I'm going to find that completely awkward, but I'm going to do it because I want to practice effective empathy. . . .

When you meet someone with cancer, it feels empathetic to tell the person how sorry you are, but my friend Kate Bowler, who actually has cancer, says that the people who show empathy best are those "who hug you and give you impressive compliments that don't feel like a eulogy. People who give you non-cancer-thematic gifts. People who just want to delight you, not try to fix you, and who make you realize that it is just another beautiful day and there is usually something fun to do." That is what caring looks like.[10]

That is what Phyllis looked like.

Her spiritual director once told me that of all the people she directed, Phyllis was the only one who would begin each session by saying, "Okay, tell me about all your kids and how you are before we begin." Most of those she directed were so focused on their own needs that they skipped right past her.

Another couple said Phyllis was the only one who would ask them, each year when we visited, how they were dealing with the death of their child who had committed suicide years before. No one else did that. But she did—every year.

Maybe other friends felt they couldn't handle such intense pain from someone else. Maybe they were afraid that bringing up the past would create pain for this couple. Maybe they couldn't face the potential for this kind of anguish in their own lives. Yet these two friends always welcomed Phyllis's visits because they felt seen and loved every time.

Another friend and her husband were widely read Christian authors with an equally prominent speaking ministry. Then the news became public that he had had an affair. He had broken off the relationship and asked for his wife's forgiveness. She courageously stayed in the marriage.

As the two of them sought to heal from this devastating crisis hundreds of friends wrote, called, or visited her husband offering support. She deeply appreciated that, but, she told us later, "While my husband received hundreds of letters, I only received two." One was from a mutual friend, and one was from Phyllis. "I think for most women," she went on, "their greatest nightmare is their husband having an affair. They can't even think about it, not even to write a note to a friend, lending support in a time of crisis."

Sometimes it takes great love to show compassion. But sometimes it also takes great courage. Phyllis had both.

She was the queen of relational risk. She took chances with people. Phyllis was willing to hazard being too intrusive to connect with people, to offer comfort, to be present with someone in need.

How was she able to do this? Certainly she had the conversational mindset and the empathy skills mentioned by Holleman and Brooks, but I think more was at work. Phyllis was able to reach out as she did because she was thoroughly grounded in who she was as a beloved child of God. She was completely secure in that. From that place, from that foundation, that solid foundation, she could take chances to reach out.

As always, I wish I could be more like Phyllis. But maybe she has helped me to at least be more willing to ask, "How are you?" and to mean it, to look for more than a superficial answer. She modeled for me how to be ready to listen, truly listen for an answer.

℘ ℘ ℘

Her courage and willingness to take risks to care for others also showed itself in crises. When our son Philip was in Little League, we were watching a game with neighbors. On this beautiful, late spring evening, we sat on the first-base side of home plate while Phyllis was fifty feet away chatting with others.

I turned for a moment but heard the crack of the bat on the ball, then a thunk nearby, and an "Ugh!" I turned back and my neighbor was doubled over, her face in her hands. Suddenly blood gushed between her fingers like someone had turned on a faucet. I responded by doing what any self-possessed, rational person would do in such a situation. I stood up, waved my arms wildly and yelled, "Phyllis! Phyllis! Get over here! Now!"

She turned toward me and casually sauntered over in our direction. After sizing up the situation she turned to the others gathered and calmly said, "Does anyone have any ice?" Sure enough, someone had some in a cooler.

"That's great," I thought. "Put the ice on her nose to bring down the swelling." But Phyllis had other ideas. She gently told our friend to bring her head up, and Phyllis then carefully applied the ice to . . . the back of her neck! In less than two minutes the gush of blood had stopped completely.

I was in awe.

Almost all the blood vessels to the head run through the back of the neck, she told me later. Ice would constrict them and significantly reduce the flow. I had always been amazed by my wife, but seeing her superpowers displayed in this way took it to another level.

Years later we were thirty-thousand feet above the American landscape when I saw two flight attendants half-dragging, half-carrying a pale, dazed woman to the back of the plane. Again I knew just what to do but now without a drop of panic. Sitting in an aisle seat, I got up, walked to the flight attendant, and calmly said, "Would you like a nurse?"

She turned to me with eyes wide and in a hoarse whisper full of alarm and hope said, "Are you a nurse?"

"No, but my wife is. Shall I get her?" The attendant nodded vigorously. I went back and told Phyllis who promptly rolled her eyes at me as if to say, "What have you gotten me into this time?"

But back she went and had the situation stabilized within (yes) two minutes with nothing to work with but her own wits. When the plane landed, they asked everyone to stay in their seats so emergency medical personnel could come on board to help an ill passenger. Afterward the flight crew showered Phyllis with their thanks.

"I may have looked calm," she told me. "But my heart was racing." Phyllis had medical competence, but she also had the courage to put care into action.

℘ ℘ ℘

Her love bubbled up irrepressibly. After the funeral of a dear friend, Phyllis told me, "I've got to make sure the kids know how much I love and respect them if I should die suddenly."

"Oh, they know, Phyllis," I reassured her. "They know, we all know what you think . . . about everything, all the time!"

"Really? I'm not sure," she said unconvinced. "I'm going to write them all anyway, just to be sure."

By this time all four were all out of the home. On a mission, then, Phyllis wrote a group email to all five of us, devoting several paragraphs to each. She named specific things about each person that she loved and appreciated, with large scoops of admiration and pride, along with hopes, dreams, and encouragement. Generous amounts of tenderness and affection were drizzled over the top.

They responded with thanks and love. Philip, however, always one to show due respect to his mother, replied with one line: "Get that woman out of the liquor cabinet!"

Though compassion regularly filled Phyllis and often drove her to action, on one baffling occasion she hesitated when someone was in need.

About ten years into our marriage, Jim and Ruth Nyquist were in a crisis. Jim was on the verge of being fired for being a whistleblower. Phyllis was distressed. Their situation consumed her. So I said, "Go over to their house. Be with them. I'll watch our kids." But she thought that might be presumptuous because even though we cared a lot about the two of them, we weren't particularly close at the time.

"No," I said, "it's fine. They'll be delighted to see you." Yet despite how upset she was about them, she wouldn't go. One of the many ironies of our marriage was that Phyllis thought (at least theoretically!) that the husband should be the head of the house, and I didn't. I thought we should be a team. Nonetheless, despite her convictions, in this case she wouldn't do what I suggested.

Back and forth we went. I encouraged her to go, and she refused. She piled up reasons—she'd be intruding; there were probably many people with them already; it was too late in the evening. Yet I knew that going was exactly what would help her even if she didn't. Not only would she encourage them, but they would also be a comfort to her. Their centeredness, faith, and peaceful strength would lift her up.

Finally, in joking desperation, I pleaded, "Phyllis, won't you please submit—just this once!"

She laughed, brightened up, and then said with stern merriment, "Okay, mister, but you've had your once!"

And that was indeed the only time in our forty-seven years of marriage that I asked. But it was so worthwhile because she came back a few hours later thoroughly refreshed. Her mind and heart were much more at ease. Jim and Ruth were also glad for her visit. They never forgot it, and the friendship of the four of us began to grow more deeply after that.

All of that, however, didn't stop Phyllis from reminding me regularly over the years, "You've had your once, Le Peau!"

18

INFLUENCING

"Phyllis loves you and has a wonderful plan for your life."

Phyllis got an adrenaline kick from helping people flourish emotionally, physically, spiritually. She simply wanted the best for everyone she met.

In a favorite scene from one of her favorite movies, *Chariots of Fire*, Eric Liddell explains to his sister that he is not going back to the mission field right away because he has the opportunity to run in the 1924 Paris Olympics. "I believe God made me for a purpose: for China. But he also made me fast! And when I run I feel his pleasure."

Likewise, when Phyllis influenced others toward God and his kingdom (or even on saving money on their electric bill), she felt a surge of his joy. It's how he made her.

Often I was the target of this loving attention. When she took on the job of area director for InterVarsity in Northern Illinois, she roped me into helping at chapter camp. These were intensive weeklong training events for students, often at Cedar Campus in the Upper Peninsula of Michigan.

Starting in the late 1990s, she had me co-leading a track with her on Christian apologetics or on a Bible overview. She always took immense pleasure in the two of us working together in ministry— the very thing she dreamed and hoped would characterize our marriage from the beginning.

By 2005 we settled into the track that went through the Gospel of Mark, using what was called the manuscript method of study. Students were given single-sided, double-spaced, typewritten copies of the Gospel with wide margins. All chapter and verse numbers were eliminated (since those were never part of the original text).

Our group met about ten times during the week, and at each session we'd take the students through a couple pages, telling them to freely mark up their manuscripts, showing where they saw paragraph and section breaks. They also used different colors for different themes as well as repeated and contrasting words. We asked them to write in the margins any questions that came to mind and any key observations they made. Then in pairs, small groups, or as a whole group we'd discuss their findings and questions.

I soon noticed how illuminating passages from the Old Testament could be. Often in our discussions when something seemed odd to the students, I asked them to look up a related Old Testament passage. Inevitably the proverbial light bulbs went on. The supposedly obscure Old Testament was often the key to clarifying the supposedly clear New Testament.

After several years of this, to help with my teaching, I started systematically noting down these connections to Mark. When I told Phyllis what I was doing, she said, "You should write a commentary on Mark."

"Oh, no," I responded. "I'm just doing this for my own benefit. There are dozens of quality commentaries on Mark. The world doesn't need another one."

"No," she responded undeterred. "You should write a commentary and get it published."

But I was the one who had been in publishing for decades, not her, right? I should know more about such things, right?

As I kept working on the project, I saw that among all those great commentaries on Mark, none of them did exactly what I wanted or needed. Doubts began to creep into my mind. Maybe Phyllis was right. To see if the idea had any merit, I decided to try writing a full-fledged sample covering the first three chapters of the Gospel.

I was surprised when, after several weeks of work, the sample convinced me that it would be possible to do a book in this fashion on the whole Gospel. When I told her, she simply smiled her knowing, Phyllis smile and said with satisfaction, "I told you so."

Phyllis had persuaded me to join her at chapter camp. Because of that I gained a wonderful appreciation for InterVarsity's tradition of focusing on Mark's Gospel as a key tool for discipleship. In addition I came to understand how essential and foundational the Old Testament is for the whole New Testament. The result was *Mark Through Old Testament Eyes* published in 2017 by Kregel Academic. A whole series of similar commentaries on the other books of the New Testament followed from other authors. All because of Phyllis's influence.

Once our church, Immanuel, had an opening for an associate minister and Phyllis thought one of our members, Annette LaPlaca, would be perfect for the job. She promptly asked Annette about it. Even though the job had been open for several months, Annette made excuses—she wasn't qualified, she'd never considered working in ministry, and so on.

Phyllis was not put off. "You ought to apply." Phyllis knew Annette was good with people, was organized and had plenty of energy. In addition, she knew Annette could use a job. It would be a win-win for her and for Immanuel.

A month later Phyllis asked Annette again if she had applied for the job. According to Annette, "Phyllis really convinced me by saying she felt the Holy Spirit was telling her that I needed to have the job. She felt she had some kind of word from the Lord!"[1] Phyllis's gentle encouragement and persistence led Annette to apply. Shortly afterward she was hired. She has been serving Immanuel happily since March 2014.

Phyllis had an ability to quickly assess the strengths people had and envision how those could be used. She was also willing to risk putting into motion ideas that popped into her mind. She didn't feel the need to brood over how people might react. She loved people and assumed they knew that. Even if they didn't follow her counsel, people could tell she only wanted good things for them.

Her strong nurse's training was never far below the surface when it came to caring for others. If friends mentioned they were having physical issues, she'd kindly admonish them to schedule and go to needed medical appointments. And, yes, they also felt cared for when she followed up with them a month later to confirm.

She left her loving fingerprints wherever she went.

℘ ℘ ℘

Often that meant showing people what God could offer them in forgiveness, freedom from guilt, healed relationships, personal growth, and purpose in life. She knew how God's grace had transformed the life of her Uncle Frank from alcoholic to preacher. She wanted that same grace for others. Talking to people about Jesus was as natural as breathing for Phyllis, and she did a lot of both.

Another love was the Bible. She often quoted George Stulac who once told her, "Saturate yourself with Scripture." Unsurprisingly, she delighted in combining her love of Bible study with her love of people who weren't Christians. "Those are great questions you are asking," she'd say to someone who wasn't so sure about this Christianity thing. "Let's get together and look at the original stories of what Jesus did and had to say."

She led investigative Bible discussions in nursing school, when she joined Nurses Christian Fellowship staff, and in Welcome Class at the Methodist church in Downers Grove. Phyllis was elated in each of these settings when someone realized they didn't have a relationship with God and wondered how they could become a Christian. She was more than happy to explain both the cost and the blessings that came from such a decision. If they were ready to go ahead, she offered a model of how they could make that commitment in prayer.

And if they didn't? Phyllis was not trying to put another notch on her Bible belt. One friend asked her, "If I don't become a Christian, will you still be my friend?"

She responded, "I want you to become a Christian because you are my friend, not to make you my friend."

Early in our marriage we invited neighbors to Welcome Class to look at Scripture. But after our involvement with the class ended, she wondered what to do next. Then in the early 1990s, some Jewish friends invited us to their house for a Seder meal for Passover.

When we arrived, we found the house transformed with large tables set up for a couple dozen people. One requirement was getting rid of any trace of yeast in the house, as was instructed at the first Passover in Egypt (see Exodus 12:15). Therefore, their home had been thoroughly cleaned, and all surfaces were covered in plastic over newspaper to prevent any further contamination. Then we, along with a mix of Jewish and Gentile friends, enjoyed the full three-hour event. Four cups of wine and all! Phyllis was enthralled.

> I watched them symbolically follow the story of the exodus of the people of Israel from slavery in Egypt with matza (unleavened bread), the bitter herbs, the blessings, and more. Clearly they enjoyed the traditions and what they meant.
>
> Then the light dawned. My Jewish friends are eagerly waiting for the Messiah. We have the good news that the Messiah has come.
>
> "I know that Messiah is coming" (who is called Christ). . . .
> Jesus said to her, "I am he, the one who is speaking to you."
> (John 4:25-26)[2]

Afterward Phyllis said, "Andy, I have an idea. Why can't we share some of our Christian heritage in a similar way?" She wanted to have a meal, of course, and have it somehow tied to the Christian calendar. Lent and Advent seemed like good options, but since Lent emphasized fasting, we thought Advent might be better for a feast. Thus, the seed of Phyllis's thought sprouted into what became our annual Advent Celebration.

Each December we invited about two dozen friends, neighbors, coworkers, and their children to our home for an evening. Since they usually didn't all know each other, Phyllis took a few minutes to have everyone introduce themselves and tell how they were connected to us.

That first time, Phyllis had invited our Jewish friends as they had invited us for the Seder. They were happy to come but wondered if, when they arrived, they could go off quietly to a separate room to light candles and say their Hanukkah prayers. "You'll do no such thing," Phyllis said. "You'll do that with all of us so we can join you!"

The house was decorated for Christmas, and the Christmas dishes were set out on red and green tablecloths. We then treated this mixed group of Christians and others to a dinner of soup and Panera bread bowls. (Once I tried to change our normal offerings of chili, clam chowder, and French onion soup—but was met with stiff resistance from the group to such an uncalled-for break from tradition!)

After an hour of good conversation and food, we gathered in our living room for a simplified version of Lessons and Carols based on what a friend from church, Carolyn Nystrom, had developed. We handed out homemade booklets which told the Christmas story through about twenty readings of a sentence or two each. Going in a circle each person could participate by reading a section aloud to the group.

This was punctuated by carols which also told pieces of the story—"O Little Town of Bethlehem," "Angels We Have Heard on High," and "We Three Kings," closing with "Joy to the World." Our good friend Jim Hoover usually accompanied us on piano though once, to our delight, we wrangled a string trio to join us!

In the middle of the readings and singing, we paused to let

people share Christmas or holiday memories and what it meant to them. Some talked about family traditions and some about their faith experiences. The evening closed with dessert and coffee, sharing cookies and other treats that our friends brought.

As we were standing around enjoying treats, the Jewish couple cornered me. "We are so curious. What's the difference between Catholics and Mormons and Baptists? It's all very confusing to us."

I was stunned momentarily. How was I going to explain all that in five or ten minutes? Besides, I'm not nearly as comfortable as Phyllis in such conversations. Yet I heard myself say, "That's a great question. But would it be okay if instead I talked about what all Christians have in common?" They agreed that would be helpful, and I summarized the story of Jesus and how he connected to the Hebrew Scriptures. When I told her later, Phyllis was delighted because that was exactly what she was hoping would come out of the evening.

Phyllis didn't want things to end there, of course. Over the thirty years we've held this event, she occasionally followed up with an invitation to a six-week study of the life of Jesus during Lent. Sometimes the invitation was just for the women she knew and sometimes it was for couples.

Asking these friends to come for a limited timeframe helped. This wasn't some open-ended activity with no end in sight. It also seemed to be a natural follow up for most. In a society that connects less and less to Christianity, Advent (and Christmas) and Lent (and Easter) are still somewhat familiar.

Phyllis not only wanted to welcome people into our home but into our lives and into a community of faith.

℘ ℘ ℘

One of the nursing school friends Phyllis continued to stay in touch with over the decades was Jane Hutchinson who still lived in St. Louis. Jane often talked about a neighbor, Amy Williams, who would ask her questions about the Bible and church. Phyllis met Amy when visiting and found her delightful. Phyllis suggested to Jane that to help Amy with her questions, the two of them study the life of Jesus in the Gospels.

Later Phyllis mentioned this to her sister Diane. Though Diane was no more proficient with technology than Phyllis, she said, "Well, why don't the three of you have a Bible study on Skype?"

Phyllis thought meeting together on a video call was brilliant, and Jane and Amy agreed. Amy dubbed their weekly meetings "Jesus School" and emblazoned that on the cover of a three-ring binder containing the chapter from John's Gospel that Phyllis emailed each week. Jane did wonder what would come of it, however. "Amy loves her Sundays," she told Phyllis. "She stays home and relaxes in her pajamas all day by herself, and I don't think she'll want to give that up."

After a year of weekly online video meetings studying the Gospel of John, in February 2017, Phyllis said, "We're getting to the end of the Gospel, Amy, and John has a point he's trying to make. He wants us to know and accept the truth about Jesus. As he wrote in John 20:30-31, 'Jesus performed many other signs in the presence of his disciples, which are not recorded in this book. But these are written that you may believe that Jesus is the Messiah, the Son of God, and that by believing you may have life in his name.' So," Phyllis continued, "next week I'm going to be asking you if you are ready to take that step."

At the end of the next week's discussion, Phyllis reminded Amy about what John 3:16 says—that God loves the world and each of us so much that he wants to give everyone abundant, eternal life. The problem is that we have walked away from God, trying to live on our own without his grace or strength. The Bible calls this separation sin. But Jesus died to bridge the gap between us and God, offering us forgiveness so our relationship with God can be restored. How does that happen? As it says in John 1:12, when we receive him and believe in his name, we become his children.

Amy said that is what she wanted. She wanted to be God's child. Phyllis offered the model of a prayer Amy could say to turn her life over to God. And Amy did.

A few weeks later Phyllis joined Amy and Jane on Easter Sunday morning at Jane's church in St. Louis when Amy was baptized. Then after everyone in the church had received communion, the pastor served the three of them. As they finished, everyone started singing, "Praise God from Whom All Blessings Flow." For Phyllis, as tears came to her eyes, it was like a taste of heaven.

19

EVANGELISM COORDINATING

After ten years as an area director, Phyllis had developed a strong, healthy team of InterVarsity staff. But each year the administrative and budgeting work became more tiresome, especially when she had to learn new software. As a well-regarded senior staff member, she had a good deal of freedom to create a new job that would focus even more on her gifts and her loves, minimizing the rest.

In 2007 she and her supervisor settled on a new role—evangelism coordinator for the region. Helping staff and students grow in their ability to talk about their love for Jesus was in her sweet spot. What could be better than talking with "not yet Christians" at camps, conferences, and major campus outreach programs like the ones at Michigan State, Ohio State, and the University of Wisconsin–River Falls?

One part of the job, however, gave her pause. That fall, when she attended InterVarsity's national gathering of evangelism champions as her region's representative, she felt out of place among all the sharp, young, creative staff. What she knew was simply helping people encounter Jesus through relationships and Bible discussions. She was not a strategic thinker like her impressive colleagues. As she prayed, however, she sensed God saying, "You don't have to do this alone. Get a team of staff together that love evangelism and are young and creative and gifted in ways that you are not."[1]

Leading a team! She loved leading teams, she loved other people, and she loved getting things done. What could be better than getting things done in a group? She was also a skilled group leader, making everyone feel welcome, valued, and special.

Now she had a vision for what to do. She would surround herself with those who were far better than she was at strategic thinking. Within months she formed the Strategic Evangelism Team made up of veteran staff which first met in June 2008 to plan for the growth of evangelism in the three-state region. They set priorities and gathered resources for staff and students. The first initiative was establishing a Community of Evangelists, younger staff in the region who wanted encouragement and training from the senior staff. This was exactly the kind of development she was hoping for.

Her capacity for work was evident. Just looking at the highlights from her fall schedule for 2009 (see box) would make most people tired. And such a schedule was typical for her during these years. Yet these highlights didn't include all the emails, phone calls, and other one-on-one meetings she had with staff, churches, or donors.

Fall 2009 InterVarsity Schedule for Phyllis Le Peau

September

10 Speak to Illinois Institute of Technology chapter meeting
    Topic: Continual Transformation: John 1

12 Training for Illinois Institute of Technology
    Topic: Groups Investigating God (GIGs)

24 Speak at Northern Illinois University
    Topic: The Power of the Resurrection

October

2-4 Speak at the Northern Indiana Area Fall Conference
  Topic: Spiritual Disciplines

8 Speak at Joliet Junior College chapter meeting
  Topic: Christian Community and Evangelism

13-15 Regional Leadership Meetings

20-22 National Evangelism Champion Team

November

6-8 Co-lead and speak at seekers track at the University
  of Illinois Fall Conference
  Topic: Invitation to a Relationship with Christ

16-18 Lead Formation (Regional New Staff Training)

30 Lead Regional Strategic Evangelism Team (continued)

December

1-2 Lead Regional Strategic Evangelism Team (concluded)

4-6 Speak with Andy at Regional Staff Marriage Retreat

8-9 Lead meeting for Regional Community of Evangelists

26-31 Staff Urbana 09 Student Missions Convention

From: Phyllis J. Le Peau, "A Note from Phyllis," August 2009 prayer letter.

Each event got her adrenaline pumping. When she returned from the November 2009 fall conference at the University of Illinois, she wrote, "I worked with Eriko Ishitsuka to lead the track, *Explore*, where I got to hang out with students, mostly internationals, who did not yet know Jesus. It is life-giving for me to look at Scripture through their eyes. They respond with a freshness and openness that excites me and stimulates my own relationship with Jesus."[2]

℘ ℘ ℘

Over that decade, Phyllis's mother had become more unstable physically. Her memory and mental capacity also declined. Louise would not tolerate live-in help nor moving to an assisted living facility. Nor did the sisters want that. They wanted to care for her. The three of them decided to rotate being with her full time. It was so seamless that Louise didn't even realize someone was with her all the time. Since Judy lived nearby, she spent two weeks a month with her mom in Fairview Heights. Phyllis and Diane each traveled there separately for the other weeks each month.

After three years of this, the strain on all of them was significant, especially for Diane who had her own physical issues. She told her sisters it would be easier on her to have Granny full time in Kalamazoo than to travel every month. But before they did so, Diane wanted to break Granny of her fifty-year smoking habit so she wouldn't have to live with smoke in her own house.

Their plan was simple. When Louise asked for her cigarettes, they simply told her, "Oh, Mom, don't you remember? You quit that habit a long time ago." And since by that time Louise's memory was a few gigabytes short of factory specs, she accepted their word.

Phyllis and Judy then travelled occasionally to Kalamazoo to give Diane a break. But after another few years of this new pattern, Diane's daughter Kim, seeing the toll on her own mother, proposed they move Granny to her house nearby. As a result, for a total of ten years, the family cared for Granny continually until the early morning of February 22, 2010, when Phyllis's mother, the outspoken woman from Shawneetown, the Judge's daughter, gently died in her sleep.

Phyllis wrote to friends: "The words, 'Girls, your dad is home,' spoken at my dad's funeral twenty-four years ago, came back to me the morning that my mom died. My next thought was, 'Mom can hear!'" Due to the severe hearing loss Louise had experienced as a teenager, her near deafness was only compensated for by powerful hear aids. Phyllis took heart that "now she could hear wonderful songs of worship and praise to the Lord."[3]

Phyllis also wrote in her journal about her profound mixture of feelings:

It has been harder than I thought since we have "been losing her" for so long. But the tears flowed freely, tears of gratitude and peace but also tears of loss. Sue Price put it well . . . "losing" is not "gone." And now she is gone. I am feeling it. The kids were all with me; ten of the twelve grandchildren made it, and I love having them with me and seeing the cousins together.

I am so grateful to you, Lord, for your bringing my folks to yourself, for the prayers of my grandmother, for my parents, generosity and hospitality and for answered prayer for a gentle death. She died so gently. . . .

I was blessed with parents that loved me, prayed for me and supported me. I am blessed with a great legacy—all the kids and grandkids are walking with the Lord.[4]

℘ ℘ ℘

As Phyllis continued leading the Strategic Evangelism Team, one idea from the group rose to the top: Why not revive the evangelistic beach projects during spring break that InterVarsity had run back in the seventies and eighties? Together, then, they created Soul Surf. Thirty InterVarsity staff and students went to Panama City, Florida, in March 2012, along with thousands of other students who were ready to party hard.

Each morning, when all the other students were sleeping in or sleeping it off, the InterVarsity group met for prayer and training in evangelism. In the afternoons and evenings, they used a variety of means to draw students in.

On the beach they took their "Red Cup" interactive display wherever they went. All the students knew exactly what to drink from their red, plastic, sixteen-ounce cups which were everywhere. But the Soul Surf display was different.

As students came to see what the big, bright board displaying four huge red cups was all about, the Soul Surf team asked them, "What are you thirsty for: love, success, fun, or purpose?" As each one identified their thirst, they could place a big colored dot on the cup that had been labeled with their answer. The team members then asked more about their thirst and introduced Jesus as one who promised to satisfy their thirst with living water.

In the evenings they extended hospitality at pool parties which advertised free food and music. They gave away hundreds of hot dogs and the Soul Surf band played classic rock—both of which were hits with the students. During the week they had good conversations with over five hundred people. More than half of these chats included an opportunity to talk about Jesus.

At a pool party Phyllis chatted with Jacob. After some small talk, she told him why they were there. He immediately went into a long ramble about how the earth developed and how the neurons in our brains randomly came together to make us who we are. About the time she decided the conversation was going nowhere, he said, "Probably there is no God involved in this at all. It just happened. But if there is a God, he is out there, distant and totally uninvolved with me."

When he took a breath, Phyllis said, "Oh, no, Jacob. God is there. He is involved. He loves you very much. He knows you by name, and he is the reason for this conversation. I have experienced his love, his forgiveness and have an intimate relationship with him."

He became thoughtful and in silence looked off to the side. She waited. He looked back at her and quietly said, "You are very fortunate. I envy your faith."

"It can be your faith too," she said. "You can have a relationship with God." Then she told him more about Jesus.[5]

Though Phyllis was several decades older than the students, she never let that stop her from enjoying them. In 2013 and 2014 Renee Richter from our church, Immanuel, volunteered to cook for the InterVarsity group during the week. She roomed with Phyllis at a beach hotel, and one night, right outside their room nine students sat with their feet in a hot tub having a blast. They were all drunk, noisy, and listening to country music.

Phyllis put on her swimsuit and without a bit of hesitation, joined them all in the circle. She laughed and talked right along with them. Renee was amazed with how at ease she was. In turn they treated her just like another person. Fellow IV staff Christine Wagoner concurred: "I stood in awe as students on the beach loved talking with Phyllis. She knew how to connect with anyone no matter their age, ethnicity, or background."[6]

At the pancake giveaway that Soul Surf sponsored one week, two young women, bare foot and in bikinis, staggered down the street. Two from the Soul Surf team, Erin and April, were afraid that one of them would fall into the street in front of a car. They invited the young women in to eat and then took them home.

As Phyllis told the story, "On their way to their hotel Erin began to tell them about Jesus' love for them and why he came. Tears flooded one of the student's eyes, and when invited to do so, she gave her life to Jesus. When they got out of the car, thirty minutes after being terribly drunk, they were both miraculously sober."[7] No doubt Phyllis remembered the story of her own alcoholic Uncle Frank so many years before.

Soul Surf continued at Panama Beach for four springs. In 2015 over one hundred fifty InterVarsity students and staff had over twenty-seven hundred spiritual conversations, resulting in twenty-nine people making personal commitments to Christ. One student said, "I came to Florida two years ago to party, and I met IV students on the beach . . . . One year ago I came back, not to party, but for Soul Surf. This year, I heard God call me to go on staff with IV and do this kind of thing with students in Europe."[8] For Phyllis, that's what it was about.

But that's not all it was about. As a friend wrote: "During one of the years we were at Soul Surf together in Florida, we were heading to swim at the beach. Many times people enter the water at the beach with caution for fear of it being too cold. Phyllis had no such fear. She full on *RAN* with her hands waving up in the air, and was yelling with the purest joy all the way into the ocean. Full abandon."[9]

Whether talking to people about Jesus or playing in the ocean, every moment was an opportunity for Phyllis to open her pores to let in life, and to let out light and joy.

℘ ℘ ℘

Whenever Phyllis held various meetings at the InterVarsity Press building in Westmont, Illinois, she'd stop to say hi to me. She could see how task oriented I was at work. Okay, very task oriented. My idea of being people oriented was to say hello in the morning and say good night when I left. Since she knew that just wasn't going to cut it for me in leading the editorial department, she appointed herself my Chief Morale Officer.

One practice she introduced during those years was calling me about every six months to say, "Ask everyone in the department what they want from Starbucks, and I'll bring it over."

About thirty minutes later I helped her pass out lattes and cappuccinos to everyone, just the way they liked it. But that special treat was just the beginning for Phyllis. She also visited with each person, finding out about their lives, laughing, and having a great time. Often a spontaneous party spilled into the editorial hallway around her.

During those meetings of hers at IVP, she'd come down the hallway at a break, and even without free coffee the same thing would happen. Whenever she appeared productivity in the department plummeted but morale skyrocketed.

℘ ℘ ℘

In addition to Soul Surf, another initiative emerged from Phyllis's team of strategic thinkers. They decided to aim to make Investigative

Bible Discussions (also called GIGs—Groups Investigating God) a priority on campuses in the region. These were right in Phyllis's wheelhouse. She loved encouraging groups of people to engage in free-flowing conversation about what Jesus was up to in the gospel stories. Questions, disagreements, doubts, challenges were all welcome in her mind. That's how people could learn and grow.

She jumped right into the program. In June and August of 2013 she made six visits to Purdue University at Fort Wayne to train students and staff on inviting their "not yet Christian" friends to investigate Jesus through the Gospels. That fall she traveled to Southern Illinois University (SIU) at Carbondale, SIU at Edwardsville, and the University of Illinois at Champaign/Urbana to do the same thing.

At the October 2013 Indiana Fall Conference she met with fifteen students in the Encountering Jesus track where ten decided to follow Jesus as Lord and Savior. "How cool is that?" she wrote. "But what makes it really cool is that each of the new believers were already connected to a Christian friend and a witnessing community."[10]

❧ ❧ ❧

Phyllis was nervous about leading that first Love That Heals seminar in St. Louis back in 1973. Though she spoke to groups hundreds of times in the following decades, she often had jitters beforehand. But they went away as soon as she got the crowd laughing. For years she began with stories of the funny things her kids said or did, like the one about Philip and the mother duck. Then she graduated to telling hilarious episodes about her grandkids.

The stories were entertaining to be sure. But she also had a point lodged in the background. Many students came from broken or less than ideal homes. They had little idea what healthy relationships might look like in a family. Phyllis wanted to paint a picture of honest, open, loving bonds with parents and among siblings, something that could take hold in their subconscious.

Some of her favorite experiences in front of a crowd were leading large groups in manuscript study. One summer she guided two hundred people over several mornings in portions of the Gospel of John at the orientation for new InterVarsity staff at the national office in Madison. She gave them time to study individually, asked them to discuss their observations and questions about the text in small groups, and then guided discussions for the whole group. And yes, she was delighted to get them all laughing.

At the Urbana Missions Convention in 2012, the 15,000 in attendance were divided into groups of several hundred each for morning Bible study. Phyllis led one such group in manuscript study. She wrote afterward, "I and my team were excited to see how the quality of the comments from students about the gospel of Luke improved each of the four days. They were focused, on task and intently listening to God. As I stood and looked over the crowd of students talking in small groups about how to apply to their lives what they had just discovered in Luke, I thought, 'I could do this forever!'"[11]

NOT RETIRING

Phyllis knew people often retired at sixty-five or seventy; however, she wondered when the right time would be to step down from her work with InterVarsity. Then on June 12, 2013, she wrote in her prayer journal:

Lina [my granddaughter] is four today.

The Lord clearly told me that my work as evangelism coordinator is finished after this coming school year. . . . It was clear and definite. This is a gift from God. I've said he will make it clear . . . which makes it so much easier to leave. Now I need to hear from him about staying around one more year after leaving the position. The main reason, I think, would be to do year two of the GIG [Groups Investigating God] project if it is moving and if it is approved for the second year for national funds. One of the things that I would love to do is to finish well—direct donors to other staff. Holy Spirit, may I continue to hear your voice. Thank you for leading me.

She longed to have such clarity. And now she had it.

She told her supervisor, saying she wanted to step down at the end of the academic year, in June 2014. But he asked her to stay one more year to make it easier to transition her responsibilities to others in the Illinois-Indiana region. She asked what I thought, and

I was fine with that plan. One reason was that since she was eight years older, I hoped we could both retire at about the same time. As a result, she retired at the end of June 2015, and I retired from InterVarsity Press seven months later.

Even though she knew this was the right time, Phyllis had mixed feelings. She wrote:

> My last prayer letter. . . . I shed tears as I say good-bye to people and a ministry I love. I am in awe of God, who has grown me over these years and has done good things on campus. I have received more than I have given.
>
> I am grateful for you. You have prayed. You have encouraged me and you have given. Thank you for your partnership in the gospel. You have influenced students to follow Jesus . . . to make him Lord of their lives.
>
> Out of your giving and praying will come missionaries, evangelists, doctors, engineers, parents, men and women who will influence the marketplace with gospel living, those who will battle against injustice and racism and poverty, and hopefully some InterVarsity staff. All of these are students who during their college years committed themselves to follow Jesus for the rest of their lives.[1]

She went on:

> As I think about the future several things come to mind. My longing for others to come to know Jesus deepens and life without evangelism would be no life at all. I want to be involved with and continue to learn from my brothers and sisters of color. I would love to somehow influence racial reconciliation and justice and work against poverty. I want to serve in my church on a more regular basis.[2]

Phyllis didn't believe Christians retired. They just moved from one phase of life and ministry to another. Certainly she wanted more time to travel and see grandkids, but she was also ready to get into something new. I suggested she take a year to see how the new rhythms of her life played out and what opportunities might present themselves. During that year I thought it would be fine to volunteer for one-time events, but that for the moment she should hold off on long-term commitments. She agreed.

Six months after leaving InterVarsity she wrote in her journal:

Life continues to move very fast. Highlights:

I am enjoying the transition even more than expected. Feeling less rushed, fewer lists (though the list is there and always will be), freer to be with people and help when needed, and time in our home.

Even so, her spiritual life was not always what she desired:

Quiet times are still lacking. Sometimes. I just don't want to have one—it bothers me that I don't long for time with Jesus. My love for him is shallow. I don't seem to expect from him in ways I used to—even to the point of wondering if prayer—at least my prayer makes a difference. I do long for corporate prayer.[3]

As soon as I retired in February 2016, we drove to Denver to see Steve, Kristen, and their girls before traveling to Tucson to be with the Phil and Dave Le Peau families for a couple weeks. A month after we got back she wrote in her journal, "We are at the lake for three weeks. The first real retirement for Andy and for us together in quiet and alone. . . . Working with Andy right across the table from him and being productive on writing tasks is gratifying. Yes, I think I am an extrovert who loves silence too."[4]

She was. Remarkably, she held strong contrasting impulses in one person. She was a Formula 1 race car driver who enjoyed sedately delivering cookies as much as running a Grand Prix. She was a task-oriented person who loved being with people. She reveled in having a full day of activity and suddenly dissolving into deep sleep at night. She was a cheerful, upbeat person with a strong melancholic streak who felt keenly the suffering in the world. It wasn't so much that Phyllis was a bundle of contradictions as that she was able to seamlessly hold together a wide breadth of human experience and aspirations.

As that year of waiting and listening to see what might come next ended, she felt guided to obey Jesus in three concrete ways—to feed the hungry, care for widows, and visit those in prison. And she did. She volunteered once or twice a week at the food pantry our church operates, which helps feed hundreds of people every month.

In addition, she began giving more focused attention to an elderly widow on our block. Even though our neighbor was not the easiest person to be with, Phyllis played board games with her and brought over meals once a week or more.

Finally, she responded to an invitation she received in her first weeks of retirement. The director of JUST, an organization that works in the DuPage County Correctional Facility, had asked her to help. They offered dozens of different classes each week on spiritual enrichment, addiction recovery, education, as well as vocational and life skills. He thought she would be great for leading Bible studies with the women. Phyllis immediately liked the idea but said she'd need to wait a year.

The positive impulse didn't fade. When the year was over, she happily signed up. Every Friday morning, as she went to lead a group of women inmates, she would tell me cheerfully, "I'm going to jail now!"

She loved meeting with these women who were awaiting trial. These were people without pretense who knew they were broken and in need. The stories she told about people at the extremities of life were remarkable. One person said she thought jail saved her life. Otherwise she would be out on the street, and likely not survive. Another put her faith in Christ, and Phyllis saw a striking transformation over the next weeks.

Then one day Phyllis came back and said that as she drove home the police had pulled her over. "Where are you coming from?" the officer had asked.

"From jail," she told him.

"Well, ma'am," he said with a half grin, "if you go any faster, I may have to send you back!"

℘ ℘ ℘

One bonus that fall came in the form of a phone call Phyllis received from her oldest son, Stephen, on the morning of October 28, 2016. We were visiting relatives in Michigan.

"Hi, Mom. Do you want to go to the World Series game tonight?"

"What? What do you mean? Do you have tickets? Are you going?"

"Yes, it will be four of us. I got four tickets in the lottery for today's game. Susan and her friend Katie, you, and me."

"Where are you?"

"I'm in Denver."

"Denver?!"

"Yes, I should get there in time for the start. But I want you to come." While Phyllis grew up as a Cardinals fan, Steve had never forgotten that his mom had cheered for the Cubs with him for thirty years, ever since their great year in 1984. She also grieved with him that year when the Cubs missed going to the World Series by just one game.

"I'm in Michigan. I'll have to talk to Dad."

"Well, call back soon. If you aren't going to go, I'll get someone else."

Unanimously, the rest of us said she should change her plans and take advantage of a truly (when it comes to the Cubs) once-in-a-century opportunity. She immediately drove back to Chicago, and met up with her daughter and Katie. With casual assurance Steve strode confidently into Wrigley Field just as the first inning was in progress, almost as if he had been planning this moment for three decades, which of course he had.

The atmosphere was electric for the first World Series game at Wrigley in over seventy years. The crowd was so excited they barely noticed that the Cubs lost to Cleveland by a score of 1-0. That was more than made up for a week later when the Cubs won four games to three for their first World Series championship since 1908. Phyllis and I topped it off a couple days later by taking the train downtown to the victory rally in Grant Park with millions of other fans.

Phyllis served several terms as an elder at Immanuel, her last term running from 2017–2019. As part of the Evangelical Presbyterian Church (EPC) denomination, Immanuel had since its founding, thirty years before, ordained women to all church offices. While some conservative Christians would see this as a sign that the church didn't believe the Bible, what Immanuel didn't believe was a particular interpretation of the Bible that limited the role of women. Instead of elevating a particular exception, Immanuel prioritized Paul's overarching theological framework: "There is neither Jew nor Gentile, neither slave nor free, nor is there male and female, for you are all one in Christ Jesus" (Galatians 3:28).[5]

One responsibility Phyllis had was working with fellow elder Harold Myra to oversee the annual reviews of the church staff. Another she was especially happy to handle was contacting those in her shepherding group every few months. She, like each session member, was assigned about ten families to find out ways to pray for them and how else the church might serve them.

She was also glad to see some initiatives in corporate prayer and how Immanuel embraced the food pantry as a way to reach the community. Yet some of her old frustrations reemerged. Evangelism at Immanuel was generally more low key than she desired. Also she could see that getting a largely white church to be more deliberate about multiethnicity was a hard nut for some in leadership.

What most befuddled her was the reluctance she saw among some elders to be more deliberate about becoming a community of disciples. Maybe they just didn't see that as part of their mandate as a group. But she couldn't understand why leaders would oppose opportunities for spiritual growth.

While that frustrated her, she found energizing outlets in the denomination. Even though she wasn't naturally a denominational person (she was a child of an Independent Fundamental Church, after all), she enjoyed all kinds of groups. She often represented our local congregation at the presbytery (regional) level and at the annual national meeting for the denomination. She also gladly offered a seminar on evangelism to the pastors and elders gathered for one presbytery meeting.

Another elder who often joined her at presbytery meetings as Immanuel's representative was Ken Wolgemuth. While traveling together, they shared personal histories. Phyllis mentioned her involvement with Youth for Christ and how her team from St. Louis won the national Bible quizzing championship in 1961.

"At Winona Lake?" Ken asked.

"That's right."

"I was there."

"What?"

"Yes, my father, Sam Wolgemuth, was one of the national leaders of Youth for Christ. The whole family went to the event. I was sixteen at the time and part of the Sparrow singing group there. I remember the St. Louis team winning." While their lives had gone along different paths in different states in the intervening fifty years, Phyllis couldn't have been happier to have a "session buddy" who was not only likeminded but also shared this unlikely connection from the past.

In 2018, when fellow Immanuel member Chris Danusiar was on the national board of the EPC, he was asked to submit nominees to join the new diversity committee for the denomination. Chris knew Phyllis was a natural choice because of her passions and gifts in communication.

She grabbed the opportunity with both hands. She had a lifetime of relationships with people from different ethnic backgrounds and had happily embraced InterVarsity's decades-long emphasis in this area. She loved a wide range of people and was always pained when people were excluded or marginalized just because of how they looked, where they were from, or how they talked.

The committee called itself the Revelation 7:9 Task Force, taking its name and inspiration from the verse in which the apostle John describes what he saw: "I looked, and there before me was a great multitude that no one could count, from every nation, tribe, people and language, standing before the throne and before the Lamb." This was a vision of heaven Phyllis and the rest of the team fully embraced.

The committee's mandate was to help churches in the denomination grow in reconciliation and to be more representative of their community within a five-mile radius. The goal was for them to more faithfully reflect the breadth of God's kingdom. Revelation 7:9 is not just about heaven or the future. It is about God's will in heaven being done on earth, just as Christians pray in the Lord's Prayer. Since his will in heaven is that people of all races and ethnicities come together to worship him, that was also his will on earth.

When we are not united here on earth, God's will is not done. Phyllis so appreciated how N. T. Wright expressed this, when he commented on Paul's passion for unity among Jews and Gentiles in his letter to the Ephesians.[6]

> It is when the Christian community comes together across barriers which divide us from one another that the principalities and powers know that Jesus Christ is Lord. And that as long as we are divided whether black and white, male and female, rich and poor or whatever, the principalities and powers smile and say, "We are still in charge here!"[7]

She thus became a member of a group of twelve committed, talented people from around the country who were experienced in multiethnic ministry. Rufus Smith (senior pastor of Hope Presbyterian Church in Memphis) and Dean Weaver (lead pastor of Memorial Park Presbyterian Church in Allison Park, Pennsylvania) were cochairs. Even though she was dedicated to the mission of the task force, she didn't feel like the equal of these highly competent people. Nonetheless, she couldn't help herself from doing two things.

First, most of the group flew into Orlando (the denomination's headquarters) the evening before they were scheduled to meet each other for the first time in mid-November of 2018. Phyllis, without any prompting from the coleaders, took it on herself to find the others in the hotel and get them together for something to eat and drink, and of course to get to know one another. That made the meeting the following morning much less awkward for everyone. She instinctively provided social lubrication for people who were sometimes stuck in their heads.

Second, she kept the team organized. Sometimes astute, passionate visionaries can't organize themselves out of a paper bag. During and after their next Orlando meetings in February and April 2019, she patiently and cheerfully kept asking at key points what the next steps for the group were going to be. What were their action items? Who was going to do what?

Cochair Rufus Smith said, "She would never let me come to meetings without saying, 'What is the agenda? And what are the assignments that you want us to have when we take it away?'"[8] For three years she provided that valuable service, helping them move forward constructively. In a low-key, non-threatening way, she acted as a third unofficial coleader.

She collected lists of resources of books, organizations, and conferences from other task force members for EPC churches to use to their advantage. She helped them set concrete goals for the work of the task force. She was key in organizing and printing the report to the annual EPC General Assembly. She also took her share of committee work by reporting on the task force to the presbytery that Immanuel was part of, asking for input and offering resources. She also met with pastors and elders from different EPC churches in the region to find out what they were already doing and where they could use help. Cochair Smith summed it up this way: "It was because of Phyllis that [the task force] has gotten traction in our denomination."[9]

To be able to put her dual gifts, of keeping people connected relationally and of helping them get so much done, in the service of her passion for bringing together people of all shapes and colors for the sake of the kingdom—it was a gratifying culmination of all God had done to make her the person she was.

As part of the task force, in September 2019, she and the rest of the team traveled to Selma, Montgomery, and Birmingham in Alabama to experience first-hand many important historic civil rights sites. These included the Edmund Pettus Bridge in Selma, where on Bloody Sunday, March 7, 1965, police attacked Civil Rights demonstrators. The key stop in Birmingham was the 16th Street Baptist Church where four young girls died in a 1963 bombing by white supremacists. Perhaps for Phyllis the most moving of these many heartbreaking places was the National Memorial for Peace and Justice in Montgomery, Alabama, commemorating the thousands of Black victims of lynching in the United States.[10]

History marks us all. It deeply affects who we are by putting us in a certain place, with certain people, in a particular set of circumstances which have their own momentum into the future. Phyllis was not someone who ignored history or pretended it never happened, even if it made her feel bad. Because she was an honest person, she wanted to face the past honestly. Because she was a compassionate person, she wanted to know how someone's family history or community history affected them—what strengths it gave and what wounds remained. She also knew that history could show us how to act, if we listen.

⟐ ⟐ ⟐

While Phyllis was deep into the work of Revelation 7:9, Immanuel announced it was making plans for a weeklong trip to Show Low, Arizona, in July 2019. Phyllis was all in. Pastor George Garrison's sister and brother-in-law were part of a Christian ministry for Apache First Nation children. The plan was for team members to lead vacation Bible school and help with some construction projects.

Going to Arizona in July didn't sound at all appealing to me, but Phyllis knew she had to go. She was committed to the national task force and had been encouraging the elders to be more involved in multiethnic ministry. Here was a chance to do just that. To top it off, she was excited that members of Roca Eterna, the Spanish-speaking congregation that meets in Immanuel's building on Sunday afternoons, would be coming too.

Two large passenger vans headed out early one morning. One was packed with luggage and equipment, and the other with a dozen people. Phyllis had great fun with those from Roca Eterna who immediately saw that she welcomed being the center of all their jokes and teasing. When people took time to sleep in the van, Phyllis was also clearly seen taking time for concentrated prayer. The group split the trip into two long days, sleeping on the floor of a church in Oklahoma both on the way there and the way back.

Phyllis was part of the team that led vacation Bible school. The first day, however, was utter chaos. Kids were running around everywhere. None of them were paying attention. That night the Roca Eterna and Immanuel volunteers met. Using the gifts that each had to offer, they came up with a plan that was better because of what both groups had to offer.

Instead of having all the kids in the same activity each hour, they would split them into smaller, more manageable groups, rotating each group through the different activities—music, crafts, storytelling, and more. It meant each team had to repeat their program five or six times during the day, but the plan worked. In smaller groups the children were much more focused and attentive. Phyllis was delighted to see that ministry with a diverse group of leaders was not just the right thing to do. It made the work and everyone in it better.

The Roca Eterna team members brought a refreshing spirit of joy and trust in what God would do. They also had great people skills and connected to the Native American children better, possibly because they looked more like them and had a more similar culture. The children listened to them more attentively. The Immanuel team members brought lots of planning and ministry experience. Both groups were incredibly flexible, changing programs on the fly as needed.

Phyllis's assignment played right to her loves and her strengths. She and Pastor George got to tell each group the story of Jesus and how each one of them could turn their lives over to him. They were assigned a small room at the back of a storage area. But it worked well because it was one of the few places they could somewhat contain the energetic children.

Sarah Holman from Immanuel was impressed with the way Phyllis gave absolute, focused attention to each child. The way she zeroed in on each as she talked and listened was palpable.

Sarah and her son, Timothy, led music in their small groups with lots of movement and high decibels. For a quiet pause, Timothy showed the children how to play the viola. When he offered to let each one try it, Diego was particularly eager. "Oh, you mean like this?" He proceeded to surprise them both by showing amazing natural ability and musical sense without ever having had a viola lesson in his life.

Afterward Sarah made sure the ministry leaders in Arizona knew that if Diego wanted music lessons, she'd be happy to provide support. Likewise for Phyllis, nothing was a one-time event. She aimed for ongoing connections and relationships.

📖 📖 📖

Back in the early years of our marriage, Phyllis had wanted to adopt but the doors we nudged open kept getting shut. Then after our kids were grown and she saw three siblings highlighted on "Wednesday's Child" on the news, her heart once again received a huge tug. At that time Ruth Nyquist had helped inject reality and hope into her world, suggesting that grandchildren might be the place to direct her passions in the future.

We didn't have grandchildren at that time, but soon all four of our children were married and soon all four had children of their own. What a delight they were. Boys, girls, birth children, adopted children, and a wonderful special needs child all gave Phyllis a breathtaking armful to love, to play with, and to brag about.

All eight of the parents were like a miracle to our eyes. They were wise, loving, and fun. We thought we were pretty good parents, but in so many ways they were even better—more patient and more consistent.

As retirement rolled around, if we could give these conscientious parents a bit of a break by periodically offering our care, so much the better. We were thrilled to spend as much time as we could with Steve's and Kristen's three (Sonal, Dhrasti, and Mitiksha), with Susan's and John's three (Lina, Luke, and Gabriel), with Phil's and Tyler's five (Eric, Corbin, Eli, Adelaide, and Ana), and with Dave's and Christe's four (Beniah, Haneul, Zino, and Dimas). We found the old adage to be so true: grandchildren are God's reward for not killing your kids!

When Steve and Kristen were thinking that another year at a boarding school might be right for Dhrasti, Phyllis and I asked if they would consider letting her come live with us instead. We had always had extra people live with us, and Phyllis was especially glad for the opportunity to support these hard-working parents.

Dhrasti, the middle of three sisters all adopted from India, arrived at our house just in time for Christmas 2019. The next month she started at Hillcrest Elementary School in Downers Grove where two of her uncles had attended. Then after just two months the Covid-19 pandemic kept her at home for online classes. Fortunately, by that time Dhrasti had made fast friends in the Immanuel youth group which was a godsend. Amidst the challenges, Dhrasti made us laugh so often.

While Covid meant online classes, Dhrasti loved the extra weeks we spent at Fremont Lake where she could still attend class remotely. When we were home, she'd often show up in our bedroom in the morning to help Phyllis pick out earrings. After Hillcrest she attended Herrick Middle School for two years before going back home to Denver for high school.

Phyllis loved grandchildren and loved adoptive families. She was disappointed when the doors closed for us to adopt early in our marriage. What a privilege, then, to have so many adopted grandchildren and to even have one live with us for an extended time. In a way, Dhrasti was the fulfillment of a dream Phyllis had had her entire life.

21

MEETING JESUS

Over the years Phyllis had several encounters with cancer. Once at Fremont in the 1980s, Phyllis had on a sleeveless top. A friend who was a nurse and had been vacationing with us noticed a purplish spot on her upper arm. "You should get that looked at," she said firmly. "That could be melanoma."

Phyllis did as she was told. It was in fact cancer, but it had not spread. The doctors got it all.

Some years later an annual mammogram revealed nodules in her breasts. Biopsies showed them to be cancerous, and a course of radiation was recommended. She was then clear for decades.

In the 2000s she began having heart issues. She had several cardioversions to correct her arrhythmia. When those stopped helping, she had ablations. When those became ineffective, she had a pacemaker implanted. Later we learned that the untargeted radiation treatments from twenty years before had probably been the cause of her heart condition.

During one CAT scan for her heart, a spot was picked up on her lung. It was slow growing, and likely not a problem. But the doctor rechecked it regularly.

In the spring of 2021, she began having back trouble and couldn't go on her regular morning walks with her neighbor, Peg Knight. Phyllis went to her chiropractor but that didn't help. Eventually Peg, who also had medical training, said she should go to a doctor. In June we received the devastating news that her lung cancer had metastasized to her spine. The slow-growing lung cancer had suddenly exploded, and we were told she had twelve to eighteen months left.

I was completely crushed, but Phyllis was not surprised. She was a nurse. She knew how these things played out. She was, in fact, flat emotionally. Whether due to the pain, the pain medication, the disease, or a combination of all those, she was never up or down much during those months.

If there was one thing she hated, however, that was it. Throughout her life she had understood the world through her feelings. She was energized when she connected with people emotionally. Her love and laughter gave her joy in living. Over the next months she certainly welcomed time with family and friends, but she was usually subdued. That seemed as hard on her as the disease itself.

Fortunately, as a result of back surgery on her tumors, radiation, and medication, she became largely pain free. That allowed her, during the next year, to receive a steady stream of loved ones who visited from around the country. Family. Friends. Neighbors. Hundreds sent cards. Dozens called. She had had such a profound impact on so many.

Being limited physically also wore on her emotionally. One of the persistent side effects of her medications was an often-fuzzy brain and inability to focus on her keyboard, making committee work arduous. The medication also affected her throat, which made talking difficult, a hugely frustrating situation for her.

Being a lifelong activist, she loathed having to step down from our church's elder board, the Session, and from her responsibilities at the Revelation 7:9 Task Force. Still she gallantly participated in as many other activities as she could, including several trips to Fremont and the house she had designed for people to be welcomed and nurtured. This time she was the one being cared for by so many who meant so much to her.

One regular commitment she kept, however, was Jesus School. She continued her regular Zoom meetings with Jane and Amy. Another friend, Cathajane, was added to their Bible study group. Their last meeting was the week she died. Jane sensed it couldn't be long for her because Phyllis said at the end of the meeting that she was too weak to pray.

Despite her limitations, her spunk and spark could still emerge. When her former InterVarsity coworker Christine Wagoner visited, Phyllis explained that sometimes she was simply unable to make it up the stairs at night. "I slept in the recliner. Since Andy wouldn't let me be alone, he put a mattress down on the floor and slept at my feet. And that's right where that man belongs . . . at my feet!"

Another time she was talking with friends about our long, happy marriage and said wryly, "When I married Andy Le Peau . . . it was the best decision *he* ever made."

𝒫 𝒫 𝒫

"I remember telling a friend," Phyllis wrote thirty years before, "'If I were dying, what I would most need would be confidence that all I believed about Jesus was true.'"[1] Phyllis knew herself well. Often, in her last months, she would ask me, "Is what we believe really true?" By which she meant: Is Jesus real? Is he waiting for me in heaven? Will I be welcomed there?

Each time she asked, I would quietly answer, "Yes. It's true."

Is dying ever easy? I doubt it. And as strong, confident, and joyful as Phyllis was throughout her life, death proved a determined enemy.

"We were never meant to die," she had often said over the years. "We were meant for life with God."

𝒫 𝒫 𝒫

When Phyllis goes into the hospital after Labor Day, our oldest, Steve, and his daughter Dhrasti come from Colorado. Our sons Dave and Phil come from Arizona. Our daughter, Susan, her husband John and their kids show up often since they live nearby. All of them come to express their love. The doctors say she won't last long.

On Sunday, September 18, 2022, Phyllis has a string of visitors. Brenna Jones, her spiritual director, with her husband, Stan. Jim and Ruth Nyquist, our longtime friends and mentors. Neighbors come as do others. Without being scheduled, they come steadily, one or two at a time. Though Phyllis is not responsive, they speak to her and pray for her.

About noon there is a lull and only family are present. John asks if it would be a good time for the eucharist. I say yes. We gather around her bed as he leads the service. He speaks briefly and beautifully to Phyllis about the faithful life she had led as a wife, mother, grandmother, and follower of Jesus. Then he serves us all communion.

By 8:00 that evening I am alone with Phyllis. The family had brought me some food before everyone else went out to eat. As I sit there with her, I remember Susan's question from earlier that day: "Have you thought about saying good-bye to mom?" I had. But how could I? How could I possibly say good-bye to the one who had loved me fully and always, the one I loved so completely, the one who had taught me so much about how to be human, to laugh, and to love?

Just a few months after we had met, Phyllis had said at the Love That Heals seminar in St. Louis that hearing is likely the last of our senses to go as we die. We should therefore talk to people who are on the verge of leaving this life. Likely they can still hear us when we express our assurances and love.

As she lies there I remember that first lesson she ever taught me, a gift I can now, forty-nine years later, give back to her. I begin talking. I tell her what an amazing, wonderful wife she has been, so full of joy and life. I tell her of all the people she has touched and influenced in profound ways. I tell her that she has been a fantastic mother, raising four wise, mature children who faithfully follow Jesus and who are now themselves terrific parents. I tell how much her grandchildren know they are loved by her, something they will carry with them always. I tell her that she has been a true disciple of Jesus, always loving him with her whole heart.

Finally, I hear myself say, "The grandkids will be okay. Our kids will be okay." Then hesitantly I add, "And I will be okay. And it's okay for you to go be with Jesus."

I kiss her and sit with her for another hour. Eventually I get ready to sleep on the couch in her hospital room.

Before I lie down, however, I sit next to her one last time to hold her hand. I realize she is not breathing. I am stunned by the inevitable. But suddenly a thought takes hold, and I look around the room wondering if I will see angels. I had heard stories of such things happening, of people seeing spiritual beings in the room where a loved one has just died.

As I look, all I see is the room. I don't know if I had been just plain foolish or if I had had a profound moment of sensitivity to the spiritual realm. What I do know is that if anyone would receive a personal escort from angels to meet Jesus, it would be Phyllis.

22

REMEMBERING

"We are here to worship God."

George Stulac opened the memorial service for Phyllis on October 10, 2022, with the same words he used to open our wedding ceremony on September 6, 1975. While our wedding was a wonderful celebration of bringing two people together for life, Phyllis wanted it to be more. She wanted it to honor God. While this fall day forty-seven years later would be both a day of grieving loss and of celebrating a life filled with love and laughter, she wanted it to be more.

For Phyllis, however, *worship* did not mean being somber or boring. It meant joy. It meant music. And not surprisingly, a friend said, "I don't think I've ever been to a memorial service with so much laughter." Phyllis would have been delighted.

At the service held at our church, Immanuel Presbyterian, her two oldest children, Steve and Susan, represented the four of them. They took the opportunity to give a bit of payback for all the funny stories Phyllis told about her children over the years when she did public speaking.

So there was this one time in our kitchen. We are all in middle school and high school, and we sat down for dinner, and someone prayed before the meal. And we had wooden chairs in the kitchen and just before the "Amen" somebody tooted, and here's how the toot sounded against the wooden chair: "Mehm." And the prayer ended, and it was definitely the first time in history that the Le Peaus let a fart go without a single comment. We looked up to start the meal and there's a second of silence, and our mom says, "Did someone call my name?" We lost it and we never let her forget it.

Through her life and her embarrassing stories, our mother taught us to have the self-confidence to be able to laugh at ourselves. What a gift![1]

George Garrison, our church's pastor, and Phyllis often enjoyed ribbing each other. George, however, was able to have the last witty word during his sermon.

It was Phyllis and Andy's desire that the meditation be based on Revelation 7:9-12, that was read a few moments ago. But before we get to that, there is one other dynamic that I need to share about the relationship that I had with Phyllis that transcended pastor-parishioner or even fellow elder. It was the rivalry between us as we supported our favorite baseball teams, hers being the Cubs and mine being the St. Louis Cardinals. There was hardly ever an email communication between us or even a short interaction where there weren't verbal barbs thrown between us as we talked about both teams and our allegiance to them.

And then one day I learned an awful truth. Phyllis was born in East St. Louis. She was raised a Cardinals fan! She was in St. Louis during their glory years in the sixties—three World Series appearances in five years; two World Championships. And for all the dynamics of the Cardinal-Cub rivalry that fans of both teams experience, her defection and her betrayal hurt. The baseball roots were painful for me. In light of that fact, it's a good thing that Revelation 7:9-12 was assigned to me, otherwise I would have been tempted to base this meditation on Revelation 2:4-5, and this is a direct quote: "But I have this against you that you have abandoned your first love. Remember therefore from where you have fallen, repent, and do the works that you first did."[2]

Phyllis would have laughed harder than anyone, and many laughed very hard. Why was she able to laugh at herself so easily and so frequently? As Greg Jao, one of her InterVarsity supervisors, put it that day, "She was confident that Jesus longed to be with her. She was confident that Jesus knew her places of beauty and brokenness and loved all of who she was. She was confident that he would never leave her or forsake her, that in his eyes, she was unforgettable and that confidence filled her with laughter."[3]

As the quintessential, loving, playful grandmother, she was unforgettable to her grandchildren who called her Mimi. They also remembered her that day.

- Cory remembered that Mimi usually beat him at *Qwirkle*. (No mercy for nine-year olds!) The first time he won she wanted to check the score to make sure "because she was very competitive."

- Beniah remembered crying after he hurt his foot playing at the lake. Everyone told him to "Go see Mimi." He did. She ushered him into her room where she broke out a Hershey bar. "Don't tell any of the other cousins," she told him. And he never did … till that day.

- Eric remembered the time she was making cookies with him and Cory. Mimi got talking and accidentally tripled the amount of salt and halved the amount of sugar and flour. The cookies had to be thrown out, but the memory lasted.

- Eli always had fun playing the Dice game with Mimi, win or lose. "Either way I still had lots of fun."

- Gabe remembered that when his eardrum got hurt, Mimi was the first one there.

- Lina recalled that at her dance recital, "She told me that I looked great and that I could do it. So as I went on stage I looked out to her."

- Dhrasti remembered watching and rewatching with Mimi all thirteen seasons of the family-oriented *Heartland* TV series about a ranch in Canada—four times!

All the rest of her grandchildren—Sonal, Tikki, Luke, Addie, Ana, Haneul, Zeno, and Dimas—knew the same fun playing games with her, the unfettered love she showed, and the many quite successful baking projects.

Her children would likewise never forget her lasting impact.

Mom made us feel like kings. She would go as far as unilaterally declaring us rulers of the random state we happened to be road tripping through. One time when we dropped Phil off at college in Arizona, she kept saying proudly, "Phil, this is your state."

Once Mom told Dave that he was such a great teacher, and I'm sure he was, but Dave's response told it all, "Mom, you've never even seen me teach." Mom believed in us more than we believed in ourselves and this is true for most of the people that she came in contact with. She believed in you.[4]

She loved influencing people with the love of God. The effect on many was profound, as profound as life and death. One friend wrote during her last illness, "Phyllis . . . you know God has used you mightily—with many. I am one of those many. I probably would not be here if God had not put you in my life."

Jane Bacon Pfeiffer from the first group of nurses Phyllis discipled right after we were married also wrote her in that last year, "You, Phyllis, recognized a new believer hungry for God and all He could give. You believed in me, offered me welcome to the kingdom of God and to share his love in serving others."

Another friend wrote me afterward, "It was her persistence that led me to Christ, along with the influence of your family."

The list of lives she touched deeply goes on and on. One of the InterVarsity staff she supervised, Michelle Graham, said at the memorial service, "There has been no one in my life who has taught me more than Phyllis about how to love lavishly and live joyfully."[5] She also wrote:

> When Phyllis became my supervisor, I was nursing some deep wounds from a former colleague. My confidence was low, and I was considering leaving ministry altogether. Phyllis lavished love on me. She saw the best in me and walked with me into healing and maturity.
>
> When I started having babies, she loved them like family. Phyllis would arrive at my home for supervision, scoop them into her arms, talk to them, sing to them, pray for them, and tell me to go take a nap or a walk while they played together. She knew I needed time to rest, or time with God, and she genuinely loved my little ones. I would return refreshed, and we would resume our day of coaching and shadowing together. Even as my babies grew into young adults, Phyllis loved on them through prayers and graduation gifts. Phyllis gave me the affection, respect, and support I had always wanted from my own parents.[6]

Dan Treier from our church noted that even her light interactions with others were memorable, lasting, and affirming. "I love how often Phyllis invaded my personal space to tell me how much she loves introverts."

I knew Phyllis for fifty years, and I knew this complex, high-energy, five-dimensional person as well as anyone. Yet I was amazed by how those who spoke at the memorial service were all able to summarize so succinctly who she was in a way I had never thought of before. In their eulogies our children Steve and Susan as well as Christine Wagoner and Greg Jao all summed up Phyllis in the same way: She loved God and loved people.

Once Jesus was asked to name the greatest commandment, something Jews had debated for centuries. Never one to be put in a box, Jesus named two. "'Love the Lord your God with all your heart and with all your soul, and with all your mind, and with all your strength.' The second is this, 'You shall love your neighbor as yourself'" (Mark 12:30-31).

Loving God and loving others are inextricably linked. We can't love God, Jesus is saying, if we aren't treating others with generosity, forgiveness, kindness, and mercy—no matter how often we go to church or read the Bible. Yet the value of others will fade in our lives or we will easily lapse into legalism if we drift away from God who is the one who gives value and worth to each individual. God's love for us makes it possible for us to love God and others in response. Our relationship with God empowers us in our relationships with others.

Phyllis combined these two loves more thoroughly, more organically, more joyfully than anyone else I have ever known. She was the most converted person I ever met.

As her friend and co-worker, Rick Richardson said, expressing the sentiments of many, "Phyllis was one of the most spectacular and magnificent human beings I have ever known. What a lover of God and people! What a loving woman who always believed in you and could challenge your socks off at any time!"[7]

℘ ℘ ℘

On July 3, 2023, over thirty members of the family gathered again on the shores of Phyllis's beloved Fremont Lake. Christe Le Peau gave a reading from *Prayer in the Night* by Tish Harrison Warren, a book Phyllis and I reread together in her last months. Christe's husband, Dave, read from Luke 24 about the disciples walking to Emmaus after the resurrection. John DeCostanza offered a few words of reflection. Then her four children and I went out to the end of the dock to commit her ashes to the water. Here, at the house she designed, is where the family she loved and bound together in so many ways would continue to gather in the years ahead.

Phyllis received one other recognition. The elders of our church, Immanuel Presbyterian, voted to posthumously name Phyllis as the church's first Ruling Elder Emeritus. Several of her children and grandchildren attended the Sunday morning service on September 15, 2024, where Pastor George Garrison explained the reasons.

> In three days it will be the two-year anniversary of Phyllis's passing, and in some ways it's hard to believe it's been that long and in other ways it's been much too long. . . .
>
> As a ruling elder at Immanuel, Phyllis's service was noteworthy on many different levels, not only the length of the many years of service, but the depth of her service as well, and it was extraordinary. Phyllis was tasked with some delicate and difficult matters as an elder, even playing an important role in a disciplinary matter several years ago.[8]

Unsurprisingly, George mentioned that Phyllis was able to use humor both to diffuse tense situations and to challenge the elders on serious matters regarding their work and the church in general. He went on:

> She had a significant impact as an elder on the presbytery level, . . . our district which includes all the EPC churches that are in Illinois and Wisconsin and Minnesota and Iowa. So Phyllis not only served as a delegate for our church at such meetings, she served on presbytery committees there and frequently gave updates with regards to the work of the General Assembly, the national body for our denomination.[9]

Rev. Andrew Smith from New York, who cochaired the Revelation 7:9 Task Force that Phyllis served on, also spoke, describing her national contribution:

> I can tell you that Phyllis was one of, it won't surprise you, was one of the ones who gave me the warmest welcome when I started and that really was reflective of how she basically served as a mother to all of us regardless of our age.
>
> Through our time on that team, it was clear from the early days that for things to get done, Phyllis had to make them get done and

that while she never served as a chair or a co-chair on that team, Rufus and my predecessor as co-chair, Dean Weaver and I would all tell you that she was the instigator to keep things moving, to keep things on track, not out of any mere administrative zeal but because she was passionate about the work of our task force as we seek to encourage our congregational churches in our denomination to better reflect the diversity, the makeup of our 1-3-5 mile radius around our churches.[10]

Finally, Elder Katherine Anderson read the resolution itself:

In recognition of her extraordinary service in the office of Elder, as well as her Spirit-led service on both the Presbytery and General Assembly levels of the Evangelical Presbyterian Church, be it resolved that the Session of Immanuel Presbyterian Church is unanimously delighted to bestow the honor of Ruling Elder Emeritus posthumously upon our treasured sister in Christ, Phyllis Le Peau. Recognized this Lord's Day, September 15, 2024.[11]

Phyllis had traveled quite a distance from the Independent Fundamental Church of her youth to a national role in a Presbyterian denomination. And yet, she had not traveled far at all. She still loved Jesus deeply. She still loved people of all shapes, sizes, and hues. She still loved getting things done in God's kingdom. She still loved talking about Jesus. And she still loved to laugh and make people laugh.

℘ ℘ ℘

Trying to describe Phyllis is like trying to capture lightning in a bottle. She was so alive, so bright, so funny, so quirky, so caring, so intense, so focused on others, so unself-conscious that clearly all these pages are not nearly enough to give a full picture.

In one of Phyllis's favorite movies, *The Sound of Music*, the older nuns complain about the problem of the uncontrollable free spirit that is Maria, their new novice: "How do you catch a cloud and pin it down?. . . How do you keep a wave upon the sand? . . . How do you hold a moonbeam in your hand?"

I have faced the same problem in trying to write about Phyllis. How do you capture the wind in a jar, or joy in a home, or love in a heart? All these seem to slip through our grasp, unrecoverable. They are of the moment—here and gone. Thus I have constantly been frustrated as I tried to write about her. I can give a snapshot. But a tangible, three-dimensional moving picture? Impossible.

I had many such transitory moments with Phyllis. Some were quiet. Some were riotous. Yet no matter how tightly I held on to any of these, whether ordinary or extraordinary, they slipped through my fingers. No matter how much I hugged them to myself, they evaporated.

It's a mystery. Though these experiences are fleeting, they are no less real, no less solid. For each has lasting power. These moments had a profound effect on all they touched. On the other hand, when we look back on a symphony after the final chord is played, where is it?

Phyllis. So extraordinary. So vital. So crazy fun. So red-headed. So loving. She could not be made to sit still for a portrait that would fit into a book. She would burst out of its pages in a blaze of energy and laughter, mocking such paltry attempts to seize her life force.

I know that in ways I've idealized Phyllis in this book. But there was much to idealize. And in reading certain passages, she would undoubtedly screw up her face in skepticism about the picture of her I have sometimes painted. She would remember her doubts, her faults, her weaknesses and be very uncomfortable with much of this.

That is not, however, what so many others remember.

ℰ ℰ ℰ

When Phyllis and I first married, we thought we would be good for each other and help each other grow in many ways. And it's true. We did. I deeply enjoyed, appreciated, and respected Phyllis. I thought we would make a great team. And we were.

But if I am honest, I probably thought more about what I had to offer. After all, she grew up in a limited fundamentalist framework while my upbringing exposed me more to the world. I would help show her a wider, richer range of ideas, of music, of literature and culture.

And perhaps some of that happened. But now I see that mostly she taught me. She taught me lessons that were far more important than what I had in mind. She taught me about life. She taught me to live.

Over the almost fifty years I knew her, Phyllis had a massive impact on me. Even as she completely accepted me and somehow even adored me just as I was, her persistent presence shaped a nerd who was always in his head into someone who gained a habit of welcoming people into our home and our lives.

Phyllis was always ready with an offer of a meal and a bed and friendship and laughter. Whenever a need arose, Phyllis would ask me about it. I'd roll my eyes (sometimes inwardly, often outwardly) wondering if I always had to stretch like this to include others into our household. But we did, and I was better for it.

Nothing is wrong with engaging a broad view of ideas and opinions and human experiences. Certainly we influenced one another. But while I may have widened her world, she widened my soul.

℘ ℘ ℘

Recently, a friend's wife was having major surgery. My initial thought was, *I need to pray.* And that was a good thought. But then I also asked myself, "What would Phyllis do?" and the answer was instantly clear. Phyllis would go to be with the friend in the hospital waiting room during surgery. So that's what I did. I showed up. My friend and I chatted for two or three hours. I stayed until the surgeon reported that his wife was stable and that he could go be with her.

Now I don't say this to pat myself on the back. The fact is that during our years of marriage I often watched her do this, many times letting her go to "represent the two of us" when someone was sick, in need, or grieving. Yes, I joined her occasionally, but certainly not always. I let her huge heart handle such situations for both of us.

Now she is no longer around, and I can't rely on her to do these things "for us." If someone is going to offer comfort "for us," it needs to be me. If someone is going to extend a bit of cheer or just be there in time of need, it has to be me. If someone is going to remind a friend about the love of Jesus, I will need to do it. Even after all these years of being taught so well by her, I'm still learning.

I think about how she would welcome people or how she would affirm others. I let her take the lead in those things for decades and supported her as I signed my name to many cards of celebration or sorrow that she wrote. Now I write the cards myself, and she is not here to sign them.

I can never be like her. She was wildly unique. I will always be the somewhat introverted, bookish boy from Minnesota. And that's ok. God made me different and gave me different experiences and gifts.

Early in our marriage, as I mentioned, we were struck by what athlete and missionary Eric Liddell said of God in the movie *Chariots of Fire*: "When I run, I feel His pleasure." When Phyllis loved and influenced others, she felt God's pleasure. When I work with words by editing, reading, teaching, or writing (or spend time with grandchildren), I feel his pleasure. While we can all feel God's pleasure, we do not all need to be the same. But we all need to grow.

When I try in my faltering way to put into practice how I saw Phyllis love God and love people, it reminds me how even now she is present with me and how she teaches me still.

ACKNOWLEDGING

Thanks go to several people who read all or part of the draft of the manuscript and gave valuable feedback. The first in importance are Phyllis's children (and mine!): Stephen Le Peau, Susan DeCostanza, Philip Le Peau, and David Le Peau who knew her intimately from their intense exposure to her over the decades. We have been so grateful to have these four wonderful people in our lives.

Thanks to Phyllis's sister Diane (Strong) O'Day for providing many documents regarding the Strong and Sanders family history as well as input on Phyllis's early life. (As she said affectionately at the memorial service: "Phyllis had a dark side. Who knew?") The pictures of Phyllis's grandparents, parents, and other relatives also come courtesy of Diane.

Special thanks also to Linda (Sauer) Floyd who gave me rich background on Phyllis's nursing school days and early nursing career, as did Jane Hutchinson and Rita (Smith) Tower. I am indebted to John Le Peau and Annette LaPlaca who each offered editorial wisdom on the whole manuscript. Other readers who gave wonderful input (and needed corrections!) include Amy Williams, Christine Wagoner, Cindy Walthour, Dan Reid, Dan Treier, George Garrison, George Stulac, Greg Jao, Jamie Wong, Jane (Bacon) Pfeiffer, Jim Hoover, Kathy Woodard, Ken Wolgemuth, Michelle Graham, Paulette Hagen, Phil Nordquist, Rick Richardson, Ruth Nyquist, Sarah Cantrell, and Sarah Holman. John Schuurman offered invaluable help with the audiobook.

As tradition requires, responsibility for any remaining errors belongs to me. As I am able, I will be happy to make corrections in future printings as better information comes my way.

I based the manuscript not just on my memory but on documentary support including our family appointment wall calendars (1975-1986); Phyllis's personal appointment books (2012-2019); family guest books (1975-2000); Phyllis's prayer journals (2000-2020); Phyllis's computer files and mine (c. 2000-2022); various letters, memory books, and other paper files. Other publications, documents, and sources are cited in footnotes.

In this book, text in quotation marks that is footnoted is reproduced from the published or unpublished materials cited. Conversation in quotes that is not footnoted usually follows the memoirist's convention. That is, these are as close as I can recall to the dialog that took place, though in some cases I may have taken a bit of license to offer representative renditions of a conversation for the sake of readability.

NOTES

Chapter 2: Beginning

[1] I may have been the first active Catholic on InterVarsity staff in the U.S. While I don't know for sure, I don't know of anyone else who had been before me. This created some issues in fundraising for me. For example, I was grilled before the elders of Grace and Peace Fellowship in St. Louis, one of the more unpleasant experiences in my life. Because of my association with the Catholic church, they could not approve helping to support me financially even though they supported other InterVarsity staff in St. Louis. I was caught in the middle because my home church didn't offer any financial support either as Catholics are not in the habit of supporting non-Catholic charities.

[2] Andy Le Peau, unpublished memo to Paul Woodard dated September 4, 1973.

Chapter 3: Becoming

[1] "World War II Research Guide," The State Historical Society of Missouri, shsmo.org/research/guides/ww2.

[2] "The central city area transformed from a white to a black area. School enrollments illustrate the speed of this transition. In 1955 Longfellow school was 0 percent black [Phyllis's 6th-grade graduation from Longfellow was in 1956] and Monroe school was 2.4 percent black; by 1967 these schools were 86 percent and 99.9 percent black respectively (Mendelson and Ranney 1967). In the ten years between 1950 and 1960 alone the racial balance in East St. Louis changed substantially. In 1950 the city was 66.5 percent white but this percentage fell to 55.4 as whites left the city (Evert Kincaid and Associates 1965)." Wendy Shaw, "A Tale of Two Cities: The Best of Times, the Worst of Times. Inequality in St. Louis' Metro-East," www.siue.edu/~wshaw/esl.htm.

[3] "Shawneetown High School 'Indians,'" leopardfan.tripod.com/id316.html. "A Brief History of Newspapers in Illinois," University Library Illinois Newspaper Project, University of Illinois Champaign-Urbana, www.library.illinois.edu/illinoisnewspaperproject/a-brief-history-of-newspapers-in-illinois/.

[4] "Lewis and Clark Expedition," The History of Southern Illinois: SCRC Virtual Museum at Southern Illinois University's Morris Library, scrcexhibits.omeka.net/exhibits/show/sihistory/expedition.

[5] Clint Cargile, "This Week in Illinois History: Moving Shawneetown (December 14,1937)," Northern Public Radio, 13 December 2021, www.northernpublicradio.org/wnij-news/2021-12-13/this-week-in-illinois-history-moving-shawneetown-december-14-1937.

6 Phyllis and Andrew Le Peau, *Grandparenting* (Downers Grove, IL: InterVarsity Press, 2017), 36.

7 This and the following paragraphs are drawn from Bertha Sanders, "Sanders Family History," unpublished paper, March 1960, typescript.

8 Phyllis and Andrew Le Peau, *Grandparenting*, 45.

9 Phyllis and Andrew Le Peau, *Grandparenting*, 16.

10 Phyllis J. Le Peau, *Caring for People in Conflict* (Downers Grove, IL: InterVarsity Press, 1991), 9.

11 Andrew T. Le Peau, *Write Better* (Downers Grove, IL; InterVarsity Press, 2019), 145.

12 Phyllis J. Le Peau, *Caring for People in Conflict*, 10.

13 "Ecuador: Mission to the Aucas," *TIME* Magazine, January 23, 1956; time.com/archive/6799360/ecuador-mission-to-the-aucas/.

14 Phyllis J. Le Peau, *Caring for People in Conflict*, 9.

15 James Bryan Smith, *The Good and Beautiful God* (Downers Grove, IL: InterVarsity Press, 2009), 25.

16 Phyllis J. Le Peau, unpublished prayer journal dated March 11, 2011.

17 Phyllis J. Le Peau, *Acts 13–28* (Downers Grove, IL: InterVarsity Press, 1992, 2002), 11.

Chapter 4: Educating

1 Phyllis J. Le Peau, *Resources for Caring People* (Downers Grove, IL: InterVarsity Press, 1991), 28.

2 Phyllis Le Peau, comments at the memorial service for Sandra Sue Links, April 1, 2017, Narberth Presbyterian Church, Narberth, PA 19072. Unpublished manuscript.

Chapter 5: Nursing

1 Phyllis J. Le Peau and Bonnie J. Miller, *Handbook for Caring People* (Downers Grove, IL: InterVarsity Press, 1991), 35-36.

2 Phyllis J. Le Peau and Bonnie J. Miller, *Handbook for Caring People*, 39-40.

3 Phyllis J. Le Peau, *Caring for Spiritual Needs* (Downers Grove, IL: InterVarsity Press, 1991), 14.

4 Phyllis J. Le Peau, comments at the memorial service for Sandra Sue Links, April 1, 2017, Narberth Presbyterian Church, Narberth, PA 19072. Unpublished manuscript.

5 "How St. Louis Avoided Riots after the Martin Luther King Assasination," St. Louis Post-Dispatch, April 4, 2024, www.stltoday.com/news/archives/collection_3dee3111-f099-5b63-b435-69c24d926e8e.html.

6 "History of NCF," ncf-jcn.org/about-ncf/history-ncf, and "Over 70 Years of Ministry," www.liloli.org/.

7 Ada McVean, "It's Time to Let the Five Stages of Grief Die," May 31, 2019, www.mcgill.ca/oss/article/health-history/its-time-let-five-stages-grief-die.

8 Phyllis J. Le Peau, *Caring for People in Grief* (Downers Grove, IL: InterVarsity Press, 1991), 23.

9 For a brief history of charismatic and Pentecostal influences among evangelicals in the 1960s and 1970s, see Molly Worthen, *Apostles of Reason* (New York: Oxford University Press, 2014), 148-172.

Chapter 7: Engaging

1 Andrew T. Le Peau, "As Different As We Think," *Books & Culture*, March/April 2010, www.booksandculture.com/articles/2010/marapr/asdifferentwethink.html.

2 Ibid.

3 Phyllis Strong Le Peau, letter to Phil and Dorothy Le Peau, August 19, 1975.

Chapter 8: Marrying

1 Robert Fulghum, *It Was on Fire When I Lay Down on It* (New York: Ivy Books, 1988), 7.

2 Phyllis Le Peau, letter to George and Barbara Stulac, July 16, 1975.

3 George (Chip) Stulac, "Family Relationships Mediated by Christ: An Exposition of Ephesians 5:18—6:4," unpublished paper, c. 1975. This document is similar to and likely the same as his wedding homily.

4 Ibid.

Chapter 9: Welcoming

1 Liz Chalberg, "Pierce Downer," dghistory.org/pierce-downer/.

2 "1846 Blodgett House Accepted into National UGRR Network to Freedom," August 4, 2023, dghistory.org/1846-blodgett-house-accepted-into-national-ugrr-network-to-freedom/. "The Lyman House," 2003, dghistory.org/the-lyman-house/.

3 "A History of Our Church," archive.dgfumc.org/history.

4 "Sears Catalog Homes," dghistory.org/sears-homes/. "Sears Catalog Homes Walking/Driving Tour," www.downers.us/corecode/uploads/document6/uploaded_

pdfs/corecode/Sears%20Catalog%20Homes%20self-tour_98.pdf.

5 "Golf Club History," www.belmontgolfclub.org/history/.

6 "The Tivoli Theater," web.archive.org/web/20170708013808/http://www.tivolistagecrew.com/history.html.

Chapter 10: Parenting

1 Phyllis J. Le Peau, "Life's Little Blessings," HIS Magazine, December 1981, 7.

2 Le Peau, "Life's Little Blessings," 7.

3 See for example *An Evangelical Commitment to Simple Life-style* sponsored by the Lausanne Committee on World Evangelization's Theology and Education Working Group (John Stott, chairman) and the World Evangelical Fellowship's Theological Commission's Unit on Ethics and Society (Ronald J. Sider, convenor), lausanne.org/occasional-paper/lop-20, March 1980.

Chapter 11: Summering

1 "Michigan Big Tree Register-Updated 07-26-2025," docs.google.com/spreadsheets/d/1uH6l1s3Sn6lEUeZMJGkrN0I4PtzTVoqf0xt3vX2pJXM/edit?pli=1&gid=392906177#gid=392906177, accessed July 30, 2025.

2 "Full Grooved Axes: Saugus Iron Works National Historical Site," last updated October 28, 2021, www.nps.gov/articles/000/grooved-axes.htm. "Axe Head Road Trip: What I Did on My Summer Vacation," August 4, 2017, Desert Archaeology, Inc. desert.com/axe-head-road-trip/.

3 "History of Native Americans in GR," March 18, 2025, www.experiencegr.com/articles/post/history-of-native-americans-in-gr/.

4 "The Three Fires," compiled by Mary Modderman, July 2024, Coopersville Area Historical Society, coopersvillehistory.org/photo-essay/the-three-fires.

5 "The History of City Hall," www.cityoffremont.net/304/Fremont-History.

6 Phyllis J. Le Peau, unpublished prayer journal dated July 31, 2009.

7 I probably first heard this phrase in the 1990s. But I have not been able to track down the original source.

Chapter 12: Home Opening

1 Paulette Hagen, email to Phyllis Le Peau, April 26, 2022. Used by permission.

2 Jaime Wong email to Dave and Christe Le Peau, October 9, 2022. Used by permission.

Chapter 13: Opposites Attracting

[1] Andrew T. Le Peau, *Write Better* (Downers Grove, IL: InterVarsity Press, 2019), 64.

Chapter 14: Joy Bringing

[1] Susan DeCostanza and Stephen Le Peau, eulogy, "Memorial Service for Phyllis Le Peau at Immanuel Presbyterian Church," Warrenville, IL, October 10, 2022, www.youtube.com/watch?v=h2QWYa50l6k [44:35—1:00:29].

[2] This was Phyllis's own paraphrase of Mark 9:5-6.

[3] Phyllis Le Peau, "Heart Prints from Phyllis," prayer letter, May 2011.

Chapter 15: Area Directing

[1] "InterVarsity and IFES History," intervarsity.org/about-us/intervarsity-and-ifes-history.

[2] For a history of InterVarsity Press, see Andrew T. Le Peau and Linda Doll, *Heart. Soul. Mind. Strength.* 2nd ed. (Downers Grove, IL: InterVarsity Press, 2022).

[3] "Our Purpose," intervarsity.org/about-us/our-purpose.

[4] Phyllis J. Le Peau, unpublished personal journal dated July 7, 2000.

[5] Phyllis J. Le Peau, unpublished personal journal dated December 23, 2000.

[6] Phyllis J. Le Peau, "I Wish I Hadn't Been Too Busy," intervarsity.org/parents/i-wish-i-hadn-t-been-too-busy.

[7] Phyllis J. Le Peau, unpublished prayer journal dated May 14, 2001.

[8] Phyllis J. Le Peau, unpublished prayer journal dated November 20, 2008.

[9] Phyllis J. Le Peau, unpublished prayer journal dated December 11, 2009.

[10] Phil Nordquist, quoted in a memory book given to Phyllis when she transitioned to the job of evangelism coordinator, 2007.

Chapter 16: People Loving (1)

[1] Christine Wagoner, eulogy, "Memorial Service for Phyllis Le Peau at Immanuel Presbyterian Church," Warrenville, IL, October 10, 2022, www.youtube.com/watch?v=h2QWYa50l6k [30:45–42:45].

[2] Jared Diamond, *Upheaval* (New York: Little, Brown and Company, 2019), 350.

[3] Ben Sasse, *Them* (New York: St. Martin's Press, 2018), 26.

[4] Sasse, *Them*, 220-221.

[5] Jeffrey Bilbro, *Reading the Times* (Downers Grove, IL: InterVarsity Press, 2021), 127.

[6] Diamond, *Upheaval*, 352.

[7] Bilbro, *Reading the Times*, 129.

[8] Sasse, *Them*, 133-256.

[9] Bilbro, *Reading the Times*, 165-169.

Chapter 17: People Loving (2)

[1] Heather Holleman, *The Six Conversations* (Chicago: Moody Publishers, 2022), 19-40.

[2] David Brooks, *How to Know a Person* (New York: Random House, 2023), 212-213.

[3] Holleman, *The Six Conversations*, 33.

[4] David Brooks, *How to Know a Person* (New York: Random House, 2023), 143.

[5] Brooks, *How to Know a Person*, 143-144.

[6] Brooks, *How to Know a Person*, 146.

[7] In Jeffrey Kluger's *Splendid Solution: Jonas Salk and the Conquest of Polio* (New York: G. P. Putnam, 2004), the author notes there were several strains of polio, each of which affected people differently. One strain, the rarest, was extremely virulent, which could quickly result in death. That was the case for Lucy Rae.

[8] Phyllis J. Le Peau, *Caring for People in Grief* (Downers Grove, IL: InterVarsity Press, 1991), 36. In the first printing of the book the author incorrectly wrote Lucy's middle name as "Ray." This was corrected in later printings to "Rae," short for Rachel.

[9] Brooks, *How to Know a Person*, 147-148.

[10] Brooks, *How to Know a Person*, 148-149.

Chapter 18: Influencing

[1] Annette LaPlaca, in email correspondence to the author, June 5, 2025. Used by permission.

[2] Phyllis Le Peau, "The Joy of Advent," Immanuel Presbyterian Church Advent Book, November 2020. Scripture text conformed to NRSVUE.

Chapter 19: Evangelism Coordinating

[1] Phyllis J. Le Peau, "A Note from Phyllis," August 2009 prayer letter.

[2] Phyllis J. Le Peau, "A Note from Phyllis," November 2009 prayer letter.

³ Phyllis J. Le Peau, "A Note from Phyllis," May 2010 prayer letter.

⁴ Phyllis J. Le Peau, unpublished prayer journal dated March 6, 2010.

⁵ Phyllis J. Le Peau, "Soul Surf 2012: The Panama City Spring Break Challenge," April 2012 prayer letter.

⁶ Christine Wagoner, eulogy, "Memorial Service for Phyllis Le Peau at Immanuel Presbyterian Church," Warrenville, Illinois, October 10, 2022, www.youtube.com/watch?v=h2QWYa50l6k [30:45–42:45].

⁷ Phyllis J. Le Peau, April 2012 prayer letter.

⁸ Phyllis J. Le Peau, April 2015 prayer letter.

⁹ Sarah Cantrell, reply to a Facebook post by Andrew Le Peau of December 8, 2022. Used by permission.

¹⁰ Phyllis J. Le Peau, October 2013 prayer letter.

¹¹ Phyllis J. Le Peau, January 2013 prayer letter.

Chapter 20: Not Retiring

¹ Phyllis J. Le Peau, June 2015 prayer letter.

² Phyllis J. Le Peau, June 2015 prayer letter.

³ Phyllis J. Le Peau, unpublished prayer journal dated January 6, 2016.

⁴ Phyllis J. Le Peau, unpublished prayer journal dated April 6, 2016.

⁵ For a book in which twenty-seven people tell their journeys on this topic, edited by a member of Immanuel Presbyterian Church, see Alan F. Johnson, ed., *How I Changed My Mind about Women in Leadership* (Grand Rapids, MI: Zondervan, 2010). Regarding the interpretation of passages in the Bible that seem to limit women in ministry see, for example, Julie Zine Coleman, *On Purpose: Understanding God's Freedom for Women Through Scripture* (Grand Rapids, MI: Kregel, 2022). Regarding how women in the New Testament participated in a wide range of ministries see Nijay K. Gupta, *Tell Her Story* (Downers Grove, IL: IVP Academic, 2023). For an academic book on the topic see Ronald W. Pierce, Cynthia Long Westfall, Christa L. McKirkland, eds. *Discovering Biblical Equality*, 3rd ed. (Downers Grove, IL: IVP Academic, 2021).

⁶ In Ephesians 3:8-11 Paul explains that it was always part of God's plan for the unity of Gentiles and Jews in worshiping Christ to reveal his wisdom to all spiritual beings: "This grace was given me: to preach to the Gentiles the boundless riches of Christ, and to make plain to everyone the administration of this mystery, which for ages past was kept hidden in God, who created all things. His intent was that now, through the church, the manifold wisdom of God should be made known to the

rulers and authorities in the heavenly realms, according to his eternal purpose that he accomplished in Christ Jesus our Lord."

[7] N. T. Wright, in a question-and-answer session after a joint lecture with Paul Barnett, "Fresh Perspectives on Paul," MacQuarie University (Sydney, Australia), March 16, 2006 (Vancouver: Regent Bookstore/Regent Audio).

[8] Rufus Smith, closing remarks, "Memorial Service for Phyllis Le Peau at Immanuel Presbyterian Church," Warrenville, IL, October 10, 2022, www.youtube.com/watch?v=h2QWYa50l6k [1:48:40–1:52:45].

[9] Rufus Smith, closing remarks, "Memorial Service," October 10, 2022.

[10] "Number of Executions by Lynching in the United States by State and Race between 1882 and 1968," Statista, September 2020, www.statista.com/statistics/1175147/lynching-by-race-state-and-race/; "Lynchings: By Year and Race," University of Missouri-Kansas City Law School, law2.umkc.edu/faculty/projects/ftrials/shipp/lynchingyear.html.

Chapter 21: Meeting Jesus

[1] Phyllis J. Le Peau, *Acts 1–12* (Downers Grove, IL: InterVarsity Press, 1992, 2002), 7.

Chapter 22: Remembering

[1] Stephen Le Peau and Susan DeCostanza, eulogy, "Memorial Service for Phyllis Le Peau at Immanuel Presbyterian Church," Warrenville, IL, October 10, 2022, www.youtube.com/watch?v=h2QWYa50l6k [44:35—1:00:29].

[2] George Garrison, sermon, "Memorial Service for Phyllis Le Peau at Immanuel Presbyterian Church," Warrenville, IL, October 10, 2022, www.youtube.com/watch?v=h2QWYa50l6k [1:28:40—1:45:30].

[3] Greg Jao, eulogy, "Memorial Service for Phyllis Le Peau at Immanuel Presbyterian Church," Warrenville, IL, October 10, 2022, www.youtube.com/watch?v=h2QWYa50l6k [1:06:43—1:22:24].

[4] Stephen Le Peau and Susan DeCostanza, eulogy, "Memorial Service," October 10, 2022.

[5] Michelle Graham, "Memorial Service for Phyllis Le Peau at Immanuel Presbyterian Church," Warrenville, IL, October 10, 2022, www.youtube.com/watch?v=h2QWYa50l6k [29:22—29:36].

[6] Michelle Graham, unpublished paper, "Reflection: Mourning Phyllis," September 23, 2022. Used by permission.

[7] Rick Richardson, reply to a Facebook post by Andrew Le Peau of September 18, 2022. Used by permission.

[8] George Garrison, "Honoring Phyllis Le Peau as Elder Emeritus," Immanuel Presbyterian Online Live Stream, Warrenville, IL, September 15, 2024, www.youtube.com/live/wh6Va5tg9Vo [38:38--51:23].

[9] George Garrison, "Honoring Phyllis Le Peau."

[10] Andrew Smith, "Honoring Phyllis Le Peau as Elder Emeritus," Immanuel Presbyterian Online Live Stream, Warrenville, IL, September 15, 2024, www.youtube.com/live/wh6Va5tg9Vo [44:36--48:00].

[11] Resolution, "Honoring Phyllis Le Peau as Elder Emeritus," Immanuel Presbyterian Online Live Stream, Warrenville, IL, September 15, 2024, www.youtube.com/live/wh6Va5tg9Vo [50:41--51:23].

COMPANION WEBSITE

The companion website for *She Teaches Me Still* includes links to articles and videos about Phyllis Le Peau as well as photographs, source documents, and many other resources. You can also leave a comment about Phyllis or the book. It can be found at:

www.sheteachesmestill.com

www.ingramcontent.com/pod-product-compliance
Lightning Source LLC
Chambersburg PA
CBHW051509150726
47997CB00001B/174